MW00427548

Mastering the Magickal
Symbolism of the
Subconscious Mind

The ESOTERIC
DREAM
Book

Designed by John P. Cheek
Cover design by Danielle D. Farmer
Type set in Louisbourg/Georgia

ISBN: 978-0-7643-4625-5
Printed in China

Schiffer Books are available at special discounts for bulk purchases for sales promotions or premiums. Special editions, including personalized covers, corporate imprints, and excerpts can be created in large quantities for special needs. For more information contact the publisher:

Published by Schiffer Publishing, Ltd.
4880 Lower Valley Road
Atglen, PA 19310
Phone: (610) 593-1777; Fax: (610) 593-2002
E-mail: Info@schifferbooks.com

For the largest selection of fine reference books on this and related subjects, please visit our website at
www.schifferbooks.com.
We are always looking for people to write books on new and related subjects. If you have an idea for a book, please contact us at
proposals@schifferbooks.com.

This book may be purchased from the publisher.
Please try your bookstore first.
You may write for a free catalog.

WE DEDICATE THIS BOOK
TO ALL DREAMERS SEEKING DEEPER
INSIGHT INTO THE LANGUAGE OF DREAMS.

We want to extend our thanks to our families for their full support and encouragement as we wrote this book. We also want to thank our editor, Dinah Roseberry, and everyone at Schiffer Publishing for all of the support we have received throughout the writing process. Special thanks go to John L. Turner, MD, who took the time out of his tremendously busy schedule to review the following body of work. Last, but never least, we gives thanks to the Divine for every blessing, big and small.

CONTENTS

FOREWORD
JOHN L. TURNER, MD

Can the so-called Lathe of Heaven be avoided? A wise man once said:

Confucius and you are both dreams; and I who say you are dreams—I am but a dream myself. This is a paradox. Tomorrow, a wise man may come forward to explain it; but that tomorrow will not be until ten thousand generations have gone by.

This remarkable quotation is attributed to Chuang Tzu, a fourth or third century BCE philosopher who argued that we should seek to live at one with nature, not imposing upon it. But what is the nature of dreams?

We spend one third of our lives in sleep and, during that time, we have up to six dreams a night, many, if not most, are not immediately recalled. When we *do* remember dreams, it is important to decode them; our subconscious mind speaks in a symbolic language that without guidance, deciphering can be a formidable undertaking.

This book is an extraordinarily well-done compendium about dream interpretation that will allow you to make sense of what I have long called "messages from our future." As if by design, these important missives are presented to us during sleep as screenplays written in an oft-times ambiguous language, forcing us to think carefully and concisely to extract meaningful information. This wonderful book will guide you, as it guided me, to understand and decode these letters from our future. You will learn techniques to foster dream recall, the mechanics of dream interpretation, the symbology in dreams that can be understood, the use of dream rituals, and magickal correspondences. Most importantly, you will learn techniques of magickally enhancing dream recall.

What I have referred to as letters are communications of vital importance! What a shame it would be to leave most of these letters unopened. With this book, you will have all the tools necessary to glean the important information that is delivered to you in your dreamtime. This book is highly recommended.

The Life of Philippus Theophrastus Bombast of Hohenheim
1896

INTRODUCTION

That which the dream shows is the shadow of such wisdom as exists in man, even if during his waking state he may know nothing about it ... We do not know it because we are fooling away our time with outward and perishing things, and are asleep in regard to that which is real within ourself.

Paracelsus
The Dream Game

The Esoteric Dream Book: Mastering the Magickal Symbolism of the Subconscious Mind will allow you to begin a serious study of dreams and the meaningful symbols the subconscious uses to communicate. This book is not a dream dictionary, but a guide on dream analysis using your personal understanding of symbols. It is ideal if you want to commit to the regular practice and mastery of dream interpretation.

This book will teach how to expand on mundane, spiritual, and esoteric dream symbolism by drawing information from the Tarot, astrology, numerology, and other magickally related sources. Yet, despite the esoteric-related references, *The Esoteric Dream Book* is ideal for all readers. It's a comprehensive guide for anyone seeking to learn and grow from the teachings of the subconscious mind, higher self, spirit, or divine.

For readers with an interest in magickal applications, we supply rituals, spells, and magickal correspondences to enhance dream work. To use the correspondences, you should have knowledge of magickal tools and safe spell casting. (If new to the art of magick, you can discover how to use magickal paraphernalia and establish sacred space in our book, *Sacred Objects, Sacred Space: Every Day Tools for the Modern-Day Witch* (Schiffer Publishing, 2013). We encourage you to take from this book what works best. Just as every dream experience is unique, the methods for dream interpretation are dependent on your comfort.

One final note: throughout this book, we share information on how to use the Tarot as a tool for improving your dream recall and understanding. Please note that in some circles, the suit of Wands corresponds to the fire element and the suit of Swords corresponds to the air element. However, our personal view is that the air element is a more fitting correspondence for the suit of Wands, while fire is the most appropriate correspondence with the suit of Swords. In taking this view, we do not suggest that alternative element/suit associations are incorrect, but that each view is equally valid.

Identifying Dream Types, Symbols, Themes, and Archetypes

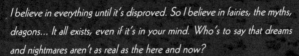

*I believe in everything until it's disproved. So I believe in fairies, the myths,
dragons... It all exists, even if it's in your mind. Who's to say that dreams
and nightmares aren't as real as the here and now?*

John Lennon

Defining Dreams

Why people dream remains a debatable subject, with some arguing that dreams are nothing more than images the mind creates as it reboots during sleep, like a supercomputer. Others argue that the dreaming mind attempts to work out the problems one experiences during waking hours. Still others contend that dreams are the subconscious mind's path of communication with the conscious mind. Some dreams are even precognitive, and these night visions have shaped the lives of historical figures, artists, celebrities, writers, and everyday individuals.

An etymological analysis of the word "dream" hints at beliefs about the origins and reasons for dreams. The word originates from the German "Traum" and Dutch "droom."[1] Additionally, "dream" originates from the Old Norse "draugr," meaning apparition or ghost.[2] This suggests that sometimes dreams are forms of communication from the spirit realm or images that haunt the mind. There is a connection between the word "dream" and the Old English "drēam" meaning "music" or "mirth."[3] This implies that dreams are the music of the mind and hints at the visual symphony of images that one experiences. If you consider symbols as the language of the higher self, soul, or divine, you can make the connection between dreaming and the potential for ecstatic or divine dream communication.

Ancient Middle Eastern societies practiced the art of dream interpretation. Evidence that the Sumerians interpreted dreams exists in passages of *The Epic of Gilgamesh*: a Mesopotamian poem written circa 1300 BC. The Babylonians and Assyrians believed that the appearance of a god in a dream was an actual manifestation of the divine being. Further, all dreams were communication sent directly by the gods who revealed themselves as symbols requiring that a priest decipher them.[4] If a dream was unsolicited, people would offer prayers in hopes that the prophetic meaning of the dream would prove auspicious.[5] Likewise, references to divine dreams are pervasive throughout biblical literature. In fact, the number of dream references in the Bible is so considerable, it would be impossible to include them all within the scope of this book.

The ancient Egyptian, Chaldean, Greek, and Roman cultures understood dreams as prophetic, holy, and sometimes of divine origin. However, the Greek philosopher, Aristotle, suggests, "The dream is of demoniacal, though not of divine nature." He also considers dreams meaningful when correctly interpreted.[6] The process of preparing for dream work is the art of dream incubation; the precise practices have been lost or destroyed, but some historical accounts revealing some of the methods of incubation still exist and indicate that supplicants searched for cures for physical/psychological discomforts, illness, and disease.

The Egyptians and Greeks erected temples or sleeping halls hosting bedchambers where one slept in hopes of experiencing divine communication through dreams.[7] The supplicant had a question in mind and took the ritualistic steps necessary to summon dream responses. For example, in Greece, people seeking precognitive dreams or divine messages refrained from eating specific foods or consuming wine before sleep. It was customary for the supplicant to wear white attire, as this lent to the clarity of dreams received.[8] The supplicant prayed to deities and made offerings to Mercury (the god of communication and the "giver of sleep") just before retiring. If dreams proved allegorical, the dreamer sought out someone knowledgeable about dreams to interpret the visions.[9] People consulted the gods and dreams about everything from disease to relationships to business to love.

Historically, there are many instances where dreams proved prophetic. Julius Caesar's mother dreamt of birthing a divine child who shapeshifted into a serpent (symbol of great wisdom), while Nero's mother dreamt of giving birth to something monstrous.[10] Calpurnia, Caesar's wife, foretold of his death; the woman dreamt she stood over the lifeless body of her husband mourning him. When Caesar considered Calpurnia's pleas not to attend the meeting of the senate, Decimus Brutus, arguing augers and dreams were foolish, persuaded him otherwise, and thusly, sealed Caesar's fate.[11]

Historical accounts demonstrate instances of recurring, prophetic dreams as well. Abraham Lincoln had recurring dreams during his presidency and just before his assassination in 1865. In the dream, Lincoln saw a ship sailing on the sea as it moved toward a gloomy, quiet, misty shore. The ship never made it to land before he awoke.[12] Similarly, in 1912, prior to the sinking of the Titanic, many people had dreams, some of which were recurring, of the ship sinking before the event.[13] Such dreams made a number of passengers forgo travel plans on the fated ship.

In the twentieth century, dream interpretation became a practice that went hand-in-hand with psychoanalysis. Sigmund Freud and Carl Jung are the pioneers of dream interpretation. Freud attributes value to dream symbolism and considers dream symbols a form of subconscious thinking.[14] He suggests that dreams have interpretative value and that when interpreted with the appropriate "psychological technique...every dream will show itself to be a senseful psychological structure which may be introduced into an assignable place in the psychic activity of the waking state."[15] Likewise, Swiss psychiatrist and psychotherapist Carl Gustav Jung considers dreams something free and independent of a person's consciousness.[16] Yet, despite all of the insight that Freud and Jung brought to the realm of dream analysis, dream origins and meaning still remain puzzling matters in the twenty-first century. Scientists are still searching for the answers to why dreams happen and if they hold significant meaning for the dreamer. Yet, major strides are occurring in the field of dream research. In April 2013, a news write up on "Counsel & Heal News" online reveals scientists have developed a way to record dream imagery based on brainwave activity.[17] It's hoped that the new recording method will provide major insights into dream function.

Common Dreams

While theories about dream origination and meaning differ, many people still share similar dream imagery and experiences. The shared dreaming experiences people have across cultures are dream themes. You should not confuse dream themes with dream types. Dream themes involve looking at the subject matter, narrative, or storyline. Dream types are classifications for dreams based on their common visual qualities or characteristics. Exploring the different types of dreams can help you to understand the messages within dream imagery.

Cosmic Dreams

Cosmic dreams are emotive, continuous narratives, and have life-altering results; sometimes called numinous, unforgettable, great, or epic dreams, these night visions are positive, colorful, and vivid. A cosmic dream is something that you will remember years after the initial experience. These dreams lead to heightened awareness or life changing consequences and can take on supernatural, magical, spiritual, or mystical attributes. Such dreams feel lucid where you're capable of influencing conditions within the dream. The positivity you experience upon waking is like none you have experienced with any other dream. You might feel as if you have deeply connected with the divine after waking from a cosmic dream.

To induce numinous dreams, meditate on The Death card in the Tarot, since you're seeking dreams with life-changing results. Consider meditating on other cards, too, like the Wheel of Fortune, representing the hand of fate in your life; The Chariot, when you want dreams to obtain a deeper self-knowing; or The Empress, for cosmic dreams involving messages on how to achieve physical/psychological/spiritual harmony. Jupiter is the planetary influence of cosmic dreams, since such visions instill you with deep, lasting wisdom. These dreams correspond with Pisces and numbers 11 and 22 (both being master numbers signifying balance and inspiration).

Daydreams

Everyone daydreams and these visions occur while you're awake but in a trance-like state. Daydreams involve real-life events and memories, the conjuring of fantastical hopes for the future, or a combination of both. Daydreams can feel so realistic, you can become engrossed in the experience and lose your sense of reality temporarily. Within a daydream, you can explore wishes, desires, or fears.

While commonly mistaken as lackadaisical behavior, daydreams involve the powerful workings of the imagination and, in some instances, can lead to new ideas or epiphanies. Napoleon Bonaparte received advice on what he should do from figures when he daydreamed. In another instance, Abraham Lincoln might very well have spotted his own ghostly double during a daydream shortly before his death.[18] If you're having repetitive daydreams, it can serve you well to assess them, since the visions can indicate your heartfelt desires or can serve as a well of inspiration. You can benefit from comparing your daydreams with your night dreams to identify a repetitious theme or any influential ideas.

Daydreams are powerful forms of visualization. Consider that continual focus on specific thoughts can lead to the manifestation of such thoughts. You can understand how daydreaming can serve as a powerful tool in helping you create reality, just as it can serve as a detriment to your physical/spiritual well-being. Focus on negative daydreams can lead to unnecessary anxiety, or worse: unintended manifestations in the physical.

Daydreams fall under the planetary rulership of Neptune and correspond to the sign of Pisces. In numerology, these dreams correspond to the number four (representing a balanced mind entering into daydreams because of contentment), seven (representing the act of hitting a plateau and reverting to imaginings in search of creative solutions), and eight (representing inward reflection leading to breakthroughs and inspiration).

If you daydream often, meditate on the Seven of Cups, a Tarot card representing dreams, goals, illusion, and fantasy, so you can engage in self-examination. Explore potential obstacles blocking success. Meditate to examine what will lead to physical/spiritual fulfillment. The Four of Cups can help you begin to explore opportunities you might have missed, disillusionments, or philosophical ideas and understandings. Finally, meditate on the Star card when you want to gain a deeper understanding of your daydreams and ideals.

Dreams and *Déjà* vu Experiences

In your dream state, you might see something that you will later see when you are awake. In such cases, when the dream proves precognitive, you will experience the sense of *déjà vu*. Conversely, in some *déjà vu* dreams, you might enter into a dream where the surroundings, people, conditions, or situations make you feel like you have seen the imagery before. *Déjà vu* dreams can sometimes involve out-of-body experiences or astral/mind travel.

Some people believe that the experience of *déjà vu* is nothing more than having already experienced something in the mundane, and reencountering the condition or situation while forgetting about the original encounter. Others assert that *déjà vu* dreams and precognition go hand-in-hand. Another explanation for *déjà vu* dreams points to reincarnation; this is particularly true if your dream does not result in a precognitive occurrence, but you have a strong sense of *déjà vu* within the dream's context; in such situations, it's possible that you're recalling experiences from past lives. Working with past-life regression techniques and combining such practices with lucid dream work might give you deeper insight into actual past life experiences.

If you want to conduct dream work involving *déjà vu* dreams, you can meditate on The Moon card in the Tarot. The card represents inner reflection, the deep subconscious, your emotions, receptive energies, time distortions, and the past/present. The planetary influence of daydreams is the Moon: a celestial light illuminating the dark. At the same time, any planet in retrograde corresponds to *déjà vu* dreams and experiences, since the planet appears to be moving backward when in retrograde motion.

The Six of Cups is another meditative tool: the card represents childhood, returning to the past, and nostalgia. Meditating on the Justice card can prove beneficial, since the card signifies personal strengths, present or future judgment evaluations, and past-life regression work. Finally, the Hanged Man can serve as a meditative tool if you want to know more about issues you can't control in the present that stem from past life experiences. In numerology, *déjà vu* dreams correspond to the numbers two (representing the past, present, and the act of seeking balance), and eight (signifying the infinite and deep understanding).

False Awakenings

False awakenings involve conditions where you feel like you have woken up from a dream when you're still dreaming. These dreams are vivid and realistic, making you feel that you're awake and have already started preparing for your day. Typically, you will see the entire room where you're sleeping and everything will look as it does in your waking life. Sometimes you might experience a sudden alarming image or a revelation that awakens you, making you realize that you were dreaming the entire time. In other cases, something in the dream suddenly appears out of place or incongruent with reality and makes you realize that you're still dreaming.

The planetary influences of false awakenings include The Moon and Pluto. These dreams correspond to the numbers seven (representing plateaus, stagnation, and the need for a new perspective), and eight (representing the false movement from dream to waking state). If you're experiencing false awakenings and you want greater clarity into the meaning of such dreams, consider meditation on The Moon, The Hanged Man, and Temperance cards. The Moon card can help you discover the deeper meaning of dream illusions. Use The Hanged Man, representing a between state, to understand how you transition from one stage of sleep to another, and meditate on Temperance to develop a more harmonious transition between your waking life and dreams.

Incorporating External Stimuli in Dreams

While you're sleeping, if there are stimuli in the environment, through the process of dream incorporation, your brain can sometimes integrate the stimuli into the imagery and sounds you experience in your dream narrative. For instance, if you're a heavy sleeper and your alarm clock is going off, even if you fail to hear it, your brain might detect the sound and present it in your dream as an alarm going off. As another example, imagine falling asleep with the television on and a popular television show about crime comes on the air as you sleep. You might end up having a dream where police are involved in the narrative or suddenly you might find yourself experiencing a dream where a predator chases you.

Dream incorporation can cause you to question the validity of the dream messages you're receiving. You might wonder if it's really your subconscious mind trying to communicate with you or if your brain is transforming external stimuli into sounds and imagery. However, you can use the process of dream incorporation to your benefit. Imagine turning on classical music before going to bed for the purposes of dream incorporation while you sleep; it could lead to a more blissful sleep state. Likewise, you can create a sleep meditation audio file that plays while you're sleeping. Through dream incorporation, you might be able to remember your dreams with greater clarity or you might even use the process to seek out answers to specific questions while in the dream state.

Meditation on the Death card might bring clarity to you about the meaning of dreams with incorporated elements, since the card represents between or transitional states of being. Clarify these dreams by meditating on the Hanged Man, representative of a state of suspension, the Hermit card, representing the search for understanding or truth, or The High Priestess signifying the preparation for understanding dreams. These dreams correspond to the sign of Pisces and Neptune. Dreams involving the incorporation of external stimuli correspond to the numbers two (representing pairings, couplings, and connections) and five (representing the Akashic element, thereby signifying the unification of all elements).

Lucid Dreaming

The term lucid originates from the Latin "lucidus" meaning "light, bright or to shine."[19] Lucid dreams involve clarity and becoming clear on the fact that you're not awake, but dreaming. Eventually, with practice, you can begin to influence or control what happens within a dream. Lucid dreaming involves working within the astral realms. These dreams can help you deal with personal issues in your waking life, and you can use lucid dream work for healing for yourself or others.

Meditate on The High Priestess card if you want to increase your awareness of the onset of lucid dreams. Meditate on The Hermit card to assist in achieving a lucid dream state. Study The Magician card to become more conscious of your actions in dreams. Alternatively, consider The Strength card if you want to gain influence over dream happenings. Work with cards hosting swords, since the suit represents action and movement, while the sword itself signifies cutting away of illusions.

Lucid dreams correspond to the numbers three and nine. The planetary influence of these dreams is the action planet Mars. These dreams correspond to the astrological signs of Cancer, Aries, Scorpio, and Pisces. Cancer, Scorpio, and Pisces are water signs, bringing receptivity to intuition and dream work. Specifically, Scorpio has to do with the depths of experience; Pisces relates to the merging of reality and fantasy, and Aries and Mars are signs of action and movement. Thus, taking control and action in a dream blends the energies of these signs.

Narrated Dreams

Narrated dreams are visions involving a seen or unseen source or someone who speaks to you and tells you what is going on in the dream. The voice might be conveying an important message. Sometimes the narration does not match up to actual happenings within the dream narrative; in such cases, you should try to remember how the events and the narration differed; the differences might lend important clues to the meaning of the dream.

When experiencing narrated dreams, pay attention to the type of narration; note whether it's in your own voice as a stream of consciousness or a recognizable voice. Question whether the voice speaks to you directly in the dream or if you merely overheard a conversation. Is the voice narrating the dream trying to persuade you? Is the narrating voice omniscient, all knowing, and telling you things that you could not possibly derive from observations alone?

Omniscient voices narrating a dream might indicate that the information is coming from a guide or spirit, whereas a dream where you're narrating the story or happenings in your own voice indicate messages coming from your subconscious or higher self. When observing the dream narrative, if a voice narrates in real time, the narrator might be reiterating the message for the purposes of emphasis so that you will give your full attention to the visual and audible stimuli you experience; thus, the voice sometimes doubles the importance behind a dream's interpretation.

Mercury, the planet of communication, is the planetary influence of narrated dreams. These dreams correspond to the signs of Virgo and Gemini, both of which indicate balance, pairings, and the self versus the higher self. These dreams correspond with the number two (another symbol of pairing and balance). Since the suit of Wands deals with communication and the suit of Cups deals with emotions, cards from both suits are ideal for meditating on in order to induce narrated dreams or to gain greater understanding from the information you receive.

If it's an adult voice narrating, the King/Queen of Cups/Wands corresponds to these types of dreams. If the voice is youthful, the Page/Knight of Cups/Wands is best for meditation purposes, since both cards represent younger people. The King or Queen of Cups is ideal for meditation since anything dream-like relates to water. The King or Queen of Wands works well, since the suit of Wands relates to communication. The Hermit is a card ideal for dream work where you're intentionally seeking guidance from the higher self or spirit. Consider working with the Judgement card during meditations to develop clarity of mind and greater understanding of dream messages.

Nightmares

The term "nightmare" is derived from the Middle English term "nightemare," used to describe a form of spirit attachment or incubus, as it was once believed that nightmares were caused by negative spirits (incubus/succubus) attaching themselves to, crushing, and attacking those that were most vulnerable during sleep.[20] The word "mare," a shortened term for "nightmare," is another term for incubus: a spirit of the night with evil intent and one that oppresses those who sleep; the term is nearly identical to the Sanskrit "māra" or "mar," meaning "killer, destroyer, or devil."[21] What's more, mare is commonly confounded with the female horse[22]; this later resulted in myriad depictions of incubi riding on a black mare when visiting those who sleep.

The content of the nightmare might lead to the understanding of the dream message; in some cases, these dreams are nothing more than visions triggered by physically/emotionally traumatic experiences from your waking life. In other cases, nightmares are conjurations of the subconscious mind and the dreams are made terrifying in order to make them profoundly memorable; if you're having nightmares with no clear physical/emotional source, you should pay close attention to every aspect of the dream since the subconscious is indicating its importance.

Some nightmares are recurring dreams. Nightmares caused by traumatic experiences or emotional issues commonly present as recurring dreams, but you can have recurrent nightmares if the subconscious is trying to get you to pay attention to its hidden message. Bear in mind that some nightmares are reflections of the shadow self: the darker aspects of the personality presenting itself within the context of a dream. If you suspect that some of the characters within a dream are merely darker aspects of your personality, you should carefully review the action of such characters to see how their behaviors, actions, and attitudes relate to you physically, emotionally, and spiritually.

Meditation on the Tower, the Devil, or the Hanged Man card can provide you with insight about the meaning of your nightmares. The Tower can serve as a tool for revealing hidden secrets, phobias, or truths. The Devil card can help in dealing with or overcoming your fears so they do not flow over into your dreams. The Hanged Man is ideal if you want to let go of phobias or irrational/rational fears. The planetary influences of nightmares include Mars, being the planet of war, movement and action, and Pluto, the planet corresponding to The Underworld, anomalies, and the unknown. For more information on the numerological correspondences of nightmares, see the section Numbers in Dreams.

Prophetic/Precognitive Dreams

Precognitive dreams are visions that provide you with information about events, conditions, circumstances, or experiences in advance. Precognitive dreams fall under the umbrella definition of prophetic dreams. There are not always cues in the dream that tell you the events will happen in the future, but when the events occur in waking life, you make the connection between the prophetic dream and the actual occurrences later on by remembering the dream.

Prophetic dreams end up happening in reality; these dreams might involve situations or people you're familiar with or they might have imagery that is foreign to you. Sometimes prophetic dreams come across as forms of spirit communication; the dreamer might see a deceased person and the spirit supplies the dreamer with information about events that later proves true in waking life. On occasion, prophetic dreams can serve as shared experiences where more than one person has the same dream experience on the same night or within a short time frame.

Documenting the dreams is a recommended practice since being able to review your dreams for potential precognitive and prophetic messages is important. As you begin to explore the types of dreams you experience you will eventually be able to note the triggers or circumstances that incite precognitive/prophetic dream narratives and imagery. Use your discoveries to increase the number of precognitive/prophetic dreams you experience in the future.

The Sun is an ideal Tarot card for meditating on when you want to induce precognitive dreams or if you need clarity on the dream message. The Sun is a card of enlightenment, awakening, and awareness. Likewise, The Moon is another card of enlightenment, one that when meditated on provides insight into the mysterious or unknown. Using The Moon card before bed or placing the card under your pillow can help trigger psychic dreams, too. The planetary influences of precognitive dreams are Mercury, the planet of communications of all kinds; Jupiter, the planet of expansion; Uranus, the planet associated with psychic senses, intuition, and insight; and Neptune, the planet of spiritual knowledge, guidance, or perception. Precognitive dreams correspond to the number eight: a number representing the infinite, infinite possibilities, and the act of tapping into universal knowledge for greater clarity or understanding.

Recurring Dreams

Recurring dreams are visions that repeat themselves; the repetition might be from one night to the next or over the course of days, months, or years. Recurring dreams happen when a person has experienced emotional/physical or psychological trauma in waking life, but also they occur when the subconscious has a message of tremendous import. The message will continue to recur until you decode it.

Once you decode dreams, you will be required to implement some kind of action or change in your waking life. If you do not initiate necessary change, recurring dreams can continue to plague you. These dreams do not have to be identical in terms of the imagery, and you might experience recurring dream themes rather than repetitious dream imagery. These dreams can be pleasant or frightening, with the more frightening dreams commonly associated with the most important dream messages.

Use The Hanged Man to explore the meaning of recurring dreams since the card represents plateaus, stagnation, and suspension in one place or position. The Hermit card is best when inward reflection on the meaning of repetitious dreams interests you, or if you hope to gain spiritual guidance. If you feel that your repetitious dreams are fear based, meditate on The Devil card to reflect on what fears are feeding the dreams and why. Alternatively, the Two of Swords can help you discover potential emotional blocks, indecisive actions, and self-sabotaging obstacles you create in your waking life that are influencing your dreams at night. The planetary influence of repeating dreams is Saturn. These dreams correspond to Leo, Taurus, Capricorn, and any of the fixed signs in the zodiac because the fixed signs imply being easily stuck, persistent, and not letting up until you see what you need to see. Repetitious dreams correspond to the number two, representing duality and the shadow self.

Spirit Communication

Spirit communications involve messages or images of/from the deceased. Such dreams may or may not be prophetic. When a spirit connects with you in your dreams, the information shared by the spirit is of the highest importance since the spirit made a considerable effort to connect with you. You might receive insight into a situation, omens, or the spirit may foretell of the death of a loved one.

In other situations, a loved one might visit you for emotional closure; these types of dreams can happen immediately following the death of a loved one. In a closure dream, the spirit might seek forgiveness for transgressions committed while alive and your forgiveness might influence the spirit's ability to rest or to continue their spiritual progression. Alternatively, a spirit might appear to give you a chance to say good-bye.

The planetary influence of dreams involving spirit communication is Pluto: an astrological body corresponding to death, The Underworld, transition, change, and the afterlife. Thus, Death is an ideal card for meditative work when seeking communication with spirits in dreams. These dreams correspond to the astrological sign Sagittarius because the sign represents communication and higher spiritual purpose. Spirit communication dreams correspond to Scorpio as a sign representing death and the occult. These dreams correspond to the number two (signifying life/death and the separate worlds of the living and the dead) and ten (signifying the act of coming full circle and the transitional stage between incarnations).

Wish Fulfillment

Wish-fulfilling dreams involve something you desire like money, sex, fame, or conflict resolution, lasting relationships, problem solving, and growth. Wish-fulfilling dreams allow you to explore all that you desire and sometimes the dreams can prove precognitive. These dreams can show you things that you might be wishing for that, if you experience or obtain in reality, would prove otherwise undesirable. Thus, wish-fulfilling dreams serve as a playground for the mind and your subconscious, allowing you to make trial runs of potential experiences and occurrences before they happen. Resolution dreams are a subset of wish-fulfilling dreams: these types of visions allow you to find solutions to plaguing problems or conditions in your waking life.

Dreams of wish fulfillment might include dreams about addictions. Some people who have stopped the baneful behaviors associated with an addiction will dream about partaking of their drug of choice. You can wake up feeling guilty because the dream seemed so real or because it triggered emotions in relation to the addiction. These types of wish-fulfilling dreams are not all about the return to negative behaviors, but more about how the brain is processing the changes and the sense of loss brought on through the necessary change.

The Star, World, The Fool, The Magician, and The Empress are all tarot cards to use to better explore the meaning and potential in wish-fulfilling dreams. The planetary influence of these visions includes the Sun, Jupiter, Neptune, and Venus, with the latter particularly influencing dreams of a romantic or sexual nature. These dreams correspond with Pisces, Sagittarius, and Taurus. Sagittarius is a grandiose, lucky sign, one corresponding to the act of confidently reaching for one's goals. Pisces corresponds with the act of wishing itself, and Taurus is a sign corresponding to the material desires or comforts one might wish initially. The numbers three (expansion), six (the act of seeking resolutions), and nine (achieving happiness) correspond to dreams about fulfilling wishes.

Night Terrors, Sleep Paralysis, and Spiritual Attack

Unlike nightmares that anyone can experience at anytime, night terrors usually affect young children between the ages of three and seven. These experiences are rare for adults. The episodes can last anywhere from fifteen minutes to an hour and the individual cannot be woken up during the experience.

The person having a night terror will show outward manifestations of the experience that include crying, screaming, confusion, physical restlessness, and sometimes the individual will react with aggression or violence. The person might open their eyes and appear to be wide-awake when in reality they are still in a sleep state; the person might not respond when spoken to or recognize who is speaking to him/her.

The person who is witnessing another who is having a night terror is typically more frightened than the person who is having the night terror. The causes of night terrors involve a person's environment, external stimuli, stress levels, sleep quality, medications, mental conditions, and genetics. Thankfully, the person who experiences a night terror usually forgets that the event happened in the first place.

Another frightening experience that might be mistakenly identified as a nightmare is the experience of sleep paralysis; this experience can occur when the person is waking from or moving out of the dream state and the episodes can last anywhere from a minute to several minutes. When dreaming, people experience Rapid Eye Movements (REM). During this time, your body is paralyzed so you will not act upon the dream imagery you experience. In some people, this paralysis remains as they awaken and become conscious of their surroundings. You're wide-awake, unable to move and the experience can induce a sense of dread. Sometimes you hear noises or sense a presence nearby.

Some theories suggest that sleep paralysis is nothing more than a sleep disorder involving the temporary paralysis of the body and hallucinations. Others assert that sleep paralysis is sometimes akin to the experiences associated with being out-of-body, and that the person experiences the paralysis just after entering or just before leaving the body during astral travel. Still others associate sleep paralysis with "The Old Hag Syndrome," a form of spirit attack.

Like nightmares, dreams involving sleep paralysis correspond to The Hanged Man, but they also correspond to the Four of Swords, signifying exhaustion and immobility. The planetary influences of sleep paralysis correspond to the planet Pluto (the act of dredging up and amplifying fears and suspension of movement), and Saturn (paralysis). These dreams correspond to Scorpio and Capricorn, with Scorpio representing poison and paralysis and Capricorn signifying structure and restriction. In numerology, the number seven corresponds to sleep paralysis, signifying stagnation, a plateau, or immovability.

You should not confuse incubi/succubi/spirit attacks with the dark dreams where you experience partial/total paralysis within the dream setting. In some cases, you might dream that you have the inability to escape a stalker or you're trying to move and cannot, this is not the same thing as experiencing an attack from an incubus, succubus, or malevolent being.

The term incubus originates from the Latin "incubo," meaning "nightmare"and "incubare" meaning "lie on."[23] The term succubus originates from the Latin term "succubare," meaning "lie under."[24] An incubus is a masculine entity that allegedly attacks females in order to have sexual intercourse with them so that they can steal the woman's sexual energies. A succubus is a female being who attacks males.

Reports of incubus or succubus attacks are in many cultures and there are several commonalities in such reports. The victim will commonly hear strange noises when they awaken and find that they are conscious but incapable of moving. The individual will often experience difficulty breathing and sometimes the sensation can feel like the individual is suffocating. The individual might feel tremendous pressure on the chest and he or she will sense a terrifying presence.[25] Some people have reported being physically or sexually attacked by such entities. While many of these attacks allegedly occur while the individual is sleeping on his back, these experiences can happen when the individual is sleeping on the side or stomach. Skeptics will assert incubi/succubi attacks do not actually occur, but for the person who experiences the phenomenon, the experience is terrifyingly real.

Spiritual Protection

Ritually cleansing the area where you sleep can help prevent spiritual attacks. You need sea salt, and sage, a smudge stick, or purifying incense. Beginning in the eastern corner of your room, walk the perimeter of the room in a clockwise or deosil direction and sprinkle consecrated sea salt as you do so. Continue in a clockwise direction. Circle the room three more times while you carry a censer containing sage or a burning smudge stick. Place protective symbols like pentacles and wards over the head and foot of the bed. You should put protective seals over the windows, doorways, and any mirrors you have in the room as well.

If you like, place one or more dream catchers in the room to help in weeding out bad dreams. Spread a circle of sea salt around your bed or place some under the bed before you go to sleep at night. In addition, you can wear an amulet for protective purposes; in ancient times, people wore fire stone pendants, an Ash tree root, or a coral pendant as a charm to thwart spirit attacks while sleeping.

DREAM THEMES

All the things one has forgotten scream for help in dreams.
Elias Canetti

Throughout the world, there is a number of dream themes people experience. Dream themes include the basic topic, subject, motif, or recurrent idea within the dream. You can have more than one theme in your dream, but you will often find that you have a single, larger theme that relates to the imagery you see.

Dreams of Catastrophe

Catastrophic dreams involve disasters of all kinds. You might dream of blizzards, fires, massive floods, earthquakes, tornadoes, or other types of natural devastation. They can involve dreams about death and war as well. The word "apocalypse" originates from the Greek "apokalyptein" meaning to reveal or uncover.[1] Thus, you can view catastrophic dreams as important messages that provide you with a revelation, epiphany, or significant disclosure of some kind. Symbolically, these dreams might indicate that you're experiencing chaotic events during your waking life, or the images might hint to troubles ahead. If you experience these types of dreams, then you should ready yourself for the unexpected in all situations.

Catastrophic dreams do not always foretell terrible events, but they can prove precognitive. If you're analyzing catastrophic dreams, especially those with natural causes, you can benefit from considering the elements and elementals associated with the type of disaster that occurs. For example, if you dream of a flood, you should look into the meanings associated with the element of water and undines, or if you dream of a devastating fire, you might want to look into the magickal correspondences with the element of fire or salamanders, the elemental associated with the element.

Dreams of Being Followed or Chased

Chase dreams depicting someone stalking or pursuing you are common. If you have been the victim of a physical attack, it's not unusual to later have dreams of being stalked or chased. These types of dreams stem from anxieties or traumatic events. Warranted or unwarranted fears can trigger chase dreams.

In chase dreams, sometimes you will see who is chasing you. A stranger or someone you know might chase you or something inhuman can pursue you in a dream. In the dream, you're stricken with fear and can respond in one of three ways. You can run away, be frozen by fear, or turn and face your attacker in an effort to fight for your life.

There are several ways to look at this type of dream and your reaction within the dream narrative gives you a good indication as to what the subconscious is trying to tell you. If you make the choice to run and hide in your dream, this could mean that you're not facing unavoidable situations or conditions in your waking life. If you're frozen by fear, this could signify that you feel trapped in a situation in which there is seemingly no escape or you might feel as if you're victimized in some way. If, however, you turn and face your attacker, this could signify that you will deal with anxiety-producing situations head on and that you will feel confident in your ability to direct the situation into a more desirable outcome. Finally, if you dream that you're searching for a safe place for hiding, but the person/thing chasing you still discovers your location, this can signify that you will not be able to avoid upcoming or existing issues in your waking life, no matter how hard you try.

If you have a dream where you're pursued, it's best to try to remember who is chasing you; if you can identify who or what you're running from, this can serve as a key to what it is you are avoiding while awake. Imagine being chased by an ex-boyfriend: this might mean that you're avoiding putting an end to old, outworn relationships, while dreaming of a current spouse chasing you might indicate that you're avoiding dealing with issues that, once dealt with, will lead to the healthier status of your existing relationship. Likewise, if a classmate or work colleague pursues you in a dream, then you might be subconsciously avoiding issues in class or at work. Meanwhile, faceless pursuits might be reflections of the darker aspect of your personality or they could represent "faceless" larger entities like corporations or a spiritual attack. It's important to consider where the chase occurs as well. See the section on Dreamscapes for further clues about your dream's meaning.

Less frequently, you might find that you're the one who is the pursuer in a dream. When you're pursuing someone or something in the dream narrative, these dreams become a subset of wish-fulfilling dreams. You should therefore evaluate what you're pursuing. Examine how you partake in the pursuit. If you're aggressive in the pursuit, it could serve as an indication that you're overly ambitious, perhaps even ruthless in your pursuit of your desires. It can mean that you are blindly seeking something without giving due consideration to all of the potential consequences associated with your desires.

Chase dreams are about balance in the physical and spiritual; they signify the need to embrace the darker aspects of the self as well as the positive aspects. If all characters within the dream become a representation of the self, then chase dreams become a representation of separation, disharmony, disconnection, and a division of the aspects of the self. These dreams prove a cryptic message that one needs to unify aspects of the mind, body, and spirit, including both dark and light aspects, in order to achieve fulfillment on physical/spiritual planes.

Origination Dreams

Origination dreams, sometimes called conception or birth dreams, involve a birth or beginnings. Both males and females can experience these types of dreams. This type of dream is common for a woman who is already pregnant, but women who desire a child might have conception dreams. Even those individuals that have no desire for a child can have conception dreams.

Birth dreams do not always manifest as a physical pregnancy and can signify the inception of a new idea, an enterprise, or an undertaking. These dreams can even signify new understandings of ideas, thoughts, concepts, designs, and plans. The notion of conception and invention or innovation go hand-in-hand, and these dreams imply that you will devise means for dealing with people, relationships, conditions, or situations.

These dreams could signify the bringing together of all the elements or components needed to initiate new beginnings in your life or in certain situations. When you have these dreams, your subconscious mind is telling you it's time for seed planting and preparation, as you ready yourself for future conditions, circumstances, and changes. You should look to your waking life to see what aspects of your physical/spiritual life you want to change, and begin taking the steps needed to birth such changes.

Birth dreams are associated with the element of air, linked by the concepts of new beginnings and future birth. These types of dreams are associated with the earth element. They symbolize fertility, the potential for abundance, and the unification of the masculine and feminine energies. These types of dreams might be telling you to take time for greater inner reflection through meditation where epiphanies, revelations, and spiritual understandings can lead to inventions, innovations, and understandings that can serve as the catalyst for great change in your waking life.

Flying and Flight in Dreams

Flying signifies being free, but it can also mean a new, elevated perspective or seeing conditions clearly. Being able to fly to great heights indicates that you might soon see success in your waking life or that you desire to be successful in an undertaking. The notion of fearlessness is important, because if you're afraid of flying, heights, and you're terrified during the dream, this takes on a darker meaning. You might fear necessary change, the consequences that follow achievement, or you might be afraid of losing control at the height of a situation when control is an absolute necessity to success.

Dreams of flying are associated with the air element and therefore signify the realm of thought, ideas, concepts, and new beginnings. These dreams can consist of you flying while in an aircraft, but more often involve the moment when you're freely flying around within the dreamscape. In the latter case, these dreams become associated with the art of astral travel and out-of-body experiences. Flying to great heights can parallel the soaring, ascending spirit. Flying dreams are all about transcendence and the conquering of bodily/spiritual limitations.

Some flight dreams are lucid dreams where the dreamer is in full control of flying and is working within the astral realms. Sometimes these dreams are out-of-body experiences; the dreamer feels as if he/she has left the physical body behind, while one's consciousness or spirit travels to various locations within physical and astral realms. Out-of-body experiences feel more realistic than a typical dream, with much of the dream proving vivid and unforgettable.

While some dreams involve flying unaided, others will involve using something to assist in the endeavor or some physical action before you can fly. For instance, if you have to get a running start before you can fly, this could symbolize that you will need to lay the groundwork for achievement of goals in your waking life before you obtain your desires. As another example, if you're holding a wand in you dream and you need the wand in order to fly, it can suggest that you might need the help of others or some kind of assistance in reaching new heights. Even bizarre tools or objects can give you a deeper understanding of flight dreams. Imagine having a dream where you're flying around and holding a pepperoni pizza in your hands. The dream can indicate that you will need nourishment that is more spiritual before you can reach your full potential.

Dreams of floating closely relate to flying dreams. When you're floating, you're moving about freely and this can signify great freedom in your waking life. However, floating is a state of suspension. If you're unable to go from floating to flying in a dream and you're stuck in one place, your dreams could be telling you that you feel stuck in a situation or that you feel as if you cannot move forward in work or relationships.

Being Lost in a Dream

If you're lost in your dreams, it could signify that you have strayed from your spiritual path or you've steered off course in your waking life. Use this dream as a cue to examine where you are and where you're heading. Begin with a reexamination of the self. In knowing yourself, you will have a greater awareness of your purpose and direction. A reevaluation of how you're approaching your spiritual development/progression is necessary when lost dreams occur; these dreams signify the need to consider your attitude, mindset, point-of-view, and methodologies. Ask yourself if you're moving forward with a closed perspective or if you're not seeing all that you need to see for clarity in situations/relationships in your waking life.

If we consider lost dreams as visions about confused directions, the dreams can be associated with the air element. These dreams are associated with blocked fire energies; when you're lost, your will cannot move until you obtain a clear perspective. Likewise, if being symbolically lost is overwhelming for you, it can mean that you're dealing with an excess of the water element in your waking life. These types of dreams should therefore point you in the direction of the earth element since they can indicate that it's time for you to partake of grounding practices; when solidly grounded, you can have a better understanding of your current position and the various directions you can take physically, emotionally, and spiritually.

Nudity in Dreams

Many people have dreams of being nude in public or in front of a group of people. Sometimes these dreams are about modesty, disgrace, embarrassment, shame, and personal vulnerabilities. In other cases, the dreamer is neither ashamed nor self-conscious, and freely parades around the dreamscape nude.

These dreams relate to the masks worn in their daily life and the different aspects of the personality the world sees; being nude symbolically suggests that you're apprehensive about being overly transparent in situations or you fear others will come to know your secrets or your secret self. When you dream of being nude, you might come to feel helpless or unprotected; these dreams, in turn, question the strength of your personal power. Since nudity is all about hiding the physical self behind attire, dreams where you're nude can be associated with your fear of being humiliated, mocked, scorned, or rejected. Conversely, if you're nude and attracting attention to yourself, it could indicate that you're excessively proud, to the point of egotism or that you're behaving narcissistically.

These dreams tend to plague the night visions of those who enter into new situations and relationships; with the boundaries of new relationships/ events still ambiguous or unclearly defined, the dreamer becomes concerned about crossing undefined boundaries and the punishment for doing so.

Sometimes the dreamer does not immediately realize that they are nude; this suggests the need for awareness and preparation for all conditions, even the unexpected. In other cases, you might dream that you're the only person concerned with your nudity and that no one else seems to mind your lack of attire; in these dreams the subconscious is trying to tell you that even in uncomfortable situations, you have ungrounded concerns, anxiety, or fears.

Being nude in dreams is related to the practice of being skyclad in magickal workings; the removal of one's clothes signifies the freedom from authoritarian or dogmatic religious doctrines as well as the freedom from societal influences. When you're nude in dreams, you cannot hide any part of yourself and it could signify that you're paying an inescapable karmic debt in your waking life. If you're willfully nude in dreams, it could indicate the transcendence over the fear of rejection or the inflexible or rigid controls put upon you by cultural/societal/religious influences. Spiritually, these dreams can indicate that you need to embrace all parts of yourself, without shame, guilt, or embarrassment, in order to maintain spiritual balance. Being naked in magickal rites is a sign of openness, unimpeded freedom, and honesty. These dreams are very much associated with physicality, making them visions associated with the earth element.

Occupational Dreams

Occupational dreams contain themes related to existing or desired employment. If you dream about a job you desire, it can fall under the umbrella category of wish-fulfilling dreams. These dreams relate to your passion, goals, and your professional achievements or desire to achieve. Occupational dreams closely relate to personal will, ambition, motivation, and your aspirations.

Positive dreams about work can signify that you're on the right path in terms of your career or that you're comfortable with your current work status. Negative occupational dreams might indicate a time for necessary change or a need to break free from the confines placed upon you in your current line of work or that it's time to try something exciting and new. When negative, these dreams relate to poor motivation and lack of ambition.

If you're having difficulty at your current job, the night visions you experience can become resolution dreams where your subconscious mind tries to offer you solutions to the situations you're experiencing. Dreams related to your job or career correspond to the concept of "survival of the fittest," and getting your basic needs met, or financial struggles and victories. Occupational dreams depict you working out a skill set. If you dream of a past vocation, your subconscious is reminding you of the strengths and limitations of your skills and talents. This can reflect the key lessons and identity markers originating from roles that you took on in past employment positions.

Drowning in Dreams

If you believe in reincarnation, you might want to consider if you drowned in a past life, especially if your drowning dreams are repetitive. Symbolically, drowning dreams relate to fears, anxieties, insecurities, and overwhelming emotions. Drowning dreams can represent overwhelming obsessions or depression. If you're holding your breath in the dream, it can imply anticipation or a period of waiting; Consider the expression "waiting with baited breath," or "don't hold your breath," as indicative of having expectations that have yet to be met. Alternatively, consider the notion that a drowning victim must save him/herself or must be saved by another; in this case, dreams of drowning might suggest that you need to be assertive and take the steps necessary to gain control of a situation or that you should stop waiting around for someone else to save you from negative conditions.

Drowning dreams relate to the element of water, and therefore, emotions, the subconscious, psychic capabilities, intuition, and receptivity; thus, these dreams can indicate that you're highly attuned to your intuitive and psychic processes or that you're "drowning out" your higher guidance and intuition. Your subconscious could be telling you that you need to be more empathic, nurturing, or compassionate, or it could be telling you that you're being too compassionate or empathic, to the point where your sympathetic and kindhearted nature is compromising your well-being. While the vision of drowning in a dream is unpleasant, the dream can symbolize positive conditions involving cleansing and healing. Consider being flooded or washed over by water, and come to understand your dream as indicative of a spiritual cleansing or healing. Drowning dreams relate to the water element in excess, indicating concepts like apathy, infatuation, sensitivity, a lack of compassion or empathy, and moodiness.

Sexual Dreams

In the most basic sense, dreams about sex are about union, but they can be about your personal vulnerability. In a spiritual sense, sex dreams can symbolize the divine marriage or the union of two perfect opposite forces or the harnessing of powerful energies to make manifest your desires. If you dream about having sex with a stranger, this can indicate that you're willing to take some risks in your life, since being intimate with someone else for the first time involves emotional risks. If you're having sex with your current partner or spouse in a dream, it could signify that you long for intimacy or the dream can represent the divine union.

If you dream of cheating on your current partner, it can indicate that you're bored with the status quo, need change, or crave adventure. Consider the taboo nature of cheating and that forbidden things are often the most desirable, and begin to understand the connection of dreams of infidelity with a desire for change or excitement. Alternatively, dreams involving someone cheating on you with another are indicative of low-self esteem or indicate the anxiety you feel over the potential loss of someone you care for or love.

Falling in Dreams

Falling dreams are sometimes associated with out-of-body experiences. The sense of falling is associated with the return of one's astral body to the physical body, and sometimes the falling can seem disturbing or abrupt. In a basic sense, if you fall, you have temporarily lost physical control of the body, so a dream about falling can indicate you're losing control in a situation or that the potential for losing control exists. Consider the fact that falling relates to unsure footing or unstable ground and see how falling dreams relate to a lack in confidence, uncertainty, timidity, diffidence, and insecurity.

Such dreams can indicate moving from an elevated state to a lower state or moving from the realm of conscious thought into the realm of the deep subconscious. The downward motion of a fall symbolically represents a fall from grace, or a sudden decline in social status or position. In addition, a fall can symbolize a change in volume or intensity, and could signify that you're about to experience dramatic changes in your waking life. Falling symbolizes a loss of innocence and is commonly associated with a push or shove into life lessons you cannot avoid or must learn through the harsh realities of experience. Consider the haphazard nature of falling and that conditions can occur at a specified time or "fall" on a particular date; this relates dreams of falling to conditions controlled more by fate or chance than by the dreamer. Thus, falling dreams can herald the entrance of fate in your waking life.

Test-Taking in Dreams

If you dream of taking a test, it could mean that you will soon face a test of your spiritual fortitude or your faith might soon be tested. This can involve initiations or rites of passage. Test dreams can indicate that something will test your skill, knowledge, or experience, or you will have to make a judgment or an evaluation. Consider the fact that you have to prepare or study for a test and see how test-taking dreams can serve as a signal that you need to prepare for upcoming challenges.

If you lack confidence in your knowledge or skills, test-taking dreams can signify your insecurity and the anxiety you feel because of your lack of self-confidence. If you dream that you fail to prepare for a difficult test, your dream is warning you about the dangers of procrastination or that you need to become more motivated or committed to your goals. Since test evaluation involves judgments, your dream can indicate that you're worried about how others will perceive you or that you will be wrongfully judged. Consider that test taking not only involves preparation, but grace under pressure and you will see how these dreams relate to maintaining self-assurance and grace in tough situations.

The concept of survival relates to test dreams. Consider that only the well prepared or those who are strongest will make it through certain situations or conditions; your dream might indicate to you the natural struggles of everyday existence or it can even indicate financial difficulties associated with meeting your needs for basic survival. Alternatively, test dreams can predict situations where you're "testing the waters" in a situation: this may signify a need to test conditions before you proceed with an endeavor. In addition, dreams involving tests can relate to the expression "testing one's mettle," meaning that you will face mental or emotional challenges that might test your conviction, will, or strength of mind.

CHAPTER 3

DREAM DOCUMENTING AND ANALYSIS

A dream is a microscope through which we look at the hidden occurrences in our soul.

Erich Fromm

Dream Journaling

Mastering the language of symbols takes continual practice. The more you actively seek and notice the symbolic tapestry in your waking life, the better you will be at recognizing and interpreting dream symbols. Begin by creating a dream journal where you document the dreams that you remember. Use a portion of the journal as an area to practice symbol interpretation so that you can become fluent in the language of symbols. Start by jotting down symbols you recognize in television advertisements, magazines, street signs, stories you have read, and of course, in dreams.

As you note the symbols you encounter, you might find it helpful to make two columns. List the symbols you encounter in one column and your immediate reactions and interpretations of the symbols in the other. Resist the urge to look up the definitions of the imagery you're evaluating; instead, document what these symbols mean to you. In order to explore dream symbols you will need to learn how symbols speak to you intuitively; this practice is an effort in retraining you to seek out meanings through your intuitive and spiritual responses.

Use some of the exercises provided in this book to help you develop symbolic fluency. The exercises can help you prepare you for the shift from thinking in literal terms to thinking abstractly. Complete the exercises in your dream journal or create a separate workbook to explore symbols.

You have the option of using an elaborately designed dream journal. Fill it out by hand, or record your dreams with a digital recorder. It's best to do both; record your dreams to capture as much of the imagery immediately after waking. Dream imagery is fleeting and soon forgotten upon waking. By using a recorder, you can record every moment of the dream you recall. If you record your dream memories, the moment you wake up, you minimize the risk of a faulty memory attempting to fill in the gaps by inserting incorrect information. Later on during the day, you can transcribe the recording and add it to a handwritten dream journal.

As you make a regular habit of recording your dreams, begin to document how you felt before you went to bed the evening before. Note what kind of day you had and how you were feeling emotionally/physically. Your emotions and thoughts prior to sleeping can seep into your dreams and play out in some intriguing dream narrative. When you record your thoughts and feelings before you sleep, you can begin to recognize how your waking state of mind influences your dreams.

When writing in your dream journal, document whether you woke up saying anything about your dream. Note if there were people in your dream; if you recognized anyone, and if so, write down the names/characters of the people you remember. Note if you felt like you wanted to go back to sleep to re-enter the dream, or if you tried to return to the dream, write it down. Make a note of what it was about the dream you were trying to recapture visually, psychologically, or emotionally. If you were successful at dream re-entry, jot down what happened after re-entry and how the dream scene/story changed, if at all. Make sure you record dreamscapes and time references as well.

Your dream journal is an ideal place to write about dreams that stay with you throughout the day and repeat in your mind. Note if your dream frightened or inspired you and document how it made you feel. Make a practice of keeping track of your dreams for the long term so you can begin to identify repeating themes, symbols, or issues addressed through your night visions.

Document any dreams that you use to work through a situation in waking life or that prove prophetic; doing so will allow you to track your dream interpretation successes and will trigger the subconscious mind into offering more dream messages. As you track your dreams, monitor psychic or precognitive successes and identify peak times during the month or year when you have many psychic dreams.

If you're serious about dream interpretation, it's not enough to simply write down your dreams and read what you have written. You have to evaluate and reflect on dream messages. Meditation is an important tool for bringing clarity to the messages from the subconscious mind. At the same time, regular meditation will help you connect with your subconscious and begin to make the dreamscape something you can work in and, in part, control.

Dream Interpretations for Life and Spiritual Growth

Dreams offer great insight in navigating daily life situations. It's important to note that not all dreams will reveal earth-shattering messages, but this should not invalidate the significance of noting every dream you remember. For instance, having a dream that warns of an unnecessary argument with loved ones resulting in hurt feeling and extreme reactions can help you weigh the pros and cons of having a debate with someone. When you avert the argument, a precognitive dream might seem like minimal foreknowledge, but you should consider the value of avoiding the undue stress. There is the element of personal transition that you need to consider when you begin analyzing your dreams too; suppose numerous dreams carry a theme of being unsatisfied at work and feeling a greater calling awaits in some other vocation. Even if the dream doesn't outline word-for-word where your new job will be and when you will get it, being confronted by your subconscious with guidance that your path carries a greater potential than what you have settled for or perhaps outgrown can be reaffirming. Such dreams can assist you in beginning to take the risks involved in exploring alternative options and preparing for a vocational change.

Some precognitive dreams will set the stage for the following day, even if it's just to let you know a change of routine is in store: traffic may be re-routed, clients might unexpectedly cancel at work, or an important letter will arrive. The latter issues might seem trivial, but bear in mind that having foreknowledge of events, even if it seems like information of little consequence, is very important on several levels. First, having some foreknowledge about upcoming events allows you to feel guided, confirms you're on the right path or, if indicated, affirms the need to make change. Second, advanced guidance through dreams provides you with one more link between the waking, conscious and logical self and the subconscious, often ignored, spiritual self. These days, the link between the conscious and subconscious is so terribly damaged that any opportunity to connect the two realms of consciousness brings strength and full awareness, making use of yet one more spiritual muscle so often left to atrophy.

By paying attention to the small stuff, you will find yourself more prepared, fully aware, and ready to take on the bigger issues in your life. If you diligently make the connections between dreams and waking life, your dream messages become clearer and more pertinent. Imagine a small child whose behavior, for better or worse, gains the attention of an adult. The child will continue the behavior that gets the adults attention because it gets results. Similarly, your subconscious might seem to throw many nonsensical images into your dreams until you really stop to pay attention. In strengthening the connection between the conscious and subconscious, both begin to work in tandem and will become stronger and sharper the more the connection is reinforced. Thus, when it comes time for dreams portending major events, obstacles, or things too important to miss, you will have a natural habit of paying attention, doubt will not be an inhibiting factor, and it will be second nature for you to take dreams seriously so you can gain from them as much as possible in the way of information. It's important not to become frustrated when your dream records yield mostly significant routine occurrences or patterns, pertaining to fears or dilemmas, of which you're already consciously aware. Such dreams prove an additional source of guidance, and in the study of your daily life, the more avenues you have to conduct research, the better.

Another benefit of tracking and recording dreams is that you familiarize yourself with the process of reflection and honest self-evaluation. Even the act of recording a dream in your journal brings the opportunity to reflect on images, patterns, and emotions inherent in the dream's story. By chronicling feelings of despair in a dream for instance, you're calling awareness to emotions that may be out of conscious awareness in waking life; this practice is valuable for synchronizing subconscious and conscious awareness, even if the dreams are not precognitive *per se*.

Looking for Repetitious Symbols in Dreams and Waking Life

Significant lucid dreams can present during times of preparation and initiation. During milestones in your life or amid uncertain times of transition, dreams might carry a powerful and repetitive message. The dream theme or pattern you encounter is significant as the details may change over time. For instance, when in the midst of maneuvering through a complex series of career moves, someone might repeatedly experience dreams of traveling over the same territory, but each time through a different vehicle and with a different goal/obstacle in mind. Another example is a repetitious set of dreams occurring over the course of two years, each with a common thread of approaching a beautiful river in which to relax and swim, only to find that there are strong currents, waterfalls, and toxic waste in the water. Each dream is a slightly evolved variation of the other, but all hold common themes. As another example, a woman might dream of opening a closet to find she had numerous animals all kept in cages in various states of neglect and starvation: all having been forgotten. This dream is repetitious and troubling, but it sends a signal to avoid neglecting the need to nurture the significant aspects of the self/life.

Consider any numbers, colors, dates, and symbols that stand out or repeat as significant. As in a quality film, only the most important elements are included in the story's depiction, so consider no part of the dream to be random filler. Consider the theme(s) of the dreams you document. As an example, think about a dream, where one is running from one path to the next only to find every door locked, such a dream can elicit verbs like "running, moving, failing, changing course, pursuing," or concepts such as being denied entry, blocked, locked out, or as participating in an exercise of futility. If this dream were a described as a single sentence, it might be something like, "I keep running and not getting anywhere." Associated feelings might include fear, desperation, panic, hope, disappointment, or rejection.

Practice viewing, not only the content of the dream, but the process woven around the images and actions. This is easier said than done. Most often, we communicate in direct and linear forms. "Running down a path and finding the door locked" can be communicated in concrete terms; you should return to the image, process it, and elaborate on it, allowing your thoughts and reflections to freely flow as you examine the dream in detail. For instance, you can view the dream where all the doors are locked as follows:

> Here, I am exerting all this energy. I am in a panic. I know I am missing something important. I am relieved to see the entrance ahead. I will make it. The door before me is large, blue, and looks just like the door in my grandmother's home where I have fond memories of spending summer vacations. I am so relieved to see this family door, but then realize it's locked, and I descend into a panic again, left out again, rejected, denied entry, failing on one more path, I run down every road I see, but always the same result.

Examining the dream in depth and also your feelings, allows you to find ways for expressing the message that is "between the lines" of your dream message. Some free association might be needed during the process, such as linking the door to memories of where the door is familiar to you in your waking life, even if the connection is not actually made during the dream itself. In waking life, logic and creativity can work together to connect pieces that might otherwise remain separate in the dream state.

Dream Interpretation Process

A dream which is not interpreted is like a letter which is not read.
The Talmud

Dream interpretation, just like dream journaling, is a process. There are several steps involved in finding the symbols in your dreams and discovering what those symbols mean to you. With a bit of dedication, you will find dream interpretation becomes easier with practice. Here are some tips on how to document and analyze your dreams:

Step 1

After you have documented your dream, break down the dream documentation into small, easy-to-work-with paragraphs. Highlight or underline keywords or obvious symbols in each paragraph. These will be your primary symbols: those that stand out the most or repetitious symbols. Primary symbols include color references, repeated words you have written, and persons, places, or things that really stand out and grab your attention. As you move through the dream analysis, make sure you document symbols one time; for example, if you analyze a paragraph and you have a symbol of an acorn and you analyze the next paragraph and the acorn symbol repeats, list it once; however, make a note of how many times the symbol appears. Write the word "acorn" and put the number of times it appears next to the word for easy reference.

Step 2

Go back over each paragraph and see symbols you might have missed or overlooked. These symbols are equally important, but their messages are more subtle. Make a note of how many times symbols recur. The number of times a symbol repeats can be indicative of a potential timeframe for the fulfillment of prophetic dreams or it can refer to the corresponding energies of specific numbers.

Step 3

Review the dream for any repeated, obvious themes, and document the theme you identify. A theme is a clear, repetitious central idea, concept, or a message.

Step 4

Make a list of all the symbols, numbers, and themes. Leave enough room to jot down notes near each symbol pertaining to meaning. Look at your list. Do any of the symbols, themes, and numbers seem to go together? Do you see a repetitious message developing? If so, make a note of it. A theme or repetitious symbol can lead to the discovery of an archetypical pattern.

Step 5

Begin analyzing each symbol for its meaning. Analyze the symbols as standalone symbols only; in other words, consider what the symbols might mean outside the context of the dream.

Step 6

After reviewing all symbols from a standalone perspective, view the symbols within the context of the dream paragraph by paragraph. Do you find deeper meaning as you review the symbols again? Note your findings.

Step 7

See if any symbols indicate a dream archetype. Review the sections of this book on archetypes to learn more about what your dream message conveys.

Step 8

Meditate on your findings. Document any epiphanies or insights you have during your meditation sessions. Later, as you record more dreams, review all of your journal entries regularly to track repeating messages, patterns, and psychic dream successes. See the meditation template provided in this book as an example of the type of dream meditation you can use.

Sample Dream Analysis

Here is a dream sample that you can use to practice detecting symbols. The purpose of this exercise is to allow you time to hone your symbol decoding skills by strengthening your ability to tune into your intuitive understandings. Review the dream once, just as you would read a story. Then, with a discerning eye, read the dream sample again as you look for symbols and archetypes. There is no pressure to get it right because the meanings you derive come from your own understanding, experience, and culture.

Sample Dream:

I am walking in a crowded grocery store in the daytime. I am looking at produce and pick up a piece of fruit that looks like a pomegranate. While I am looking at the fruit, I notice a young man wandering around looking lost. He is very disheveled, but has a big smile and looks harmless. He asks me a question I cannot remember, but elaborates to ask me what I think of a toy horse he is going to get for his young son. He explains he needs to get his son a very nice gift to make up for the fact that he spontaneously left the boy to go to a different part of the state, where he was supposed to meet a man he connected with through the Internet. He traveled to meet this man, but the man never showed up. He is now returning and wants to make up for lost time by buying his son a very nice gift.

The man wants to know if I were a kid, would I think this toy horse would be enough to compensate for the son's hurt feelings over his (the father's) sudden disappearance. As he tells me the story, a young woman walks over to us. She is disheveled and has blond hair extending to the floor. She is wearing a ragged, long, green dress. She reminds me of a hippie. She is smiling and starts to share her opinion with the young father.

I am distracted from what she is saying because I am thinking I want to tell this man to put the horse away and get some food for his son, and to earn his trust back by being stable and doing things with him, not by giving him toys. I am trying to sort this thought out to tell the man, when I become aware that I am thinking this man must be pretty unstable to just suddenly take off on a quest to meet a stranger. I begin to explain my views to this man, in a nice way, and the three of us are standing around having a discussion about this man's path, when I realize it must look absurd to see three people standing around in the corner of the produce section, next to the entrance door, talking about our personal affairs. Then I wake up.

Now Process:

Highlight or underline any image, word, or section of the dream sample that seems significant to you.

Jot these in your journal, and begin listing each symbol.

Now look at the same dream documentation, only this time note the highlighted words as these are the symbols that you might consider choosing for analysis after documenting the dream.

Compare your findings with the symbols highlighted here.

Following this dream sample, you will find a listing of some of the symbols and the potential messages.

Take time to write out responses and surfacing reactions as you work through the guideline questions.

After working through the dream analysis and choosing identifiable symbols, view the sample dream analysis for comparison. It's best if you do not move ahead and look at the sample analysis before you do the exercise: this will help prevent the symbol identifications from influencing your own work.

- Use the following questions as an explorative guideline to connect to your personal bank of symbols and their meanings:
- What comes to mind when you think of the symbol you are viewing?
- How does the symbol make you feel?
- Does the symbol remind you of anything or is it similar to other symbols you have seen?
- Do you encounter the symbol often in your waking life and if so, what does the symbol mean to you when you do encounter it?
- What are the initial bodily responses you have when viewing the symbol?
- What colors or shapes does the symbol contain and what significance does the colors/shapes have for you?
- What meaning would your cultural or religious group give to the symbols and does the meaning differ from your personal interpretation?
- What are the normal and extraordinary attributes of the symbol, if any?
- Do specific symbols repeat throughout the dream or are there similar symbols that you can identify that might provide you with a running dream theme?

- Do you see any numbers in the dream?

Now that you have begun identifying symbols and exploring what they mean to you, here are some ideas on how you can elicit deeper meanings by considering the multiple layers a symbol can represent. Here you will find a few of the symbols in the sample dream and ways to look at the symbols from a different perspective. Once you review how to analyze symbols, return to the sample, and work on the remaining symbols in this exercise as a way of further instilling the lesson.

WALKING implies freedom, independence, and transition as one is traveling while he walks. Walking signifies a slow, intentional transition or progress without intervention or outside assistance, such as a vehicle. You might link walking with enjoyment, excitement, flexibility or being on a quest or mission. Walking requires self-motivation, self-direction and so, it implies control. The act of walking outside exposes one to the elements as well as other external dangers, and implies vulnerability, risk, earth, nature, and walking.

If you detest walking and associate it with poverty, hard work, pain, or difficulty, the dream carries a different message. The act of walking would be a symbol the subconscious would use to convey a different message to you. This is why it's essential that you become well versed in eliciting meaning from your cultural, personal, and subconscious databank of symbols in order to develop greater dream understandings.

Now look at more symbols from the sample dream. Remember, the meanings listed here are a result of the authors' interpretations and your own meanings will be quite different. The goal is not to have the same associations, but to recognize how to form the associations.

A CROWDED GROCERY STORE signifies constriction, discomfort, awkwardness, and the lack of desire to share your personal space, especially if you're uncomfortable in a crowd. The crowded store represents infiltration of privacy, the unwanted observation of others, and feelings of uneasiness and confinement. Your own reactions to crowds will play a key role in determining what a crowded store means. Consider that the grocery store is a place that can be associated with nurturing, exploration, close connections to nature (since you're standing in the produce aisle), and the harvest, which implies the cycle of death and rebirth. Sustenance through sacrifice of others, maternal energies, feeding, and nourishment are subtle associations with grocery store symbolism. The store is a place of display, images, perusing a variety to explore options to nurture one's self, and a marketplace infers community, a hub of action, trade, commerce, connection between natural processes, and social structures.

DAYTIME signifies growth, visibility, obviousness, ideas, and exposed truths. Being a period of light, the day represents illumination both in the physical and spiritual, clarity of thought, and understanding. This time period in dreams signifies public appearance and activity. Solar energies also suggest fatherhood, health, and personal identity.

PRODUCE has a double meaning, suggesting fruit and vegetables as well as the ability to "produce." Thus, produce is a symbol of fertility, abundance, natural cycles, nurturing, the mother goddess, productivity, harvest, fruits of one's labors, the peak of the cycle of life and growth (productivity at its peak before the temporary "ripeness" of one's fruits begins to "decay"), height of strength, health, healthy choices, feeding, and restoring to health through correct choices in foods.

POMEGRANATES corresponds to the goddess Persephone and, therefore, to the Maiden aspect of the feminine divine. The pomegranate represents something deceptively sweet or seductive, as in Persephone's confinement in the Underworld after eating the fruit before her return to Earth. The fruit corresponds with the color red, passion, excitement, natural sources of sweetness, or the seduction by something appearing harmless or innocent. The pomegranate connotes innocence, youth, new beginnings; the quick return of an estranged lover, temptation, and attraction both harmless and fatal. Finally, the pomegranate corresponds to the Roman goddess Concordia, a deity ruling peace, harmony, concord, and union; the seeds of the fruit are many and packed close together, and come to represent unity.

LOOKING is an act that signifies physical senses of observation and surface or superficial assessment, but it can also represent psychic vision, seeing beyond the surface, taking in one's surroundings, and increased awareness.

YOUNG MAN WANDERING signifies youth, independence, freedom, self direction, free will, journeys, quests, the Fool archetype, virility, strength, and wandering. It represents the failure of channeling one's ability toward a direct goal or the misuse of energy.

BEING LOST signifies adventure, lack of guidance, being closed off from divine guidance, squandering time and opportunities, or the lack of productivity. The condition of being lost signifies spontaneity, the act of stumbling onto new opportunities and can signify lost dreams.

BEING DISHEVELED signifies rejection of social norms, independence, carelessness, and the lack of consideration for social responsibility or societal expectations. It can signify the lack of observation or care of the self, the lack of attention to the physical body and, likewise, the lack of attention to the mundane or physical realms. The act of being disheveled signifies too much time spent on impractical tasks.

A BIG SMILE signifies joy, happiness, and friendliness. Sharing a smile with someone suggests that you're amiable, approachable, and that you're not a threat. However, a smile can be deceptive and seeing a smile in a dream can signify lying, the hiding of one's true intentions or the act of trying to prove one's innocence. A smile can represent the act of trying too hard to appease others, possible illusion, assessing for a potential threat, relying on the physical senses, or missing important cues that would otherwise allow you to spot "a wolf in sheep's clothing."

A QUESTION OR THE ACT OF QUESTIONING implies trust, consultation, seeking sage or expert advice, connecting with another or connecting concepts, or seeking guidance from an authority. The act of asking questions implies authority given to the dreamer, responsibility, being entrusted with guidance, and mentorship.

A SON signifies youth, innocence, male energy, new beginning or potential, possibilities coming into form, and undirected energy. This symbol represents impressionability, and being sought out for guidance on how to treat the son can imply partial or full responsibility for a coming up with a plan. This symbol within the context of the dream sample represents the act of molding new beginning or potential outcome that, in the immediate moment, needs your judgment or that requires that you weigh in to direct important matters.

A GIFT implies appeasement, but also manipulation. The gift, in this dream sample is used to disguise irresponsible behavior and to soothe hurt feelings. Thus, this type of gift is much like the Trojan Horse: a gift disguised as a diversion or distraction.

LEFT THE BOY is an action signifying abandonment, renouncing an idea early in its inception, forsaking responsibilities, and abandoning one's work or obligations.

NEGLECT signifies of the loss of a parent, immaturity, and the lack of social or ethical responsibility. However, this symbol might be a subtle repetition of the message behind being "disheveled," and might therefore be repeating the message of the lack of self-care as well.

A DIFFERENT PART OF THE STATE is a dream reference with a double meaning. A state is a location, but also references a state of mind or being. In this dream sample, a person did not go to a "different state" but to a different part of the state. Perhaps this signifies accessing a different level of consciousness or awareness. In addition, moving to a different location or establishing distance suggests the movement away from one's responsibilities or obligations.

A MAN signifies maturity, animus, active and projective forces and development. A man represents a level of growth beyond the son. In this case, the "man wasn't there or never showed up," so the theme of abandonment is repetitious and could imply karmic repercussions. The father who abandons the son is also abandoned, and has to return to the beginning (son).

Now that you have completed your own process of compiling symbols and meanings from this sample, and gotten a view of some alternative symbolic interpretations, you might be getting more comfortable with symbolic language. To promote fluency in the language of symbols further, try the following exercise.

Metaphorically Speaking

Below is a list of words that are not literally connected. In your journal, experiment with these words, first individually, then as a group.

To start, take each word and complete the sentence:

"_____is a_____."

For example, the word "dog" can appear in a sentence like: "A dog is a loyal guardian." There is no right and wrong answer. This exercise is practice in accessing the subconscious through free association. Experiment with the following words:

Dog	Pickle	Sister	Stamp
Trolley	Dollar	Railroad	Ring
Hammer	Movie	Bed	

After you experiment with forming associations with the individual words, try to weave them into a sentence by connecting as many words as you can in whatever order you choose. For example, "My sister's dog jumped out of the bed and chased a trolley." Play with making several sentences so you can explore word variations and different meanings. Put several sentences together to make a brief paragraph.

Next, pretend this paragraph is a dream narrative. Now you can see why it would not need to make logical sense, as dreams can seem illogical, change, and use unusual references. For the sake of gaining greater skill at discerning symbolic language, go back to the paragraph you created. Pick out words or references that have symbolic meaning as if it were a dream. For each, consider the metaphors listed above and add further depth to your symbolic interpretation of the paragraph. As this example is a fictitious dream, it will be most useful to elicit the process of interpreting and linking symbols together. Complete this exercise in your dream journal and you will be closer to recognizing and analyzing symbols more easily!

Finally, do not forget to practice interpreting dreams you have while reading this book. It's never too early to start recording your dreams. You can always complete the in depth interpretation steps later, once you write your dreams in your journal.

Recognizing Symbols and Archetypes

Yet it is in our idleness, in our dreams, that the submerged truth sometimes comes to the top.

Virginia Woolf

A symbol is an image or a pictorial representation of an idea or concept. For instance, the image of a bald eagle might represent the idea of freedom or the color red symbolizes danger or rage. Symbols appear in dreams because the subconscious speaks to the dreamer through images and sound presented through the dream narrative; this allows the subconscious to convey rich imagery with intense, symbolic meaning quickly. Dreams are much like visual and audible poetry; people can interpret dreams, and every interpretation varies depending upon the interpreter.

The analysis of dream imagery can sometimes provide subconscious messages that can warn of potential dangers. You can receive lessons from the subconscious that can educate, illuminate, inspire, and lend to spiritual growth. Decoding dream messages can prove a cumbersome task, especially for those who have a strong focus on the intake of messages in verbal or written expressions in literal forms because dream messages, particularly those that are not clearly prophetic, are not always literal. Analyze symbols, images, storylines, settings, situations, and words you see in your dreams so you can use the wisdom of the higher self, the universe, and divine for the betterment of your waking life.

Symbols are an abstract language, and just like oral and written languages, symbols have meanings profoundly shaped by usage, cultural influences, social context, and the context in which the symbols appear in your dreams. Therefore, learning how to interpret dreams is a practice that you should approach as if you're learning a new language.

The first mistake that many people make when new to dream interpretation is turning to dream dictionaries for symbol definitions. While dream dictionaries are helpful in offering some universal understandings of dream symbols, it's far too easy to become overly reliant on the use of dictionaries in an effort to analyze dream imagery. A sole dependence on dream dictionaries results in the abandonment of the opportunity to master the unique and exclusive language that your subconscious mind uses to communicate with you. At the same time, you're missing the chance to tap into your intuitive understandings of dream symbols.

While symbols have universal meanings that you can easily uncover in a quality dream dictionary, those meanings are not absolute; all dictionaries will prove beneficial in learning meanings derived from language, but they are just one tool for discovering meaning. Another disadvantage you face when you become dependent on dream dictionaries is that you're really getting a definition of a symbol defined by someone else. Ultimately, you're sometimes accessing a diluted version of a symbol's meaning or the bare bones definition of what a symbol might mean instead of a personalized, more informative definition of the symbols you're evaluating. If you want to take dream interpretive work seriously, you're going to have to prepare for hard work ahead of learning about the idiosyncratic, sometimes eccentric methods of communication your subconscious mind uses to communicate with you.

Dreams will present you with major and minor symbols. Major symbols are those that are repetitive or are symbols that exist within recurring themes within the dream, with several symbols that contain similar meanings working as major symbols. Minor symbols within a dream's contexts are those that seem less significant than repetitious symbols or are those symbols that only appear one or two times within the entire dream narrative.

The best way to improve your dream interpretation skills is to practice interpreting symbols each day. The more you work with symbols, the greater your awareness of symbols and their subtle meanings becomes. Interpreting dreams is a lot like interpreting the symbolism in short stories, movies, art, and books. That being the case, you can improve your ability to identify and interpret dream symbols by spending time viewing art, watching movies, and doing more reading and writing on a regular basis. Start your own journal of dream symbols where you document what symbols mean to you and only you. Do not rely solely on the symbol interpretations of another. Symbols are a lot like poetry. You're the best person to interpret the symbols you see.

At the same time, you should dedicate yourself to improving your vocabulary; doing so will improve the word and image arsenal that your subconscious mind can use for communicating with you. Bear in mind that language is limiting, especially when you're trying to describe the often-abstract symbols you will encounter in your dreams. That being the case, you will want to have a strong hold on a good vocabulary so that when you're documenting your dreams, you will have an easier time of describing what you see.

Understanding Archetypes

So what is an archetype? Suppose the magickal practitioner sees a circle with a dot in the center and knows this image to represent the Sun. The graphic is the image meaning the Sun, but the term Sun then has symbolic associations that are not limited to the magickal practitioner, but are also widely understood, transcending cultures. The symbolic meanings that span numerous cultures include light, health, vitality, success, luck, growth, strength, and life-giving heat as well as danger in excess. Since humans the world over have experience with the Sun, its symbolism becomes more universal than any ordinary icon. It transcends cultural limitation and becomes an archetype.

An archetype is a symbol that has such universally recognized meaning that it crosses cultural boundaries and speaks to the spirit of human experience. The word archetype comes from the Greek "arkhetupon" meaning "primitive model."[1] Psychologist Carl Gustav Jung, during the early 1900s, describes imagery and symbols derived from the collective unconscious and used the term. An archetype is a prototype; the symbol can be a character, idea, situation, setting, image, plot, or theme. Archetypes consist of imagery, situations, or conditions that all people can easily relate to because the symbols represent conditions that almost everyone experiences; the archetypical images presented in dreams are symbols you can interpret, extrapolate, and apply in your waking life.

Archetypes are symbols or patterns consisting of universal, common, or shared meaning; the archetypes you derive from dreams have a general meaning that is similar for many people, but the meaning can be a bit different for you personally. Consider when you are reading a book that the story includes symbols with universal meanings. You bring your own knowledge and experience to the story and this allows you to take away a personalized meaning from the story you have read. The same rule applies to dream interpretative work; your dream imagery presents you with symbols that are universal with common meanings that anyone can decode and use in a meaningful way, but it's your own knowledge, life experiences, and the meanings you assign to specific symbols that are what personalize your dream interpretations.

Archetypes persist as immutable symbols; their general meaning does not change over the course of time. These symbols have profound meaning richly condensed in the form of themes, imagery, settings, situations, ideas, and characters. When you connect with or encounter archetypical energies, you can immediately empathize with the energies, even if you have not actually directly endured the experiences, situations, or conditions represented by the archetypes in question. Connections with archetypes are easy to make because of the ubiquitous nature of the symbols: cultures share these symbols as they persist unaltered through the generations. Archetypical patterns reside in the collective unconscious where anyone can tap into them at any time. The universality of archetypes is what makes these symbols so pervasive and so easily understood by those who identify with them.

For the novice dream interpreter, the best time to start working with symbols is now. Start by purposefully looking for symbols and archetypes. After reading this section, put this book aside for a moment and grab the nearest newspaper or magazine. Scan the document for pictures you would consider icons. Whether you choose a company logo or the image/photo of a celebrity, try to become conscious of the visual symbols and images used to convey a message.

When you have identified several symbols, reflect on what you associate with the images you have chosen. If you have chosen the image of a celebrity, is the person someone you admire and would consider a hero or is the individual a symbol of excess and self-destruction? If you have chosen a corporate logo, is the image a symbol of faith in a good product? Do you associate the logo with greed-based or environmentally harmful practices? Consider the reactions you have to the images so you can begin to sense the subtle system of communication that exists between your conscious and subconscious. Make note of your bodily reactions; do any of the images you're viewing make your breathing more rapid and shallow? Does your body tense up or recoil when viewing the images chosen? Do you lean in closer to the image because it's visually pleasing?

After noting your bodily reactions to the images, note your emotional responses. It's a good idea to note your mood before viewing the images and comparing your notes with how you feel after you view certain symbols. Consider whether they conjure up specific emotions or memories.

Practice looking for symbols daily. You might want to keep a small memo pad with you at all times so you can take note of symbols that catch your eye, call to you, or repeatedly appear. Work with the symbols you find most meaningful and continue to document what the images mean to you and how they make you feel. The goal is to connect with the symbols and to increase your awareness of their pervasiveness.

All symbols contain two levels of meaning. For example, a broom might make you think of things like cleanliness or, on a conscious level, you might remember the need to sweep your kitchen. On a subconscious level, the image of a broom might come to mean sweeping or clearing away negative energies, cleansing and the purification of space or the self. The two levels of meaning associated with symbols remain separate, but parallel until you, through proactive and mindful processes, connect them.

Make a habit of noting symbols in your notebook or dream journal. You can identity icons, such as logos, a pictorial image of the caduceus, or the symbols can be those you discover in stories, movies, books, and other media. Begin the process of noting symbols and calling forth their meanings and personal attributes from the subconscious.

Connecting Dream Symbols and Waking Synchronicity

Dreaming or awake, we perceive only events that have meaning to us.
Jane Roberts

If the subconscious conveys meaning through symbols, then learning to comprehend the sentence of symbolic communication requires the recognition of synchronicity. Synchronicity refers to encountering information (in this case symbols) in a manner that may seem coincidental on the surface, but which yields a greater depth of meaning by assuming that all encounters are intentional and not random.

To understand this, let's assume a young man has a dream that he is playing bagpipes. Assume he has no Celtic heritage in his family and disregards the dream from having any personal value. Let's imagine that he does not care for the sound of bagpipes, they remind him of the noxious alarm of a fire engine. Assuming this young man does not know the value of thinking symbolically (if he did he may stop to consider what type of "alarm" his subconscious is cuing by sending him an image he associates with deafening alerts) and that he quickly forgets this dream. The next afternoon he is browsing channels on TV and sees a commercial for a Scottish festival, featuring someone playing bagpipes. Perhaps he takes notice and recalls his dream. Later that evening, he hears bagpipe music while flipping radio stations. The next day he overhears a conversation among coworkers having to do with a marching band and his coworker's father playing the bagpipes.

By now if this individual were inclined to think symbolically, he could follow his initial symbol, the bagpipes, and begin to elicit some meaning like loudness, alert, disruption, emergency, alarm, or annoyance, based on his associations with this symbol. He mentions this chain of events to his mother on the phone that evening and she informs him that her brother, his uncle, played bagpipes as a young man. The subject of our story then shares that he never cared for this instrument as it reminds him of a loud fire engine. His mother tells him, "Speaking of fire engines: your uncle's apartment had a small fire last night, but no one got hurt." An instance like this is representative of synchronicity, where two apparently concurrent events prove to hold more meaning than mere coincidence can otherwise explain.

Note any synchronicities you experience: these events are the universe's way of communicating with you through symbolic images, conditions, situations, and events. Document them in your dream journal. You may even find that you begin to experience more synchronicities the more you pay attention to them.

CHAPTER 5

COMMON DREAM
ARCHETYPES

*All human beings are also dream beings. Dreaming ties all
mankind together.*

Jack Kerouac

With practice, you will begin recognizing that
archetypes are, and have been, all around you, from
the time you heard your first fairy tale, right up to the
classic literary works, to the current fiction you enjoy. In esoteric circles,
the archetypes live in the Tarot, astrology, myth, elemental magick and
animal totems, as well as other forms of creative representations of
common human experiences.

Throughout the symbols shared in this book, you will see a reference
to the shadow of an archetype. The shadow, most easily considered the
negative side of an archetype, is not so easily defined. This makes it vital
for us to explore the concept of the shadow as well as the symbolism
associated with light and darkness. Light carries significant symbolism,
ranging from awareness or enlightenment, knowledge, sight, vision,
inspiration, understanding, and the transcendence to health and vitality.
Light is often considered good or positive, while darkness is considered
bad or negative, but the latter associations form a narrow, limiting view.
In fact, both light and darkness can have positive and negative attributes,
and the same is true for an archetype and its shadowed aspect.

Light is helpful because it brings the comfort of full view, but can be
blinding, burning, or too concentrated, as is the case when one has plenty
of knowledge, but lacks the wisdom or ability to apply the knowledge
in useful ways, or when one seeks illumination in service of their own
mission only, while blocking out a more holistic perspective. Likewise,
darkness implies the need to rely on internal processes like intuition,
faith, and in a literal and figurative sense, feeling one's way through the
dark, in order to perceive information and guidance.

Light is projective, bringing it a masculine, active, driving force.
Darkness is contemplative, receptive, subtle, intuitive and in that sense,

feminine in energy. Darkness yields information on a subconscious and subtle level: information that one must cultivate or work harder to attain, while light provides information directly, but requires little effort on the part of the seeker. Darkness requires rumination, interpretation, and individual intuition. The darkness brings deception and illusion as things can appear different than they are with limited light. Thus, the forces of light and dark, like the archetype and its shadow, work together to bring awareness of a full reality. At the same time, light, and dark, the archetype and the shadow, complete each other.

The Hero, Warrior, and Quest

The hero is a legendary figure appearing in stories and myths originating from all cultures around the world. Many types of heroes exist, including the warrior, romantic, unwilling, and tragic. Your dream symbols indicate the kind of hero archetype you're connecting with from the collective unconscious.

The hero is a brave individual who faces challenges. The hero usually endures dramatic changes and faces major obstacles. As the hero's journey progresses, the simplicity of life is lost; the hero must embrace the new complexities he faces willingly or he will be compelled to deal with the encumbrances presented along the way: in this way, the hero is much like a child transitioning from youth to adulthood.

The hero must ready himself to confront challenges with unwavering will, lest his challenges persist or reappear with even greater intensity. The journey of the hero usually results in the individual coming full circle and gaining wisdom through experience. However, the quest does not always result in positive outcomes, since there are heroes both celebrated and tragic.

Most heroes have supernatural or unusual conditions involving their engendering and are sometimes of divine or royal blood. An individual taking on the attributes of this archetype will often separate from friends and loved ones as they enter into new situations with new people or surroundings: this puts the hero in the uncomfortable position of a stranger in a strange land. Heroes enter into a quest after physical and/or emotional trauma, while others enter into the quest through circumstance or obligation. Individuals serving as this archetype commonly have powerful weapons or preternatural powers and/or receive assistance from supernatural or divine beings. In some cases, special guardians, animal companions, and mentors come to the aid of the questing hero.

Sometimes the hero serves as a scapegoat as imposed obligations or inherited difficulties compel the hero to partake of a quest involving atonement from the transgressions of others from earlier generations. If the hero is compelled to rectify past transgressions, especially those committed by others, the hero might feel victimized; however, he can find power in developing a willingness to complete the quest and can thereby eradicate the sense of victimization.

The warrior hero is more aggressive than the hero who takes on a quest for love, self-discovery, or to fulfill inherited obligations; yet, the warrior can harness violent actions for positive means. The hero as warrior is highly disciplined; the individual has mastered skills essential for survival, and the warrior fully understands his own physical/psychological boundaries or restrictions. Nevertheless, the goal-oriented warrior fearlessly proceeds with the quest and is not afraid during the attempt to transcend imposed human limitations on the body, mind, and spirit.

While on the quest, a hero sometimes faces unforeseen interruptions or temptations, and the disruptions or enticements will seemingly threaten the hero's forward progression or success. The enticements or distractions the hero must contend with are typically tests of determination, wit, ethics, or physical/spiritual fortitude. The journey can involve an array of enterprises including tests, trials, and tribulations resulting in purgation, atonement, and a symbolic awakening, reawakening, or rebirth. When the quest concludes, the hero returns to the place where he began, bringing with him new insights, blessings, or revelations serving, not only the hero, but the entire tribe, village, town, city, or community.

The Shadow Hero encompasses the individual as a social pariah, recluse, and the individual that society expels due to unforgivable transgressions or physical/psychological differences. Thus, society often marginalizes the Shadow Hero. The hero in pursuit of vengeance or self-punishment also represents the shadow aspect of the hero archetype. Likewise, the warrior who channels physical aggression for baneful purposes is yet another example of the hero colored by the darkened aspects of the shadow. Even the hero as the lover has a darkened aspect, particularly if the lines between love and lust or passion and obsession are crossed.

One of the most well known heroes in the Greek mythos is Perseus, the son of the Greek god Zeus and Danaë, the daughter of King Acrisius.

According to some stories, Acrisius consults Pythia, the Delphian oracle, who tells Acrisius that if his daughter has a son, the boy will grow into a man and kill him. Acrisius decides to lock Danaë up in a building made of stone and brass to keep her from having a child, but Danaë gains the attentions of Zeus, who appears to her and impregnates her.[1] Danaë gives birth to Perseus and when Acrisius discovers this, he casts his daughter and grandchild into a chest, and out to sea, so the hand of fate is a significant role in Perseus' life.

In some accounts, Perseus's mother marries Polydectes, the King of Seriphhos,[2] and this results in Perseus being raised in Athena's temple. Later, when he is grown, Polydectes hosts a gathering where all guests are to bring him horses. He invites Perseus to the event, knowing he has no horses to offer him.[3] Perseus attends the gathering, but he cannot give him the gift he requests and promises Polydectes Medusa's head.[4] Perseus embarks on a quest fraught with peril and danger, but receives supernatural assistance through the helmet of Hades, Hermes' sickle, Athena's mirror, a bag, and winged sandals.[5]

The Shadow Hero is in the story of Oedipus, who is the son of Lacius and Jocasta: the king and queen of Thebes.[6] Prior to his birth, the oracle at Delphi warns Lacius that he would have a son who would one day murder his father and marry his mother. To avoid the prophecy, Lacius and Jocasta have the boy's feet pinned and bound and have a servant abandon him in the wilderness.[7] Oedipus is found and is raised by the King and Queen of Corinth. When he becomes a man, he consults the Oracle of Delphi and is told of his evil fate.[8] In an effort to avoid fulfilling the prophecy, Oedipus decides to leave Corinth and heads for Thebes. On the way there, he encounters a stranger who enrages him and he kills him: in doing so, he unwittingly kills Lacius.[9] Later, without knowing Jocasta is his birth mother, he marries Lacius' widow, and the prophecy is fulfilled.[10] The story of the tragic hero serves as a warning of, not only the powerful role of fate, but of the danger in allowing the full emergence of the uncontrolled shadow self or in not finding a balance between the self and the shadow.

Dream Meaning

Since heroes have remarkable or questionable conditions involving their births, the transference of this idea to dream interpretations indicates new beginnings on the horizon, particularly of an unexpected origin. You should keep alert and watch for sudden or surprise opportunities. Likewise, the iconic representation of seeking out one's origins in this archetype could signify that a journey of self-discovery is in the offing: this journey may lead to a greater understanding of the self and a deeper connection with the universe or divine. Bear in mind that the journey you face will most likely be fraught with obstacles, tests, and challenges along the way. When entering the quest, you might feel like a hero who is the stranger in a strange land, as it's not unusual for new opportunities to present new conditions or to bring about the entrance of new people in your life.

The Hero archetype serves as a symbol suggesting that you will have an opportunity to enter into a state of becoming. Since this archetype represents those who endure physical or emotional trauma, you should prepare yourself for change, bearing in mind that not all change is comfortable. If your dream symbols are pointing to heroic archetype energies or patterns, then you will face a quest in the near future or you stand at the precipice of dramatic change in your waking life. Like the hero in myths and folklore, you will have unexpected or unforeseen assistance, either from others around you or through spiritual avenues. Consider that any resistance to the coming change will only cause you greater difficulties. While the journey you're about to embark on may prove trying, you can move toward successful outcomes provided you move ahead by taking the moral high road and accepting the sudden appearance of beneficial assistance along the way.

When the Shadow Hero connects with you in dreams, it's a call to question your motives and to examine whether or not the cost of the quest is too high for you or others. It's time for you to determine if you're creating situations for the sole purpose of getting even with someone or if you're seeking to punish yourself by enduring unnecessary tests or trials. Vengeance serves to poison the one who carries it. Likewise, self-punishment through self-imposed penance is a futile endeavor: one that will ultimately offer little to no relief of guilt, self-reproach, or remorse.

When the Shadow Hero shares its message with you in dreams, it's a good time to reflect on fate/destiny and its role in your life. If you feel connected to the dark aspect of the Shadow Hero as warrior, you should take care not to confuse the positive use of assertiveness and aggressive action with unnecessary hostility and abuse as you proceed through your journey. If connecting to the Hero as the lover within the shadow aspect, you would do well to monitor existing and future relationships for hints of obsession and codependency.

MUNDANE DREAM MANIFESTATIONS: This archetype may appear in dreams of leadership or visions involving focus on the self or a single character in the dream. Dreams of quests (desired or not) and dreams where you star in your own narrative are additional examples. If a character is the sole focus of the dream, note what traits/role this person embodies, as it might indicate what you should invite into your life.

Connecting with the Archetype

What obstacles are you struggling with in your daily life?

Are you at the beginning of a rite of passage or initiation?

Are you ready to face new challenges as a willing hero or are you trying to avoid immanent change/transition as an unwilling hero?

Are you afraid of change?

Are you ready to fight for what is rightfully yours?

Are you prepared to meet with your destiny?

Will you be the ethical hero in your own life and keep your morals intact or will you move forward by overcoming obstacles at the cost of your own dignity, self-worth, or at the cost of others?

Magickal Correspondences at a Glance

COLORS: Red, white

CHAKRA: Root

DAY: Tuesday, Thursday, and Sunday

DEITIES: Ares, Mars, Odin

ENERGIES: Masculine

ELEMENT: Air, Fire

HERBS/INCENSE: Ginger, rosemary, sage, anything spicy/aromatic

MOON PHASE: Waxing

NUMBERS: 0, 6, 7, 8, 12

PLANETARY: Jupiter, Mars, Sun

STONES: Carnelian, white/fire opal, pyrite

TAROT: The Fool, The Devil, The Hanged Man, Knights

TOTEMS: Lion, dog, ram

ZODIAC: Aries, Leo, Sagittarius

The Judge and Critic

The archetype of the fair, understanding, and compassionate mediator is The Judge. The judge weighs all sides of an issue before making a decision. A judge examines, considers, and formulates an opinion, and the decision made will induce consequences. If this archetype is rising up from the collective unconscious to connect to you in dreams, you might soon face a decision that will have intense ramifications or you might be the subject of someone else's judgments.

Tied to the archetype of The Judge is The Critic, who bears the message of cynicism, one that either is tolerated due to absurdity of appearance or performance, such as the court jester, or is viewed as on the fringe. The Critic tends to hold an unpopular place in myth and stories as this person communicates what others may fear or believe, but do not want to say, and likely expresses views that question authority or challenge the *status quo*.

This archetype is associated with King Solomon, a figure honored for his wisdom and fairness. For example, a biblical story about the king reveals his discernment and ability for uncovering the truth. Two harlots approach Solomon, both claiming to be the mother of a child, so Solomon demands that someone bring him a sword to split the child in half so that one half of the child could be given to each of the women.[11] While the judgment seems unjust and cruel, Solomon's ruling causes the biological mother to concede to giving up her child to the other woman to prevent the child's harm; this helped Solomon determine who was telling the truth. The child was spared and returned to his birth mother. In the latter story, it's easy to see why The Judge archetype represents individuals who are cunning, clever, witty, and highly intelligent.

In myth, you can identify with Judge archetypical energies through depictions of the Egyptian god, Anubis. In ancient Egyptian funerary scenes, the deceased's deeds are judged by several judges, including the jackal-headed God, Anubis, who weighs the heart of the dead against the feather of Ma'at, the Goddess of Truth.[12] If the deceased's heart is lighter than the feather, then the individual is judged as one who has lived a righteous life and joins the god Osiris in the afterlife. If the heart is heavier than the feather, it indicates that the deceased lived a life filled with evil deeds, and Ammit, the Eater of the Dead, would consume the heart and soul of those deemed unworthy for eternal life.[13]

The first cynic, Diogenese, was a Greek philosopher and extreme ascetic who rejected all mainstream traditions and social graces to live, what he considered, a sincere life. He roamed the cities questing after an "honest man" and had no problem voicing his cynical and critical views to all he encountered, including Alexander the Great. Other critic/cynic archetypes in history include Jonathan Swift and Mark Twain. In legends and myth, the critic is typically the court jester: the only one allowed to criticize the king, because after all, one could rationalize, he is mad.

Mundane modern critics are bloggers, whistleblowers, and documentary makers who expose and criticize injustice. Spiritual and esoteric critic voices exist in the doubting messages emerging from the subconscious and from archetypical characters who bring messages of doubt or harsh reality, like the rational-minded onlooker from the story of the "Emperor's New Clothes" who rains on everyone's parade when proclaiming the nudity of the Emperor.

The Shadow Judge is in stories like the "Judgment of Paris"; Zeus hosts a celebration honoring the marriage of Thetis and Peleus, but does not invite Eris, the Goddess of Discord.[14] Feeling slighted, Eris decides to attend the banquet anyway, bringing with her a golden apple inscribed with the words "for the fairest one."[15] She tosses the apple into the midst of the celebration where the gods are gathered; the goddesses Aphrodite, Athena, and Hera, all believing they are the fairest, try to claim the apple.[16] Zeus is asked to judge who is fairest, but he decides to pass off the role of judge to Paris, a mortal; the three goddesses stand before Paris on Mount Ida, all of them nude so that their physical beauty can be judged.[17] All of the goddesses try to bribe Paris, but Aphrodite is the most persuasive, promising him Helen, the wife of Menelaus, and Paris chooses her as the fairest of all goddesses.[18] As agreed, Helen falls in love with Paris and he takes her to Troy; the result of this agreement leads to the Trojan War.[19] Through this myth, you can begin to understand the true nature of the Shadow Judge: one who makes decisions that are not necessarily fair, but those formed through manipulative means or for the purposes of personal gain.

Dream Meaning

Prophetically, this archetype might indicate an impending litigation or legal action. It might suggest that situations will arise that will call for your sound judgment. When your dreams indicate The Judge archetype is connecting with you, it's time to look at the type of energies you have been fostering in your waking hours. You will want to begin to question your integrity in given situations and to make sure that you're progressing forward while putting out the most positive energies possible.

The depictions of the Judge can serve as a message that truth will be questioned or that decisive action is necessary. In contrast, the shadow aspect of The Judge becomes one who wields his or her power unfairly, violates ethics, or offers biased and unfair decisions. In the lens of the inner critic, the Shadow Judge is one that is overly critical or too harsh with personal judgments of people or situations; in this darkened aspect, the Shadow Judge iconic energy is one that heralds the misuse of authoritative power to the detriment of the self or others. If your dream points to the dark energies of the Shadow Judge, your subconscious mind could be warning you to be wary of flattery, promises, persuasive actions, and to wrongly influenced judgments.

MUNDANE DREAM MANIFESTATIONS: Court proceedings, evaluation, being weighed or critiqued or dreams of receiving feedback or using analysis are some of the types of dreams that invoke the meaning of The Judge. Cleaning, sorting, organizing, labeling, categorizing, discarding things, or dreams of judgmental acts or critical people represent The Judge archetype in dreams.

Connecting with the Archetype

Are you judging a troubling situation fairly in your waking hours?

Are you ethical and forthright about the judgments you make?

Are personal biases tainting your judgment?

Are you compassionate in your judgments or when dealing with others?

Are you being too quick to judge yourself or others?

Are you too lenient or strict in a given situation and are you ready to impart an unyielding action, decision, or forgiveness when required?

Should you be in a position of judgment at all or should you cast aside your judgments and go with the flow?

Are you being too self-critical to the point of hindering your own success or spiritual evolution?

Are you critical of others?

Magickal Correspondences at a Glance

COLORS: Purple, blue, black, white
CHAKRA: Third eye
DAY: Thursday
DEITIES: Anubis, Ma'at, Zeus, Venus
ENERGIES: Judge/Feminine, Critic/Masculine
ELEMENT: Air, Earth
HERBS/INCENSE: Apple, hazel, laurel, lily, oak, Solomon's seal
MOON PHASE: Full Moon
NUMBERS: 2, 7, 9, 11
PLANETARY: Jupiter, Uranus, Venus, Saturn
STONES: Agate, lapis
TAROT: Justice, The Chariot, Judgement
TOTEMS: Owl, fox, serpent
ZODIAC: Aquarius, Libra, Sagittarius

The Hunter or Huntress

The Hunter or Huntress archetype symbolizes sustenance and nurturing; this might seem contrary to the image of hunter as one who kills, but often the chief goal is gathering food. The hunter and huntress represent great skill, knowledge, and cunning, since hunting involves understanding how to survive in the wild. The hunter/huntress is brave, since the individual must step outside of civilization and enter into the wilderness: a place of mysteries and danger. The hunter/huntress faces potential death.

If the Hunter archetype has a positive nature, he kills only when necessary and wastes nothing of the kill. If dealing with the shadow aspect of the Hunter, he kills for the thrill of the chase, not for the need for the life-sustaining gift that the hunt provides. The movement from civilization's boundaries into wilderness heralds change and symbolizes the willful/ unwillful transition from innocence to experience. The hunter/huntress leaves the protective confines of what is known or knowable and enters into the dangerous world of the wilderness or unknown.

This archetype is a symbol of balance, as hunters are necessary to ensure that animal populations do not run rampant or out of control. A loss in this essential balance can result in the wilderness encroaching on civilization.

Likewise, when a hunter kills too many animals (not for sustenance, but for the sake of killing), a substantial loss of wildlife results. For centuries, hunters have valued, not the kill, but the animal killed, going as far as to identify with the prey by valuing the prey as sacred. Thus, the Shadow Hunter/Huntress is one that takes without consideration of fairness, balance, or need; this dark aspect points to the myriad hazards associated with the hunt, whether the risks are physical or spiritual.

In Greek mythology, Artemis, the goddess of the hunt, encounters the Theban hero and hunter Actaeon, who discovers her in the woods while bathing. Amazed by her immense beauty, Actaeon stops and watches her bathe.[20] When Artemis discovers Actaeon watching her, it infuriates the goddess, and she curses him, turning him into a wild stag so he cannot speak of what he saw.[21] Actaeon does not immediately realize his transformation until he sees his reflection in a nearby body of water.[22] As Actaeon gazes at his reflection and wonders what he should do, his own hunting dogs spot him, hunt him down, and tear him to pieces.[23] Having not heeded the words of the goddess, Actaeon falls victim to a self-induced punishment.

The story suggests the need for the individual to remain ever self-aware; Actaeon did not recognize his own physical metamorphosis until seeing his reflection, suggesting a disconnection between the physical self (body), and internal perception (mind). The myth indicates how quickly the hunter can become the hunted or just how fast desire sours. Conversely, the archetype of Hunter does not have to suggest a literal hunt; in many myths, there are stories abound of heroes that hunt for their origins or solutions to challenges. Thus, the Hunter/Huntress archetype can suggest the inward or external search for the self or the act of hunting for origins, knowledge, or resolutions.

Dream Meaning

When the Hunter/Huntress archetype appears in dreams, it could connote an upcoming rite of passage or initiation into the mysteries. The dream symbols may indicate a need for courage or bravery or the willingness to step out of one's comfort zone to ensure mundane/spiritual progression as well. Hunter energies can indicate physical/spiritual seeking. Hunting involves exploration, inquest, and scrutiny. It's time to reflect, not only on what you're searching for, but also on how you're searching. An evaluation of your heart's desire is necessary and your assessment should include an examination of whether what you hold sacred is all that it appears to be.

Question whether the hunt is one for the purposes of physical/spiritual nourishment and sustenance or for the personal quest for power. To hunt for something suggests the pursuit of excitement and adventure. There is a play of power involved in hunting as the hunter seeks to dominate prey. The appearance of this archetype in dreams may therefore point to power plays in waking life or it might indicate the desire for fun and adventure. When the Hunter/Huntress archetype connects with the dreamer, it might be a calling for the individual to develop greater self-awareness, to listen to the intuitive guidance of the higher self or divine, and to consider whether the hunt will result in all consuming or destructive ends or not.

MUNDANE DREAM MANIFESTATIONS: Dreams of pursuit, chases, hiding, hunting, shopping, or acquiring food, resources, or knowledge are visions originating with the Hunter archetype. This archetype appears in vision of wild animals, forest settings, interacting with hunted animals, or dreams of being wanted by the law. Further, the Hunter/Huntress archetype exists in dreams of pursuit from a law enforcement standpoint as well as the act of pursuing others.

Connecting with the Archetype

What do you need in your life for spiritual/physical sustenance?

Are you being "called to the hunt" in a situation where you must act for the greater good of your friends, family, or community?

Do you doubt your ability to survive a particular situation, despite your level of skill and knowledge?

Are you fearful of necessary change?

Are you being resourceful, wasting nothing available to you?

Are you pursuing something for the wrong reasons?

Are you pursuing your desires in a balanced way?

Do you have a strong sense of self-awareness?

Magickal Correspondences at a Glance

COLORS: Red, green, brown
CHAKRA: Root, third eye
DAY: Mondays, Thursdays
DEITIES: Artemis, Diana, Cernunnos

ENERGIES: Masculine
ELEMENT: Fire
HERBS/INCENSE: Cedar, cinnamon, yarrow, sage
MOON PHASE: Waxing, Full, Waning
NUMBERS: 3, 4, 13
PLANETARY: Jupiter, Moon
STONES: Hematite, moonstone, onyx
TAROT: Temperance, Death, Knight of Swords
TOTEMS: Dog, fox, stag, wolf
ZODIAC: Sagittarius

The Devil and Trickster

In many traditions, the Devil is the ideal Trickster because of his deceptive nature. He is as an entity that seeks to obtain the human soul or to prevent one's salvation and usually does so by either tempting the individual to sin or by offering the individual favors with the soul as payment. Conversely, in some stories, deities that have been demonized and identified as devil-like figures are often beings of light and enlightenment.

The Devil is one of many identities, including Satan, Lucifer, Mephistopheles, and The Beast. He is intelligent, sly, shrewd, and calculating, with one of his most frightening features being his charismatic and alluring nature, since human beings are oft tempted in one form or another by what encompasses their own undoing. In his dark guise, he is the nemesis, archenemy, adversary, foil, or antihero. This archetype embodies seduction, allure, addiction, enslavement, delusion, and destruction. It's the antithesis of what compromises one's values and identity. This archetype signals the lost mission; a committed quest or venture becoming a detour of pleasure and gratification, or the ultimate distraction from our larger purpose, much like the crack in the foundation or the termite that eats away at the structure of a home.

The Devil or Adversary as an archetype is not limited to Satan or any specific figure. It's the very energy of rebellion, challenge, and compulsion. The Devil represents the quest for more money, fame, pleasure, and the gratification of the ego, not the fabric that connects one to the Divine and to society. In the mundane, this archetype is the energy of addictions of all kinds: from drug and alcohol, to food, sex, and money—anything desired insatiably. It's the lust that drives greed, compulsion, or obsession, manifesting in business, relationships, material acquisition, and in any realm where you seek to have more, only to lose track of why having more of anything is so important in the first place.

The Devil is insidious, the enemy within, the Shadow and the repressed side of the personality that represents our darkest longings and desires, even those we do not want to face or acknowledge. While the Devil's archetypical energy can be a creative, generating force, it's boundlessness and its repression can cause greater turmoil and havoc.

In many ancient stories, humans and divine beings are not portrayed as wholly good or entirely evil, but a mixture of both; it was under this paradigm that the concept of evil was understood and ultimately shaped the modern understanding of the Devil's characteristics; representations of the devil are based on a merging of pre-Christian and Christian beliefs. Thus, there are a number of representations of devil-like beings in cultures from around the world.

Your view on The Devil will shape the meaning of the symbols that you associate with the archetype. In Judeo-Christian beliefs, the name Lucifer is the proper name of Satan before the fall, but in Greek mythos, Phosphorus (Phosphoros or Lucifer) is the light bringer, the Morning Star, and the planet Venus when it appears in the sky before the morning sunrise. In some cases, the name appears as a surname for goddesses of light, including Hecate, Diana, and Eos.[24] In myth, Phosphorus is Astraeus' and Eos' son;[25] Thus, he is the child of two Titans: the god of the dusk and the goddess of the dawn.

In the *Encyclopædia Americana*, Edward Wigglesworth and Thomas Bradford write:

> All the conceptions of evil spirits which had been entertained before the Christian era—the impure Beelzebub whose breath scattered pestilence; Belial, the prince of hell; Samael, the seducer and destroyer, Lucifer (the Phosphoros) of the Greeks who lives in the fire; Asmodeus the devil of marriage – were now amalgamated with that idea of the evil principle which the Jews had acquired in Babylon."[26]

The Trickster

The term trickster immediately conjurers images of playful and sometimes destructive deities, but there is much more to the Trickster archetype. The concept of the Trickster not only includes deities, but also the magician, the shadow, monsters, anomalies, misfits, and superhumans. The Trickster brings chaos, enforcing life's momentum and forward progression. In an interview on ISIS Paranormal Radio, George P. Hansen, the author of *The Trickster and the Paranormal*, defines what he calls "the Trickster constellation of characteristics:"

> There's a lot of Tricksters ... Hermes of the Greeks, Mercury of the Romans, Eshu, Legba, Spider...Hare, Coyote of the North American Indians...Loki of the North... The interesting thing is that they seem to crop up in virtually all mythology, which suggests they are important. Sometimes they are kind of humorous figures and for us Westerners, we kind of tend to dismiss them.... There are a number of characteristics they seem to share in common.... They tend to be deceptive; they might be shapeshifters; when involved with other people they tend to disrupt things, causing mischief or worse. They also tend to break and violate sexual taboos... and sometimes are associated with psychic or supernormal abilities. [Tricksters] are sort of marginal, sort of outsiders' they don't hold the highest position in the ranks of the gods; but they are pervasive, found virtually in all societies.[27]

Often times, the Trickster is viewed as negative or "devil-like," but such characters have positive attributes. Tricksters implement necessary change, desired or not. The Trickster archetype can serve as a needed catalyst, one that appears when stagnation occurs.

Dream Meaning

When The Devil archetype connects with you, it's time for the dreamer to recognize the things one finds seductive, but that will ultimately prove consuming. You should examine inner desires, get in touch with the shadow self, and examine improper, forceful drives. Your dream suggests that you need to harness and modify greed, jealousy, and anger so that you can transform the energy into positive motivation.

When you dream about the Devil, you can view the archetype as an internal or external adversary. As an internal adversary, consider the expression, "You're your own worst enemy," especially if you're hindering your own growth. Reflect on whether overwhelming emotions, fears, or anxieties are controlling your actions. Consider if you're remaining in a negative situation, despite the ability to escape it. The appearance of the Trickster in your dreams indicates that it's time for dramatic change.

Often times, devil imagery is about self-imposed limitations. As an external enemy, consider if, in your waking life, you have unrealized enemies or if you sense hostility from another. An external adversary can represent someone in your waking life: A person that does not have your best interests at heart.

Mundane Dream Manifestations: The Trickster archetype corresponds to addictions, lust, taboo ideas and concepts, infatuation, enslavement, toxic relationships, and compulsive acts. This archetype can also manifest in dreams as seduction, temptation, acts of greed, enticement in business or pleasure, and material gains. Sometimes the archetype will manifest in dreams as contracts, characters with shapeshifting abilities, and animals with tricksterish qualities like the raven, blue jay, or fox.

Connecting with the Archetype

What forces represent adversity to you?

Do people in your life characterize these forces?

What motivates you, but also hold seeds of destruction?

Are you imposing limitations on yourself?

Do you feel trapped in a situation where you really have the ability to escape?

Are your emotions limiting or trapping you?

Are there unexpected, chaotic forces in your waking life?

Are you experiencing stagnation in your life, only to discover that something has served as a catalyst that stirs things up again?

Magickal Correspondences at a Glance

Colors: Orange
Chakra: Sacral
Day: Wednesday, Saturday
Deities: Phosphorus, Hades, Hermes, Mercury, Eshu, Legba, Loki
Energies: Masculine/Feminine
Element: Earth, Air, Water
Herbs/Incense: Basil, cedar, lemongrass, sage

Moon Phase: Dark Moon
Numbers: 0, 6
Planetary: Saturn, Mercury, Pluto
Stones: Smokey quartz, amethyst, sunstone, abalone
Tarot: The Fool, The Devil
Totems: Spider, hare, coyote, raven
Zodiac: Gemini, Pisces, Capricorn

The Magician

With the power to shape reality, The Magician archetype represents the power of will and mental discipline to affect change in the physical world. Often this archetype is associated with some type of alchemical or supernatural study. The Magician sometimes appears as a scholar of the occult or magick, pursuing such subjects as science and art. The Magician is sometimes seen as a trickster, having the ability to mold reality and influence outcomes to his own will, all while adhering to the fine lines between wants, needs, and the greater good at large.

The Magician relates to the Scientist as well: both attempt to transcend boundaries by harnessing natural forces to create outcomes where their wills and actions are a generating force. Both the Scientist and Magician have been feared or viewed as individuals trying to play the creator's hand, and both have great responsibility to temper their desires with ethics since they wield great power. The archetype exists in modern reality since scientific discoveries bring both miraculous results coupled with unintended consequences. The power of the Magician must be weighed against the consequences of what such power produces.

The Magician is not only a scientist in the spirit/physical realm. He is an archetype of transformation and metamorphosis. The Magician's role is to expand and transform. He serves as a reminder of the constancy of change. The Magician is a facilitator of energy, communication, and evolution, extending his reach beyond the physical, without the barriers of the mundane.

The archetype seems to be in service of humanity, but remains at a distance from real crisis, more detached and intellectual. This carries connotations of power and prestige, but in some cases, of disconnection from feeling or lack of empathy. It's no wonder that just as the modern archetype of scientist-turned-mad exemplifies one who crosses the boundaries between using knowledge and power to serve humanity versus to control, manipulate, or even enslave humankind. The Magician is an archetype of great power that is not always positive. The evil Magician or the Sorcerer whose quest is to use power to benefit him/herself only is a potent Shadow archetype and provides a warning against consuming power or the engaging in the quest for extreme, self-serving ends.

Some argue that the magician delves into territory belonging only to the divine and therefore is tempted by the power easily, succumbing to narcissism and self-destruction and thereby proving the breach in boundaries. The Magician enters a realm in which great personal responsibility and ethics are required, just as the scientist has tremendous obligation to embark on their research with ethics intact and to the always consider unintended consequences of their discoveries or inventions. There are stories abound about the Magician who exerts his power and will to create what he wants. Such stories reveal that overexertion of will in creative acts yields unintended, often undesired, results (the story of the Golem or the "Sorcerer's Apprentice" for example), so can be found in stories of scientists achieving the miraculous and deadly, like Frankenstein's monster. (See the Monster archetype for more information).

The Magician signifies scholarly learning, study, and academics, as alchemy, astrology and other supernatural arts. In history, the Magician is in figures like John Dee, the scholar of astrology, alchemy, and other metaphysical arts, who served as court magician/astrologer to Queen Elizabeth I. He was a refined academic, scholar, and mathematician as well as occultist; Dee paired with Ed Kelly who mastered the art of necromancy and successfully made contact with angels and spirits. Later, some said that Kelly was a con artist who confabulated the results of his experiments in spirit communication; the representation of the archetypal Magician nonetheless exists in Dee, who constantly sought understanding of the mundane world through psychic experimentation, scholarly research, and occult study, thereby forming the blend the Magician embodies.

Contrast the Magician to the witch who is typically associated with intuitive understanding and the natural ability to work magick using resources available from the garden or kitchen. The Magician is often associated with higher status in society, as even queens and emperors would consult magicians and alchemists, but would simultaneously condemn witches. Thus, The Magician was given access to libraries and was supported by powerful figures in government, while the witch was feared and shunned.

While the witch is often seen as having a natural connection to magick and the elements of nature, the Magician is often portrayed as one whose study and education has fostered his occult knowledge. Thus, there is a link between The Magician and mental discipline. The magician is seen as one who is inspired to become adept at using the forces of self/nature/divine in order to serve humanity, but is in a class apart from a healer or teacher *per se*, as The Magician may wield power to heal, but is not filling the role of the medicine man or spiritual healer.

Usually, stories of self-serving magicians end with the magician receiving some form of karmic payback for their single-mindedness or misuse of knowledge, as seen in stories about the downfall of the powerful people of Atlantis. The dark magician walks on the threshold of using power initially for benevolent purposes, but in some way succumbing to the allure of the quest, either power for power's sake or to gain power over others. The shadow of this archetype echoes the quests for the philosopher's stone, immortality, love, wealth, fame, or the control of others. This archetype includes depictions of the benevolent Magician (such as the god Thoth who intervenes on behalf of other gods) or more sinister examples like the dark wizards from modern stories like *The Lord of The Rings* or *Harry Potter*. Consider reviewing the similarities between The Magician and Devil for greater understanding.

The Magician exists in gods like Hermes and in the legendary figure of Hermes Trismegistus or Hermes Thrice Great, the legendary pre-Christian prophet whose existence is shrouded in mystery and speculation and who brought the teachings of Thoth and Hermeticism.[28] The Magician archetype is in figures such as Taliesin, the Merlin in the King Arthur stories, the god Mercury, and in numerous contemporary stories and legends.

Dream Meaning

When The Magician archetype appears in dreams, consider whether magickal or superefficient means are being sought to accomplish your goals and whether these means seem possible or unrealistic. Consider if you're manifesting your desires while being open to synchronistic, positive opportunities, or if you're expecting grand results with little effort. Reflect on whether you're expecting an outcome that your efforts do not support. In addition, consider manifestations of the negative mirror image of The Magician, the Mad Magician or Evil Sorcerer. Are you seeking power for the sake of power, or are you looking to exert power over others for personal gain? Look to clues from your dream that may speak to possible misuse of power or dynamics of control.

The number eight and reflective circumstances or surfaces ("as above, so below") are indicative of The Magician's power.

MUNDANE DREAM MANIFESTATIONS: These can include dreams of sculpting or carving or manifesting refined product out of raw materials. Dreams of innovative new technology that makes the impossible possible is the energy of The Magician. Dreams in which one wields power to overcome obstacles: for instance, a dream where one is faced with a dead end only to suddenly possess the ability to walk through walls if certain ritual or behaviors are enacted first, or instances where mere desire causes manifestation in the dream are all imagery connected to the powerful magician. Such examples are The Magician at work, even if a robed, monk-like scholar does not appear wielding a magick wand. Dreams of manifesting what is needed in the moment, overcoming obstacles, asserting one's will to overcome blocks and limitations, and demonstrating the power of the mind are all connected to this archetype.

The Magician may appear as wizard, magician, sorcerer, scientist, inventor, supernatural power manifesting in mundane situations, superhero, shape shifter; transformations of the identity and physical form such as healer, miracle worker, electrician, builder, craftsperson, or cook. The archetype may manifest as a process, such as turning one substance to another, the transformation of the self or surroundings, or the act of making something from nothing. A sudden transformation that suggests increase in value (spinning straw into gold) or a decrease in value (a king or deity becoming a pauper) is indicative of The Magician archetype and its message. Alchemy, magick, synchronistic events, energy healing, or dreams containing magick tricks, spells, rituals, laboratories, technologies, short cuts, or conveniences are all associated with The Magician.

Connecting with the Archetype

What is your ultimate goal, and what means are you using to manifest your intent?

Are you making the best use of opportunities?

What are you doing to bring your dreams into manifestation?

Are you pursuing goals efficiently?

Are you keeping yourself open to new possibilities?

Are your goals and expectations reasonable?

Are you pursuing your goals actively or expecting results without putting in the effort necessary to make manifest your dreams?

Are your aligning your efforts with the outcome you intend?

Are you using your talents, skills, or efforts ethically?

Are you too controlling in relationships or have you given up your will to conform to the will of another?

Magickal Correspondences at a Glance

Colors: Orange, purple, gray
Chakra: Solar plexus, third eye
Day: Wednesday
Deities: Thoth, Isis, Mercury, Cerridwen
Energies: Masculine
Element: Akasha
Herbs/Incense: Mugwort, mandrake, peyote, salt, any herb that relaxes or opens the mind
Moon Phase: Waxing, Full
Numbers: 1, 8
Planetary: Mercury, Jupiter
Stones: Magnets, hematite, pyrite, gold, green stones, malachite, jet, onyx, smoky quartz, snowflake obsidian
Tarot: The Magician
Totems: Snakes, rabbits, doves, cats
Zodiac: Virgo, Gemini, Sagittarius

Monsters, Anomalies, and Misfits

Any monster, anomaly, or misfit you see in a dream will most likely frighten you or leave you with an unsettled feeling, but some of these images might even appear humorous or evoke pity. The word "monster" originates from the Latin *monstrum* meaning "prodigy, an omen, something unnatural, or a sign from the gods."[29] A monster is anything that has defects, whether physical, psychological, or both and it can be human or inhuman; it's image and/or actions can be upsetting, startling, disturbing, and terror-invoking.

The Monster archetype represents a distortion of nature that seems grotesque. Contrast this with the Superhuman who portrays excess or unnatural ability positively. In some cases, the Monster/Superhuman represent two sides of the same coin, as in modern comic book characters who are perceived as hideous until the hidden value of their special abilities is revealed.

Sometimes the Monster is an ally and this holds a powerful message as well. Consider "Beauty and the Beast" or the story of the Golem, in both cases the common reaction to the monster is fear, but those who are patient and wise enough to subdue their emotional response are able to tame the monster or at least recognize its benevolent nature. Perhaps the fear of the Monster is really a projection of the fears of humanity's potential in the worst extremes transferred onto another being who then becomes the focus, thus, reviewing the Martyr archetype might supply insight if monsters appear in dreams.

Bear in mind that human perspectives define what is and is not monstrous; for instance, actions or behaviors considered acceptable in one culture are wicked, inhumane, evil, or monstrous to another culture. Something or someone that is monstrous does not always have to have a terrifying outward appearance. In fact, some of the most frightening monstrosities are those that have attractive external appearances with deficient or malformed internal characteristics.

Something or someone that behaves monstrously is behaving in a wicked, cruel, or evil manner. Strangely, what is monstrous is oddly attractive in some way. For example, people enjoy the horror genre because it allows them to experience the monstrous while remaining at a safe distance from monstrosities. Stories are a way of exploring the darkest nature of the human experience without ever encountering any real danger. Thus, what is considered monstrous has a dual nature: it's attractive yet repulsive, disturbing but appealing, dark but stirs curiosities, thereby inspiring fear and awe simultaneously.

There are many monsters in myth. Medusa is one of the most well-known monstrosities. In some stories, Medusa is a once-beautiful woman celebrated for her luxurious hair. After gaining the attentions of Poseidon while in Athena's sanctuary, Athena becomes outraged at the violation of her sanctified temple. To punish Medusa, Athena turns her lovely hair into serpents.[30] According to Apollodorus, Medusa is the daughter of Ceto and Phorcys and one of three gorgons; however, unlike her equally frightening sisters, Eurayle and Stheno, Medusa is mortal. All of the gorgons were born with serpents on their heads, hands made of brass, gold-colored wings, impenetrable scales, long tusks like a wild boar,[31] and with a single glance, could turn those who looked upon them into stone.

Medusa, being the only mortal gorgon, is eventually killed by Perseus. The Greek hero cuts off her head, and stories tell of Medusa's blood having the ability to produce more serpents. Her head retains the power to petrify those who look upon it, even after death.[32] Later, the head of Medusa is placed upon Athena's shield, therefore becoming a powerful weapon of protection.

Medusa's depiction extends well beyond the superficiality of her macabre physicality. First, because Medusa was once a beautiful woman, her depiction points to the deep beauty that lies beneath something that otherwise appears frightening or objectionable. Second, the gorgon's image represents the existence of feminine wisdom and the power of shared knowledge to create permanent change: snakes symbolize wisdom, extending in all directions from Medusa's head, and the gorgon's ability to petrify those she encounters with a single look, even after her death, symbolizes the awesome, life-altering power of wisdom when it's shared with others. Sharing wisdom is even reiterated in stories where drops of Medusa's blood fall from her head to create more serpents that are later spread throughout other parts of the world.

Apollodorus' depiction of the gorgon as having impenetrable scales makes Medusa's image one that is superficially undefeatable, but Perseus overcomes the seemingly impossible obstacle anyway when he kills her. Thus, the story conveys one's ability to sometimes overcome what otherwise seems impossible, but also depicts the act of bravery in the face of superficially impossible obstacles. Finally, when her head becomes part of Athena aegis, the goddess of wisdom, Medusa, represents the protective power of wisdom obtained.

Other monstrous images in myth include creatures like Cerberus. The child of Echidna and Typhon, Cerberus is a three-headed mastiff (sometimes depicted with more heads), who guards the gates of Hades; the beast is said to be submissive to those who enter, but consumes those who attempt escape.[33] Hercules, who brings Cerberus up to the earth, conquers the mythical beast. According to some stories, during the struggle, the great beast, foaming at the mouth, is dropped to the earth and gives rise to the herb wolfsbane.[34] While the image of Cerberus is at first frightening, again, deeper meaning can be derived from the superficial dark imagery. As gatekeeper of Hades, the creature serves as a necessary evil to maintain order in the face of potential chaos, and the beast ensures the continuous protection of clearly defined boundaries. When Hercules drags Cerberus from the entrance of Hades up to the earth, he essentially drags the beast from the darkness into the light, thereby demonstrating that light overcomes darkness or good overpowers evil.

Dream Meaning

When monsters appear in a dream, it might represent what frightens you the most: use this to gain greater understanding of your night vision. In considering Medusa's image and the appearance of monstrosities in your dream narratives, you will find that what appears grotesque on the surface is often an image rich in important symbolism. When you see something monstrous in a dream, you need to look beyond the superficial appearance or physical construction of what you see. Your dream images might encourage you to dig deeper and to seek the beauty that lies beneath the physical.

Your subconscious is attempting to make you pay considerable attention to the images you're presented with; by showing you frightening images, you're much more likely to remember the dream. Dreams of monsters might represent what you view as unconquerable, unsurpassable, or undefeatable in the way of challenges. As in the story of Hercules and Cerberus, your dream could be challenging you to become "enlightened," to "face your demons," and to bring whatever issues psychologically tormenting you into light.

To gain greater insight into the messages behind monsters in dreams, it proves helpful in examining what different types of monsters convey. Here we provide different examples of how the Monster archetype manifests in dreams. The list includes creatures that you can examine in order to begin to understand the subtle subconscious messages such imagery implies. Some suggestions on how to interpret specific creatures is available as well.

Anomalous Figures

Anomalous figures are distortions of the physical body of humans or animals. When you dream of anomalous figures, it implies excess or too much emphasis on the qualities that the specific body parts represent, and a dysmorphic view of the self or others. The appearance of anomalies is indicative of the feared loss of accessible talents. If, in the dream, body parts are missing, it suggests that there is not enough emphasis on the qualities that the missing body parts represent. Consider the meaning of the excess formation or body parts or the areas of the body that disappear, aren't there to begin with, or that take on other shapes. Review the section on body parts in this book to gain a deeper understanding of the potential message your dream is sharing.

Anomalies can manifest in dreams of witnessing your own body morph into a distorted appearance, seeing limbs or features appear, disappearing limbs or features, or in visions where parts or features of the body turn into unnatural objects. Dreams of encountering others whose physical form is unusually distorted or appears frightening due to the exaggeration or lack of formation are ways anomalies appear.

Beasts

Beasts include unnatural or unlikely creatures from myth. Unicorns, dragons, centaurs, or any infinite combination of creatures the subconscious conjures in the dream are good examples. Note the qualities of the animals in the image as well as the feelings the creature calls to mind. If you have a particular affinity for the creature in your waking life, consider what the creature means to you. Extrapolate meaning by exploring the qualities, features, and characteristics associated with these creatures.

Demons

Varying by culture, demons are the embodiment of negative energy. Whether perceived as evil, misguided, trapped, or void of conscience, these beings symbolize the energy that thrives in the complete absence of spirit. The foil to deity figures, the demon represents chaos, negativity, and acting without conscience. Demonic imagery can refer to inner demons, too, thereby suggesting unresolved issues, or ambiguous, sinister drives and motivations.

When demons appear in your dreams, it represents the loss of spiritual connection and threat of lost hope or depression. Carnal desires threatening spiritual integrity or the immersion in negative energy or atmospheres are represented by the appearance of demons in dreams. Demons manifest in dreams as humans or animals possessed or in dreams of antisocial behavior, anarchy, chaos, disruption, or acts of cruelty. Demonic imagery is in dreams of depression or of having joy, love, or spirit threatened by entities that appear as people or in abstract forms as well.

Hungry Ghost

Monstrosities might be inherent, acquired or karmic, or a combination of the three. Consider for example the Buddhist image of the Hungry Ghost: a being whose lust, greed, and insatiable appetites are an afterlife manifestation of the consequences of a life of addiction, desire, and the emphasis of instant gratification. The Hungry Ghost has a large belly, but a small head and wanders through its realm always in a state of longing. Thus, a karmic link between the Hungry Ghost and the human mistake involving ego emphasis and instant gratification is woven. The large belly of the creature represents its insatiable desires, while the small head signifies the reliance on instincts instead of logic or reason.

Vampires

The Vampire reflects cultural fears. Consider the cultural significance of a being that lives forever, but also in bondage; a creature that carries magnetic power over others, but destroys what it lusts after. The vampire will typically present as charming, but whose seduction of the unsuspecting results in bite/blood drinking. The latter action initiates the victim into immortality along with the plague of blood thirst and aversion to light. Numerous other qualities vary by culture and time, such as the ability to shapeshift into the form of a bat, and various methods of killing/repelling the beings (for example, a stake through the heart, crucifix, exposure to sunlight, or beheadings). Note similarities between the Vampire and the Devil archetype: both hold the power of addiction, enslavement, seduction, and are often romanticized. There are numerous connections between vampiric beings and addictions of all kinds. For example, note the connection between vampire characteristics and sedative/opiate addictions where one might be undetected among others, sleep excessively, and follow their drug even as it drains them of vitality and spirituality.

There are commonalities between vampires and cultures where fear or oppression surround sexuality. Consider the sexual undertones of vampire legends. Of all possible ways that you can be initiated into the vampire's lifestyle, it's typically portrayed as a courtship, and a sexual encounter in which a victim is inflicted with the transformative bite. Vampires are forced into a nocturnal existence, thus, the symbolism of being forced into the awareness of darkness. The result is the shunning or hiding from conscious awareness and the ability to thrive in a world of shadows, darkness, illusions, and hidden or arcane mysteries. Like the initiation from virgin to sexually active, the parallel in courtship, seduction and the irreversible lifting of the veil of innocence into the dark, ageless world of full awareness with its sorrows and pleasures, the initiation of the vampire is the dark or taboo nature of the power of sexuality. The magnetic draw it can foster between two people or the longing it can create results in unrequited love, and the victim is forever changed by this encounter. Interestingly, in the act of becoming addicted to a substance a similar progression occurs, from flirting with, abusing, then becoming addicted to a substance with irrevocable consequences. One is initiated from a state of innocence to a life of insatiable longing and pursuit.

Vampires in dreams signify the longing for power or control or desire for satisfaction that you're not perceiving in waking life. This figure can appear to alert you to behaviors that are becoming compulsive or addictive, or the presence of a powerful illusion in waking life. To drink blood is to intrude on the boundaries of another and take on their essence. Perhaps people in your life are draining you, or situations you're facing are infringing on your personal privacy or vitality. The vampire suggests you're giving away part of yourself that holds your core energy and, that if patterns do not change, you may lose yourself in another, a job, or a toxic behavior. Sexual desire may be an issue when the vampire presents. Consider what you're courting in waking life and whether the desire for pleasure is distorting your view of the danger present. The vampire can represent initiation, death, and rebirth and so these archetypes should be reviewed as well. However, there may be pain and loss involved in this initiation.

Dreams of vampires manifest in images of Dracula, vampire-like figures, vampire bats, being bitten, having blood taken by another, or in dreams where another drains your energy, blood, sweat, urine, or other bodily fluids.

Dreams portraying sexual taboo such as rape, incest, or other forbidden sexual practices relate to vampire imagery and messages.

Werewolves and Shapeshifters

The werewolf is a monstrosity acquired through the misfortune of the bite of another werewolf. Similar to the vampire, the contagious quality of this transformation suggests crisis, initiation, and disruption in an otherwise normal life. The third example, an inherent monstrosity, can be represented in the popular comic book figures born with unnatural qualities that lend special abilities for good or ill, but at first stand out as mere anomalies. Consider that these characters rose in attention during a time in history in which humanity delved into scientific discoveries that proved both miraculous and destructive, such as the exploration of nuclear material. It's no surprise, then, that a number of these monstrous figures were the conception of natural beings altered as a result of toxic waste or science gone wrong (an example of this would be Godzilla).

The appearance of a werewolf or were-coyote or other shapeshifter signifies duality. Unlike the vampire, the werewolf is not confined to unconsciousness by day and free only to roam at night. The werewolf lives a double life and it's most strongly subject to this fierce transformation at the full moon. Therefore, you should consider 28-day cycles and the Moon archetype.

Seeing werewolves and shapeshifters in dreams signify a loss of control of the logical senses and loss of civility or humanity. Such dreams suggest strong emotional undercurrents that might explode if not acknowledged. Cyclical gain and loss of control is implied. Consider the nature of the shape-shifting creature for additional clues to its message. Study the attributes of wolf, coyote, or other creature. Question whether the Hunter or Trickster archetype comes into play and consider how these qualities are manifesting in waking life. Too much oppression of instinctual or animal drives might cause periodic eruption and the act of yielding to one's animal nature. The moon is linked to both wolf and mental health, so consider your emotional life and mental well being. Reflect on whether too much stress is causing outbursts of anger or overindulgence in carnal desires during your waking life. Examine whether confinement is resulting in cabin fever or binges on shopping, eating or other "hunting" behaviors.

Actual werewolves or shapeshifters, but also dogs, wolves, or other humans who assume animal qualities represent the Werewolf archetype. Dreams of double lives, of rapid changes in temperament, the loss of civility or dreams in which civilized or constrained settings are contrasted with wild and uninhibited behaviors signify the message of the werewolf. In contrast, despite the animalistic, aggressive nature of the werewolf, the archetype can signify the positive attributes of wolf-like creatures too, including loyalty, empathy, commitment to the pack or mate, and the adherence to the hierarchy or ranks within a pack. Thus, consider the context of the dream and the feeling it invokes for interpretative clarity.

Zombies

The monster in dreams brings the opportunity to confront fears. It may represent the inner drives you hope to hide from the world and can indicate the aspects of life that you fear will take over and distort your true essence. Monsters exemplify the fears of specific cultures and times in history. For example, certain Native American tribes feared monstrous beings called skinwalkers; likewise, in Haiti, a belief in zombies exists. In fact, zombies are such a significant part of the Haitian culture that numerous reports of zombie phenomenon exist and ultimately form the tapestry of cultural expectations. Thus, when one is cursed with the "zombie powder" through someone else's magick, the afflicted will not only succumb to the effect of the powder (slowed vital signs and a brief period of death—mimicking slumber), but will also be presumed a lost cause by their loved ones. The afflicted may be seen later on by family and shunned, for it's believed that once afflicted with the zombie curse, the individual actually dies, is brought back to life by the magickal practitioner who inflicted the curse upon them, and then is enslaved by that person. The afflicted will thus enact the role of slave and the community will respond to them as a pariah to be avoided and mourned as dead.

The zombie is a representation of eternal enslavement, void of conscious thought or volition, as a result of a curse bestowed by a magician. Typically, revenge and political/cultural factors are involved. Consider for example the correlation between the powerful Magician inflicting a curse of death, and eternal enslavement on an unsuspecting victim with the reality of life in an unstable dictatorship, with the ton-ton macoute capable of removing people from their homes in their sleep to face enslavement, torture, or death. It becomes apparent that the monster is the parallel of monstrosities performed by humanity. The zombie represents the loss of will and life force. The zombie becomes an empty shell forced into eternal servitude.

Symbolically zombies indicate a loss of ambition or motivation. Zombies signify "going through the motions" without actually thinking about what you're doing, relying on instinctual drives alone without reason for support, or performing everyday actions on automatic pilot. Delegation of control to an outside authority, by force or perceived disempowerment are representative of the Zombie archetype. Consider what aspects of waking life are intruding on your will and personal energies. Consider the role of the zombie in the dream. Is there pursuit or mere observation? The dynamic between you and the zombie can give clues to enhance the meaning of the dream. Likewise, dreams of becoming a zombie yourself or of one known to you becoming a zombie can give clues as to perception of loss of power and autonomy in a relationship. To what forces are you or your significant other enslaved?

Connecting with the Archetype

What can you learn from what frightens you?
What is at the root of what scares you?
Can you look at a disturbing issue with a new perspective?
Are you looking beyond the superficial surface of an issue to examine the deeper issues beneath?
Are the issues/obstacles you face truly insurmountable?
Is your perspective skewing your view of an issue erroneously?
What is the nature of the aberration in the dream?

Magickal Correspondences at a Glance

Colors: Black, white, gray
Chakra: Root, sacral
Day: Saturday
Deities: Medusa, Hephaestus, Kali, Chiron
Energies: Masculine/Feminine
Element: Akasha, Earth
Herbs/Incense: Wolfsbane, mandrake, bat's claw root, garlic
Moon Phase: Dark Moon, Full Moon
Numbers: 0, 3, 8
Planetary: Pluto, Jupiter
Stones: Garnet, turquoise, quartz
Tarot: The Tower, The Devil, Death
Totems: Snakes, wolves, dogs, frogs, cats
Zodiac: Sagittarius, Capricorn

CHAPTER 6

MORE COMMON DREAM ARCHETYPES

Superhumans

The Superhuman as archetype represents an individual who defies boundaries and in doing so, transcends limitations. In myth, we see the superhuman image in depictions of Hercules, son of Zeus and Alcmene. In myth, he is "a human hero, a conqueror of men, and cities ... a subduer of monsters and is connected in a variety of ways to astronomical phenomena."[1] Today, the name Hercules has become synonymous with strength, courage, and bravery.

Superhumans are those who set records with exceeding skill and talent: exceptional athletics, genius or other commendable assets of personality or achievement; however, such conquests serve as double-edged endeavors. Attempting to meet expectations or to be super or the demands of superiority can drive one to obsession with perfectionism, drawing on the more negative sides of the Devil/Adversary or Dark Magician archetypes.

Emphasis on superiority implies elitism. If one is to excel, it means that others will have to fall short or will have to meet average standards. Thus, an implied value or judgment of superiority comes with superhuman views and energies. Such a perspective can lead to false pride, condescendence, and, as history has illustrated, dangerous consequences; for example, the moment when humans have sought to refine themselves into superior beings or a superior race. The latter example is an illustration of the Shadow Superhuman, the dark aspect of human nature and pride, a form of alchemy turned sour; it's like the act of seeking an exceptional and refined golden element, only to find the complete opposite of enlightenment or refinement in situations where the ends do not justify the means.

There is a fine line between an exception to the rule being considered superior or exceptional versus being an anomaly/monstrosity, especially if one considers the phenomenon of unusual characteristics like gigantism, genius, or other atypical physical features. A culture may define such features as unique and exceptional that provide added talents or enhancement, or such characteristics can be perceived as abominations. Whether applying this concept to creative genius, mental illness, or even left-handedness, the only difference between something unique being refined and exceptional or feared and reviled is one's subjectivity. Thus, when interpreting superhuman features for dream meanings, it's a good idea to review what the Monster archetype conveys as well.

Dreaming Meaning

If the archetype of the Superhuman appears in dreams, you might face a situation that requires you to rely on your exceptional talents and skills in your waking life. The appearance of this archetype implies the need to explore your extraordinary abilities and to put them to use for the betterment of the self or for the community. If you connect with the Superhuman archetype following adversity or a loss of some kind, your subconscious could be stirring you to discover talents unexplored previously. Finally, this archetype could also imply the need to put all of your efforts into an undertaking to ensure a positive outcome or that you will find your greatest power in your courage, bravery, and inner strength.

MUNDANE DREAM MANIFESTATIONS: Superhumans appear as superheroes, celebrities, or giants in dreams. Excess of talent or abilities, or unnatural abilities triggered by the presence of special tools, and dreams of exceeding one's typical capacity, signify the message of the Superhuman archetype. Meanwhile, the shadow aspect presents in dreams where excessive talent or positive abilities backfire or hide a weakness that leads to the dreamer's downfall. Mundane hero manifestations can occur in the form of larger than life personalities or heroic acting individuals, such as soldiers, firefighters, or those who defy typical boundaries in their mundane work. Dreams of discovering secret belongings, possessions or treasures or uncovering talents/qualities not possessed or considered strong in waking life all fall under the domain of the Superhuman archetype.

Connecting with the Archetype

What allure is in exceptional abilities from legend, myth or literature, and pop culture?

In what ways do you emulate the stories of exceptional or superhuman characters?

What are your humble beginnings?

What can you learn from overcoming adversity?

What are your exceptional talents and how can you develop them?

In what ways do adverse situations demonstrate your inner strengths or hidden potential?

Magickal Correspondences at a Glance

Colors: Purple

Chakra: Crown, solar plexus

Day: Thursday, Sunday

Deities: Any demigod, giants, Jupiter, Kwan Yin or other Ascended Masters

Energies: Masculine

Element: Akasha

Herbs/Incense: Blessed thistle, juniper, laurel

Moon Phase: Full Moon

Numbers: 1, 3, 8

Planetary: Jupiter, Uranus

Stones: Diamond, bloodstone, agate

Tarot: Strength, The World

Totems: Snake, lion, leopard, eagle, hawk

Zodiac: Sagittarius, Aquarius, Aries

The Wanderer and Fool

The Wanderer is an archetype that represents the quest through the lens of one embarking on a journey. The reason for The Wanderer's search can involve the pursuit of spiritual awakening, or it can stem from basic inquisitiveness. The Wanderer is in the vagabond or the solitary, noncommittal rogue. Freedom is part of this archetype as is the lack of connection with others or with society. This archetype engenders the Buddhist philosophy of non-attachment and the Wanderer typically travels with minimal weight: both emotionally and that brought on by attachment to material objects. The Wanderer is often materially poor, but spiritually rich. The stereotypical image of the American Hobo, free to ride the rails and outwit the police at will; the footloose, and the unattached all relate to The Wanderer.

Those representing this archetype might prove curious as well as fickle. They do not settle down. They are flexible and adapt to any condition. One of the best examples of The Wanderer archetype in myth is the story of Odysseus, the hero in *The Odyssey* by Homer, who faces myriad challenges and obstacles in his journeys.

The Shadow Wanderer is one who wanders aimlessly without a point of reference or direction; with the Shadow Wanderer energies in play, the individual may feel that he or she is lost, subjected to the cruel hands of fate, and one might even take on the victim role. There is no way around the energies of the Shadow Wanderer, only through, and in some cases one may feel like an actual wanderer, moving from one situation to another, from one moment to another, helplessly wandering without relief or rest in sight.

Dream Meaning

The Wanderer signifies a loss of connection from the self or others. When this archetype appears, it represents a disconnection from what is important or it signifies a need for greater socialization. The Wanderer implies excessive flightiness or an excessive air element. You might find yourself lost in your thoughts, stuck in the middle of a project, or experiencing a sense of being ungrounded or lost.

When the Shadow Wanderer appears in dreams, it's a warning to forgo settling for the role of victim, but to hold strong as you regain a sense of orientation. The Wanderer appears as one who is lost or in transit. Consider the means of transport when interpreting dreams where the Wanderer appears.

Dreams of being lost in a large house or a home that seems to have endless attachments, doors, hallways, or rooms are indicative of Wanderer energies. The latter type of dream suggests a search for the self or an uncertainty about the self, particularly if the rooms and attachment in the home are new, hidden surprising or unexpected in appearance. A dream of being lost in a home signifies a need to rediscover your deep emotions, yourself, or it suggests the need to better integrate the mind, body, spirit connection.

MUNDANE DREAM MANIFESTATIONS: This archetype appears in dreams involving a vacation or commuting, but not arriving at your destination; travel of all kinds, walking, being lost in a building, or in dreams of floating, or not having a sense of purpose. Dreams where scenery changes rapidly; dreams in which you're at a distance from others or not committed or connected to other dream figures; dreams of loss of security such as eviction or being fired or dreams of being discharged from a hospital, military, or other structures are other manifestations of the Wanderer. Visions involving school graduation; dreams suggesting disconnection, release, and then lack of reconnection; visions of prison breaks, being on the run, breaking up a relationship or quitting a job, dropping out of structured settings or rejecting family or cultural tradition in a dream all present the message of the Wanderer.

Connecting with the Archetype

How can you embrace spontaneity?

Are you yearning to break free from expectation or tradition?

Are you flexible or adaptable or do you prefer structure and control?

Have you considered spending time exploring your surroundings without a predetermined agenda?

Have you considered deeper self-exploration?

Are you looking for your purpose?

Are you wandering with a purpose or aimlessly?

Consider ways to begin challenging your need for control or perfection.

Magickal Correspondences at a Glance

COLORS: White, red

CHAKRA: Solar plexus, third eye

DAY: Wednesday

DEITIES: Mercury, Hermes, Isis, Nephthys

ENERGIES: Neutral

ELEMENT: Air

HERBS/INCENSE: Ivy, vines, lily of the valley, pine, sea salt

MOON PHASE: Moon Void of Course, Waxing

NUMBERS: 0, 1

PLANETARY: Mercury

STONES: Apache's tear, quartz, pyrite

TAROT: The Fool, The Hermit

TOTEMS: Wandering mantis, wandering albatross, turtle, any migrating animal or bird

ZODIAC: Gemini

Ghosts

The Ghost represents an essence existing in absence of physical form. Due to the association with ghost as spirit of the deceased, this conjures the feelings of grief, loss, and unfinished business or of messages or warnings transmitted from the afterlife, from a being presumed to have acquired wisdom from experiencing their own shortcomings as a mortal. Thus, the Ghost as an archetype connoting settled scores, finding closure, offering guidance and perspective, but also of hints at the concepts of residual emotion or being "haunted" by mistakes, loss or by past situations.

When appearing in dreams, a ghost could be the essence of a person or place that remains and has a profound emotional impact on the dreamer, even if the dreamer is not experiencing the physical aspect of what remains "haunting" them. The Ghost suggests being in contact with the ethereal residue, the emotion, essence, and spirit of a person or situation that has not fully been brought to closure and so insinuates that transition is in place; the spirit has not crossed over yet, or the loss has not been fully accepted and so remains. It's the energy lingering between two places/times/dimensions and so suggests both flexibility, motion, fluidity, but perhaps confusion, lack of commitment, or remaining stuck in one realm when belonging in another. Dreams of the deceased or of ethereal beings; dreams of residual presences; dreams of spirits, a haunting, or a feeling of being watched or haunted, or even powerful dream imagery can have a ghost-like quality, haunting the dreamer and lingering in the mind for the rest of the day.

Consider in the story "The Aeneid" where Aeneas journeys to the underworld and encounters Queen Dido: the lover he left behind to pursue his quest. He encounters her in spirit form, a reminder of his loss, but a phantom with which he can no longer interact. The Ghost is then the Shadow or illusion that remains both in memory, and spectral form, and can bring sadness, fear, and the burden of past issues needing resolution.

When examining The Ghost archetype in myth, consider the story of Artemis and Actaeon; after the goddess Artemis turns Actaeon into a stag and his hunting dogs hunt him down and kill him. Yet, this myth has a ghostly element; a rumor had spread abroad that a ghost haunted a rock in the woods and caused a great deal of destruction in the area. People consulted the oracle who suggested that the bones of Actaeon be buried, and that they build a brass image and chain it to the rock in the woods; doing so would allow the dead hunter's spirit to rest.[2] The story of Actaeon suggests that spirits linger because of a traumatic death, the sudden loss of life, or because of anger at the fact that one's life is cut short.

A similar myth tells the story of the restless spirit of the Roman poet, Virgil, who some medieval writers suggest conducted a rejuvenation ceremony in an effort to regain his youth. Virgil is said to have built a castle in an isolated area where the ceremony could be performed. Virgil asked his servant to kill him, to cut his body up into pieces and to place it in a barrel of brine; the servant was to keep a perpetual lamp lit, replenish the lamp daily, and to allow the oil to continuously drip on the barrel holding Virgil's body.[3] The servant agreed and performed what was asked of him; the Emperor, favoring Virgil, missed him, and upon the threat of death, demanded that the servant tell him where Virgil was located; the servant brought the Emperor to the castle, confessed to participating in Virgil's death, and the Emperor killed him on the spot.[4] At that moment, witnesses saw Virgil's ghost appear as a male child who ran around the barrel while shouting, "Cursed be the time that ye ever came here." The lamp oil suspended, the ritual was incomplete, and Virgil disappeared.[5] The story of Virgil is much like the story of Actaeon, where Virgil is angered that his chance at eternal life has been destroyed, but there is a subtle hint, through Virgil's own dismemberment, pointing to the pervasive human desire to be *re-membered.*

Dream Meaning

The Ghost may appear in dreams without appearing as a spirit or deceased person. For example, a dream in which a man sits in the comfort of his living room only to see his boss from work walk across the room, realizing in the dream alone that the boss has actually moved in and now lives with him, is experiencing the ghost of his job, the boss or both. He is thus being haunted by his work or boss and may be taking his work home with him. Therefore, the ghost does not only represent the spirit, but being haunted, the interference of one sphere of life infiltrating another, just as a ghost appearing oversteps the boundary between the world of the living and that of the dead. Consider if dreams of boundary invasions, intrusion, or abnormal crossing of one realm into another implies feeling haunted by something overextending its territory in the life of the dreamer.

MUNDANE DREAM MANIFESTATIONS: The ghost archetype appears as a spirit, dreams where boundaries are crossed, residue, dreams of personal belongings of one who is deceased or cut off from the dreamer. Even dreams of reminiscing past memories suggest the ghost. Shadows, vague impressions or appearances, or the portrayal of incomplete scenarios suggest unfinished business; veils, haze, loss, regret, or sadness may accompany this archetype.

Connecting with the Archetype

What is haunting your thoughts/heart?
Do you have unresolved business?
Are you clinging to what no longer serves you?
What do you want to be remembered for the most?
Are you grieving a loss?
Are you crossing boundaries unnecessarily?

Magickal Correspondences at a Glance

COLORS: Gray, indigo
CHAKRA: Crown, heart, throat
DAY: Any day, particularly during dusk or dawn hours
DEITIES: Osiris, Anubis, Pluto, Hades, Persephone
ENERGIES: Neutral
ELEMENT: Akasha
HERBS/INCENSE: Basil, sage, dragon's blood, frankincense
MOON PHASE: Waning, Dark
NUMBERS: 7, 13
PLANETARY: Pluto, Neptune
STONES: Quartz, amethyst, emerald
TAROT: Death, The Chariot
TOTEMS: Butterfly, caterpillar, hibernating animals, loon, swan
ZODIAC: Scorpio, Pisces

Priests and Priestesses

Priests/Priestesses are the initiated clergy of a religious sect or group; these individuals hold sacred the mysteries and understand divine truths. The Priest/Priestess makes an oath to serve the God/Goddess, and they are spiritual healers, educators, and those who lead by example and sound spiritual instruction. Those who take on this sacred role seek to protect the interests of the spirit.

The individuals fitting this archetype view the spirit realm as co-existent with the mundane world, walk between both realms, and nurture the growth of the spirit through administration of tests and interventions via sacred rituals and rites of passage, all of which assist in guiding and healing the self and others. Thus, the individual is the preserver of spiritual tradition, and their responsibilities may include keeping the confidence of others and the mysteries secret from the uninitiated.

Priests/Priestesses are the moderators of sacred tasks including birthing, marrying, and healing. They preside over rituals initiating others into the deeper mysteries; these rituals can include, but are not limited to sex, death, and transformation through the life cycle. In some cultures, the Priest/Priestess might be first "married" or "wedded" to this dogma or lifestyle, holding the duties of their role above all else. Other responsibilities or actions the Priest/Priestess embody include the interpretation of omens, signs, and dreams; consultation on mundane and esoteric issues; advisor to political leaders, gatekeeper of mysteries; moderator between divine and mundane authorities, and keeper of balance between mundane and magickal realms.

One example of the Priestess archetype includes the Lady of the Lake from Arthurian Legends, Morgan le Fay, who is sometimes mortal, sometimes demi-goddess. Other examples include the Merlin, also of Arthurian legends, or Pythia, a priestess, prophetess, and the Oracle of Apollo at Delphi, who interprets omens. The Pythia, sometimes virginal and sometimes a crone, would ritually cleanse her body in the fountain Castalis, and retrieved laurel leaves from a nearby tree to make a wreath that she could wear during divining practices.[6] Before sharing visions, the Pythia entered the sanctuary in the Temple of Apollo and stood in front of Apollo's statue while burning a mixture of barley-flour and laurel-leaves; she would descend into the oracular vault, drink water from a sacred spring, and chew on laurel-leaves before sitting on a tripod with a branch of laurel in her hand.[7] Thus, Pythia served as a mediatrix between humankind and the gods, delivered messages to those seeking divine guidance.

Dream Meaning

When the Priest/Priestess archetype appears in dreams, it signifies spiritual authority and calls for you to consider being responsible for, protecting, and moderating spiritual energies. This archetype challenges you to overcome mundane limitations so that you can excel spiritually. Your super ego might challenge your ego and an initiation might be on the horizon. This archetype suggests the need to focus on secrets, culture, or important traditions. You might enter into a situation where you must connect with your higher aspirations and core values. The Priest/Priestess archetype calls you to act as mentor, teacher, or guide as well, and the appearance of this archetype in a dream suggests the sharing of knowledge and wisdom for the betterment of the self, spirit, or the spirit of others.

If the Priest/Priestess appears in dreams, it suggests that you need to seek out balance in all things. This archetype is indicative of upcoming initiations or rites of passage and sometimes implies a call to engage in self-healing or the healing of another. Consider the role tradition plays in your life as well, and reflect on the sacred tasks for which you are responsible. Finally, this archetype might be signaling a need for secrecy, or that a situation will arise that calls for the utmost confidentiality.

MUNDANE DREAM MANIFESTATIONS: The Priests/Priestesses appear as spiritual or mundane guides, chauffeurs, drivers, pilots, and others who appear in dreams as subtle guides. Consider the vehicle you see in the dream, if applicable. Teachers, mentors, mediators between the dreamer and mundane authority figures are representations of the Priest/Priestess archetype.

Connecting with the Archetype

What subtle intuitive guidance is arising?
Are you being challenged enough spiritually?
What unorthodox mentors are surfacing for you?
In what ways can you lead, teach, or inspire others through spiritual practices?

Are you following your deepest values?

What traditions or rituals are lacking in your life?

Who/what fosters the connection between your individual consciousness and divine power?

Compare your spiritual evolution to progress in your mundane life.

Magickal Correspondences at a Glance

COLORS: Purple, silver, gold
CHAKRA: Crown
DAY: Monday
DEITIES: Isis, Athena, Apollo, Horus, Osiris
ENERGIES: Feminine
ELEMENT: Water, Earth, Akasha
HERBS/INCENSE: Star anise, camphor, poppy seeds
MOON PHASE: Full, Waxing
NUMBERS: 2
PLANETARY: Neptune, Pluto
STONES: Lapis, moonstone, sunstone
TAROT: High Priestess, Hierophant
TOTEMS: Birds of prey, goat, fox, raven, vulture
ZODIAC: Sagittarius, Scorpio, Pisces

Shaman

The Shaman is similar to the Priest/Priestess as the traditional wise man or woman of a people, tribe, or group; the Shaman's practices tie to natural cycles and the world of spirit. The Priest/Priestess is one who is dedicated to and initiated in a specific religious system, while a Shaman may stand independent of a socially recognized system of religious dogma. They are typically identified as maintaining traditions of the original people of their culture, regardless of where they are found in the world. A tribe or community often identifies a shaman as a medicine man or woman and this is due primarily to involvement in the healing arts.

The Shaman seeks the wisdom of spirits in order to learn from them or to request assistance in magickal workings. The Shaman is skilled in practices like astral projection and trance, as these are the primary methods for walking in the astral realm. Through trance, the Shaman seeks levels of higher consciousness, takes vision quests, or communes with spirits in order to seek out solutions to mundane issues, and like the Priest/Priestess, the Shaman interprets omens and dreams and sometimes works with spirit or animal guides. Shamans often have shapeshifting abilities, a skill that associates the Shaman with the Trickster archetype. The raven and the shaman are closely connected, both of which have connections with the Trickster and that interact with the physical and spirit world. In the case of the Shadow Shaman: this might represent the individual who uses his or her powers to seek out even greater power, or one who uses spirits for malevolent purposes.

Dream Meaning

The Shaman signifies messages relating to parallel lives, reaching into unorthodox realms, flexibility, dual vision, mediation, and the responsibility to uphold tradition. The appearance of the Shaman is a message about transcending mundane limitations. The Shaman archetype may appear as one who stands apart, but is also granted passage through territories not typically open to outsiders. To dream of a Shaman or a person with shamanic qualities signifies passage, submersion, and initiation into greater mysteries.

The Shaman beckons you to seek natural methods of healing. This archetype speaks of the power of sound, herbs, trance, music, rattles, drumming, and even dance. This archetype can teach you how to walk through the darkest passages of your life in safety, even when you feel you're moving through situations blindly or without physical or spiritual guidance. The Shaman is a nurturer or sorts, nurturing the people with his ability to heal and elicit harmony. This same archetype might suggest the need to tap into ancestral knowledge, energies, wisdom, and power, or the need to connect/reconnect with ancestral spirits.

MUNDANE DREAM MANIFESTATIONS: The Shaman archetype appears as dreams of dual citizenship, membership in inner circles; membership status extended to an outsider, a loner, a medicine person or folk healer, a preserver of traditions, and figures with dual origins. Someone who is communing with spirit or animals, or nature or people whose appearance suggests wildness are alternative representations of this archetype. In addition, people appearing from caves or venturing into caves or tunnels;

aboriginal people, shapeshifters or people who seem to have an uncanny connection to nature or the spirit world are all Shaman representations. Finally, dreams of unorthodox healers or natural medicine; dreams of communication across cultures or times, and dreams of soul retrieval or time travel all relate the message of The Shaman.

Connecting with the Archetype

Are you aware of your environment and your spiritual or cultural roots? Are you feeling disconnected from the Earth or your cultural origins? How can you reconnect with ancestral spirits?

Consider ways to connect with Earth energies, like seeking out natural healing remedies or including more plant-based foods in your diet.

Consider how you can become more grounded and connected to plants, trees, the elements, and Earth spirits.

Magickal Correspondences at a Glance

Colors: Brown, black, green
Chakra: Root, crown
Day: Friday
Deities: Thoth, Bast, Green Man, Gaia
Energies: Feminine
Element: Akasha
Herbs/Incense: Sage, sweet grass, peyote, mugwort
Moon Phase: Dark Moon, Full Moon
Numbers: 3, 9
Planetary: Venus, Saturn, Pluto
Stones: Moss agate, fossils, amber resin
Tarot: Hermit
Totems: Raven, bear, turtle, coyote
Zodiac: Taurus, Pisces, Gemini, Scorpio

Healer/Wounded Healer

The primary focus of this archetype is the support of life processes and death when no other options remain. The Healer is more like The Shaman in that he or she may operate independently of a spiritual or religious philosophy. The Healer tends to the progression of the soul as the afflicted subject contends with physical illnesses that signify personal initiation, not just disease. For example, a broken arm is not just a limb in need of repair. The Healer regards the treatment of the limb, but also considers the global recovery process of the individual who now experiences transformation in their abilities and routines. Emotional and physical healing are unified. The Healer will help the afflicted cope with the spiritual meaning and ramifications of the symptoms, experience, and the process of recovering.

Healers are deified, as is the case with Apollo, a deity synonymous with healing arts and medicine. In myth The Healer can be portrayed by a god or goddess figure, thereby suggesting the divine nature behind the healing arts; take for example, the story of Isis, the Goddess of Medicine, bringing restoration to Osiris by collecting his scattered body parts from the desert and bringing them back together for the purposes of resurrection.

The Healer archetype is exemplified in the legend of Chiron, the centaur who taught healing arts to others, only to become mortally wounded himself. His story of self-sacrifice gives way to a more complex archetype as well: The Wounded Healer. The latter archetype has become linked in astrology to the meaning of the placement of the asteroid Chiron in the natal chart, designating a place of crisis that prompts healing for the self in a way that is natural to heal others, but which one finds personally elusive. The snake symbolizes The Healer archetype traditionally, as is seen in the continued use of the caduceus. The Sun is symbolic of healing and the restoration of vital energy; thus, it's a sign associated with the Healer archetype as well.

Dream Meaning

It's time to nurture and repair the effects of imbalance to physical, emotional and spiritual systems. Consider the type of healer portrayed in the dream, their ethics, and motivations. Consider the theme of healing and whether you are on the giving, receiving end, or both. Reflect on the role of The Healer in facilitation of growth or perhaps in doing damage control. Look to the dream for clues; a dream of easing pain in the chronically ill suggests a long-term path of maintenance, but not full recovery. Nonetheless, it may tell you to continue your efforts. You may find that your energy is not producing the results you would like, but is still beneficial.

A dream in which a Healer provides a diagnosis suggests news of the need for attention to whatever system is represented by the body part afflicted in the dream. Dreams where the healer completely cures the subject suggests full recovery, emergence of success, resolution and reparations made in the system or traits the afflicted body part represents. A dream where The Healer gives a false diagnosis, unethical or ineffective cure or does harm intentionally may suggest waking life resolutions sought by the dreamer that will be ineffective or cause more damage than relief. Consider the motives and other dream clues for further layers of information.

MUNDANE DREAM MANIFESTATIONS: The appearance of The Healer includes doctors, medical personnel including nurses, technicians and aids, medical offices, medical ailments, first aid kits, and the administration of medical interventions: from surgery to medicine, to the dissemination of medical knowledge, to the provision of healing foods, and teas, or substances of an unusual nature. Resolving illness, but also initiating death or easing into death in the dream is the work of The Healer as well. Emergency responders, folk healer, medical paraphernalia, but also the exposure to illness, injury or medical complaints appearing in the dream relate to this archetype, along with dreams of pain, or non-medical figures administering medical advice.

Connecting with the Archetype

Consider the dream context: is the healer providing emergency, rescue, acute or long term/preventative maintenance?

What body parts/systems manifest the ailment in dreams?

What is your reaction to the healer's diagnosis/treatment?

Does the treatment seem effective?

Are you resisting an honest appraisal of the health of systems affected in the dream?

What can you do to improve the functioning of these areas?

Is the dream calling you to administer healing to yourself or others?

Are you resisting healing changes or interventions?

What relationships require mending and what interventions are you willing to take to heal the relationship?

Consider the symbolic meaning of the afflicted areas and reflect on whether this corresponds to imbalances in those areas of life.

Magickal Correspondences at a Glance

Colors: Purple, white, blue, gold
Chakra: Root, solar plexus, heart
Day: Sunday
Deities: Isis, Apollo, Gaia, Asclepius, Chiron
Energies: Masculine
Element: Fire, Water
Herbs/Incense: Echinacea, basil, thyme, ginseng, chamomile
Moon Phase: Waxing, Full
Numbers: 0, 1
Planetary: Sun, Mercury, Venus
Stones: Unakite, clear/rose quartz, moonstone, moss agate, or any blue stone for emotional healing
Tarot: Hanged Man, Death, Sun
Totems: Guinea pig, snake, cat, dog, honeybee, and domestic pets
Zodiac: Virgo, Leo, Sagittarius, Pisces, Scorpio

Weavers

Weavers teach that there is no coincidence and that all events, meetings, encounters, situations, and happenings serve to weave life experiences together as a large, universal tapestry. With this in mind, it must follow that certain people or beings are charged with the responsibility for being catalysts for fate. Weavers are facilitators of change and growth.

In Greek mythos, the Three Fates are Clotho the spinner, Lachesis the allotter, and Atropos the unturnable, and these Goddesses are commonly confused with the Graeae, the three Grecian Goddesses or gray witches, Deino, Enyo, and Pemphredo, who share one eye. According to this myth, Perseus, son of Zeus, encounters the Graeae who have something to teach. Perseus steals the eye from the Graeae in order to force them into revealing information on how to defeat Medusa; when the single eye is taken from the goddesses, an eye that gave them a shared, singular perspective of the external world, the truth is then revealed. If the Three Fates set into motion new opportunities, the Graeae loosen the perspective one needs in order to see the new opportunities for what they are.

Weavers are commonly associated with silk worms and spiders. The Grecian goddess Athena is a masterful weaver. The maiden Arachne, whose name means spider, is a talented spinner and weaver, who learns her skills from Athena.[8] Pride gets the best of Arachne when she claims that she learned her weaving skills on her own, without assistance, and that there was no one that could rival her spectacular abilities, not even the goddess herself.[9] Athena heard of Arachne's claims and went to her in the guise of a crone who kindly told Arachne that her claim of being greater than the goddess Athena was dangerous and something she should willfully recant while requesting forgiveness.[10] Arachne adamantly refuses to recant her claims and boldly challenges the Goddess to prove she is the best weaver. Athena transforms herself, accepts Arachne's challenge, and the weaving competition ensues.[11] Arachne angers Athena despite her lovely weaving, and the Goddess repays Arachne's disrespect by cursing her to forever weave as a spider.[12]

In an alternative account, Athena is the goddess who "wove the robe of the universe"; she creates her own robe, Pandora's attire, and she gives Jason a cloak she makes herself.[13] Arachne, a proud and skillful weaver, challenges Athena to a weaving competition and the goddess finds Arachne's work flawless.[14] Nevertheless, Athena destroys Arachne's weaving, causing the maiden considerable upset; so much so, she hangs herself.[15] Athena rescues Arachne from the rope, but the rope becomes a web and Arachne transforms into a spider.[16] The story of Athena cursing Arachne by turning her into a spider, serves as a reminder that even in events where student surpasses the teacher in terms of knowledge or skill, it remains necessary and appropriate for the student to remain respectful of the teacher. Likewise, the story serves as a warning about the dangers of excessive pride, and such a warning, along with the lesson of respecting your elders might be coming through to you in dreams if you connect with the Weaver archetype.

Dream Meaning

This archetype is one that calls on the dreamer to stay alert and brace one's self for what is about to occur, whether it be fortuitous or not. The dreamer can be sure of one thing and one thing only, that change will occur and in a way that you will not anticipate. This archetype challenges the dreamer to think outside of the box, to forego one's own limitation and to let the universe take control. While being urged to prepare for the unexpected, you should also take on a new perspective and to see things for what they actually are as personal expectations are sometimes blinding.

When this archetype appears in dreams, be open to the collaboration with a team or the experience of others. Sexuality is also suggested here and the creative force of combination, alchemy and submersion is suggested. Potential immersion of plans, skills, dreams and creative vision with another or group may be necessary. Creativity of all kinds especially crafts, writing, or speaking are indicated. In a negative sense, the weaving of a web of lies or confusion may be implied but review the dream for context.

This archetype suggests events surfacing at present forming a broader, longer reaching net than you might realize and so be mindful of the projection of current energies and plans. Complex systems and consequences may be forming around the dreamer and consider that nothing is occurring in a vacuum at this time. Fateful interventions or twists of fate may be arising in waking life.

Weaving can quickly become a catalyst to meditation and trance. If weaving symbols appear in your dreams, this can be a calling to be more attentive to meditations. The Weaver archetype signals the need for engaging in trance and walking in balance between the realms.

MUNDANE DREAM MANIFESTATIONS: The Weaver appears in dreams involving weaving, sewing, knitting and textile crafts, braids or braiding, the Internet, networking, spiders, webs, bees and beehives, communes, and relays. This archetype comes through in imagery involving construction sites, construction workers, farmers, teachers, stitching, fate, twists of fate and divine intervention, conveyor belts, factories, currents and tides. Finally, visions of collaboration, teamwork, and group projects signify the message of The Weaver.

Connecting with the Archetype

Consider the role fate is playing in your waking life.

Are your actions revisited on the broader community?

Are you proactive in fellowships, communities, or groups or do you disengage while still expecting to reap benefits?

Are you being asked to share the effort of collaboration?

How can you benefit from surrendering full control and allowing for the formation of relationships that have a greater degree of interdependency?

Practice artistic or creative expression.

Practice collaborating in groups and being open to the input of others.

Take advantage of opportunities to let your skills mix with the skills of others.

Magickal Correspondences at a Glance

Colors: All colors, particularly those created through blending

Chakra: Heart

Day: Thursday, Friday

Deities: Fortuna, the Graeae, The Fates, Athena

Energies: Feminine

Element: Akasha, as a weaving of all elements

Incense/Herbs: Sweetgrass, flax, hemp

Moon Phase: Waxing Moon, Full, Waning

Numbers: 1, 5, 10

Planetary: Venus, Jupiter

Stones: Any stone that is a blend of color, brown/blue turquoise, bloodstone

Tarot: The Fool, Wheel of Fortune, Temperance

Totems: Spider, bee, ant, beaver, communal or networking animals

Zodiac: Taurus, Sagittarius, Libra

Witch and Sorceress

The Witch appears in various roles. This archetype often encompasses the power of female energy and women's wisdom. The Witch is a combination of healer, secret keeper, teacher, herbalist, magician, and scapegoat. Through magick and mystical dealings with both the natural and spiritual realms, she is a facilitator, a conductor of energy, and catalyst of growth and change. She connects the spiritual realms with the natural and mundane worlds.

The Witch is associated with unorthodox lifestyles or outmoded/primitive ideas. The witch posed a threat to the early medical industry and propaganda intending to discredit the wisdom and skill of the witch as healer ensued. The association with rejection of urbane and civilized lifestyle is evident in historical connection between witches and unconventional and powerful women. At one time in history and even in some parts of the modern world, widows, opinionated women, or women who are independent or in any way nonconformist are presumed witches.

In Greek myth, the child of Perseus and Sol, Circe, is a witch known for her understanding of herbs and magick; After the Trojan War, Odysseus and his companions visit her and she uses her magick to turn his companions into pigs.[17] Odysseus demands the return of his companions to their former state. Circe acquiesces.[18] Thus, the witch uses her ability to transform her external environment at will via magickal applications.

The Witch can use magickal powers and the healing arts for good or bane, thereby altering the neutrality of magick through the careful direction of will and intent. She has knowledge of the interconnectivity of the mind, body, spirit, and how to strengthen or weaken the connection. She therefore acts as weaver and unraveler. The Witch archetype is often demonized or villianized, since the individual embodying this archetype stands on the fringe of society, often escapes the binding force of conformity, and is therefore marginalized by the larger community.

Dream Meaning

The appearance of Witch imagery in dreams represents feminine or hidden power, intuition, natural magick, and women's mysteries. You might be experiencing a pull away from conformity. It might suggest that unorthodox beliefs, primitive or naturalistic influences are surfacing. If you're getting intuitive messages through the dream and these messages threaten power, the witch might be emerging as symbol of this energy. Empowerment, sacrifice, reclaiming and communion with natural forces within and around you are indicated. There may be an uncanny talent or force emerging within you that threatens your status or intimidates those in authority, or what the authority in the dream represents in your waking life. Alternatively, your dream might signify your own fear in relation to unrealized or unexplored talents.

MUNDANE DREAM MANIFESTATIONS: This archetype appears as the witch, crone, elderly woman, seductress; power perceived as dangerous, scapegoats; individual power being invalidated by others, connection to plants, animals and nature, unusual magickal abilities presenting in the dream, spells, magick, ritual in the dream, working in secret, or being driven into secrecy. Additional manifestations related to the Witch archetype include dreams in which thought exerts control over nature (for example, storms), female authorities in dreams; struggling with own abilities and power in dreams, and supernatural talents. Power displayed by those easily underestimated in the dream, and grass roots and resistance movements fall under this archetype.

Connecting with the Archetype

How do you perceive your personal and/or feminine power?

How do you exert power?

What is your reaction to the witch?

What is your view of authority and how is it playing a role in your life?

Spend time outdoors under the full moon.

Express yourself fully: draw, paint, write, and invoke divine feminine energies into your life.

Spend time in the garden or nature and connecting to animals.

Magickal Correspondences at a Glance

COLORS: Black, gray, white

CHAKRA: Crown, throat, third eye

DAY: Monday

DEITIES: Hecate, Aradia, Isis, Diana

ENERGIES: Feminine

ELEMENT: Earth, Water

HERBS/INCENSE: Nocturnal flowering plants, rose, lotus

MOON PHASE: Waxing, Full, Waning, Dark

NUMBERS: 1, 2, 3, 13

PLANETARY: Venus, Moon, Uranus

STONES: Lapis, hematite, moonstone, amber, garnet

TAROT: High Priestess, Moon, Hermit, Empress

TOTEMS: Cat, raven, owl; nocturnal animal, sea, and mystical creatures

ZODIAC: Taurus, Cancer, Aquarius, Pisces

The Martyr

The Martyr is the archetype of change brought on through self-sacrifice. Although this archetype is commonly recognized by modern society as invoking the image of Christ on the cross, it's actually an archetype that spans back further in antiquity. In ancient pagan lands, it was tradition in matriarchal pagan society for the female ruler to be both spiritual and political leader and, as such, it was believed that survival of people and the stability of nature depended on her rule. It was necessary for her to choose a healthy consort to complete the cycle of birth, growth, death, and rebirth. It was known that after this time her mate would be sacrificed, thereby returning royal blood to the land. Long after this tradition ceased to involve literal sacrifice, the concept of limited-term rulership followed by the giving up of one's power or status in sacrifice so that new fresh power could emerge continued.

In viewing The Martyr as a change agent rather than a victim, one is liberated and can appreciate their role in facilitating powerful transitions through their own sacrifice. In ancient traditions the sacrifice of one's comfort, luxuries, or even life, was seen as a righteous act. What little remains of this archetype in modern mundane affairs exists in the act of donating precious belongings or even blood so that others can benefit from one's loss, the act of everyday heroes such as firefighters who are often hurt in their mission to help or save others, or even the act of childbirth, in which one sacrifices individual dreams and ambitions to promote the growth of new life altogether.

This cycle is repeated in the Arthurian legends, This theme is deeply ingrained both in Arthur winning power through the Wild Hunt reenactment, then solidifying this power through the Great Marriage to Morgan le Fay, and then losing power to his son, Mordred. The sacrifice, in an archetypal sense, facilitates change through the noble act of acquiescing to newer, often younger, fresher potential. It's seen in modern US politics when presidential or other political terms come to an end and new ideas are allowed to surface, and as such, rejuvenating the arena.

Another example of The Martyr archetype exists in a Norse myth describing the creation of the runic alphabet. In a story suggesting that wisdom often follows the greatest sacrifices, Odin, the Norse god of wisdom, hangs himself from the sacred Yggdrasil tree.[19] Odin remains on the tree all while looking upon the depths of Niflheim, in deep reflection and "self wounded with his spear.[20] In his role as martyr, after the passage of nine days, the god obtains the wisdom he seeks and knowledge of the mystical runes.

Dream Meaning

This indicates being called on to sacrifice short-term for long-term gain and that you may be called to release part your identity no longer serving the greater good. You're being challenged to consider service in its many forms and to be of service to something greater than yourself. You may be facing challenges that force you into powerlessness so that a new perspective can be gained. You may be awakening to see your larger path rather than focusing on instant gratification. Depending on context the dream, the vision might suggest the intrusion of boundaries/ privacy, self-pity, or expecting others to do for you what you should be doing yourself.

MUNDANE DREAM MANIFESTATIONS: Scapegoating, figures known to the dreamer who exemplify Martyr archetypes, sacrifice, being left out, giving blood, volunteering, providing service at cost to yourself or sacrificing an element of time, and resources or money. Being scapegoated by others, and being stuck, confined, or powerlessness is suggested when The Martyr archetype appears.

Connecting with the Archetype

Do you feel like a scapegoat?

In what ways do you feel stuck or powerless?

What sacrifices are you willing to make for larger causes?

Do you feel like life has turned upside down?

How can you harness a new perspective to your advantage or for the benefit of others?

What lessons can you learn from powerlessness?

What do you have to accept that feels intolerable and what lessons can this situation impart?

Examine any relationships that you feel you're sacrificing something for and to what end this sacrifice is helping/hurting.

Meditate, breathe, and engage in gentle stretching exercises.

Practice acceptance and letting go.

Magickal Correspondences at a Glance

COLORS: Blue, black, purple
CHAKRA: Solar plexus
DAY: Saturday
DEITIES: Osiris, Odin
ENERGIES: Masculine
ELEMENT: Fire
HERBS/INCENSE: All perennials, rose
MOON PHASE: Waning
NUMBERS: 3, 12
PLANETARY: Saturn, Neptune, Pluto
STONES: Apache tear, obsidian, jet, onyx
TAROT: Hanged Man
TOTEMS: Snake, beasts of burden, horse, and animals commonly eaten to sustain life
ZODIAC: Pisces

Mentor

The Mentor refers to an advanced guide or teacher who may not be a career educator, but is nevertheless a personal guide or advisor to one or many individuals. A mentor has knowledge and experience and uses knowledge to guide another through trials and transitions. In modern society, examples would be various forms of wellness and life coaches, scholastic tutors, or senior members of a workplace who help guide novice employees through their adjustments. A mentor can also be an established member of a spiritual group who extends their knowledge informally (not a priest/ess) to teach or train others.

The Goddess Athena, holder of wisdom, was also known as Mentor and would appear intermittently to guide Odysseus in Homer's epic *The Odyssey*.[21] Like Athena in *The Odyssey*, the mentor is often hidden in plain sight or appearing as on or near to the same level, not separated by numerous lofty titles or markers of status. The mentor is also portrayed as a coach not an aggressive teacher, but the coaxing voice of the conscience. The Owl has become synonymous with knowledge and education as well as with the Mentor due to the affiliation with Athena.

Dream Meaning

Seeing a mentor in your dream signifies guidance from sources outside of you or your higher consciousness. Instruction, role modeling, and challenging the behaviors and beliefs of the dreamer are indicated. Consider the context of dream for details. Pay particular attention to the guidance you receive. Meditate on the guidance for further instructions on how to apply what you receive in your waking life.

When the mentor appears in dreams, it could be signaling you to become a mentor as well. Your dream could be trying to tell you it's time to reach out and assist others. The main message of this archetype expresses the importance of giving and receiving, or paying forward that which you have been freely given. If the mentor appears in your dreams, it might be time for you to consider how you can serve your family or community better.

MUNDANE DREAM MANIFESTATIONS: Images of the Mentor archetype include any teacher, instructor, or the process of being taught, any institution of learning, written instructions, hearing instructions or factual information announced in the dream. Information presented in the dream as factual regardless of its authenticity; tutors, instructors, and teachers presenting in the dream, or reference to school, education, books, tutorials or workshops, seminars or trainings all fall under this archetype's manifestations. Scholastic processes or components, report cards, school buildings or uniforms and references to learning or academics correspond with this archetype as well.

Connecting with the Archetype

Who in your life is acting as your mentor?
Are you resistant to change or guidance?
Are you listening to the guidance you receive?
Are you in the position for mentoring another?
Are you of service to your family/community?

Magickal Correspondences at a Glance

COLORS: White, yellow
CHAKRA: Third eye
DAY: Friday

DEITIES: Athena, Thoth, Sarasvati
ENERGIES: Feminine
ELEMENT: Air, Earth
HERBS/INCENSE: sage, lotus, apple
MOON PHASE: Waxing Moon
NUMBERS: 3
PLANETARY: Venus
STONES: Quartz crystal, amethyst, aquamarine, sapphire
TAROT: The Chariot, The Magician
TOTEMS: owl
ZODIAC: Libra, Capricorn

Messengers, Angels, Guides, and Guardians

The general role of Messenger in various stories and myths exemplifies transiting information. Deified, the Messenger role is identified in the god Mercury or Hermes. Mundane examples include workers within communications systems, postal workers, announcers, broadcasters, receptionists, public relations workers, and process servers. Additional examples include prophets, seers, and those who spread spiritual messages as psychics or diviners. Systems and abstract processes carry Messenger energies and this can include one's Internet connection, phone service, or cable service in the mundane or one's subconscious—dreams, or intuition in the esoteric. Hawks and other birds have become synonymous with Messengers due to their ability to reach great heights and transfer communication over vast distances. Horses, as well, are symbolic Messengers, carrying people and information at great distances.

Angels are called "ministering spirits" and are an order of immortal spiritual beings; in Judeo-Christianity, Angels are messengers of God's will, but in other ancient cultures, there are beings similar to angels, including the Roman lares or genii and the Greek daemons.[22] Angels are spiritual guides or messengers. In fact, this archetype carries a role bridging spiritual leader with Messenger, while typically associated more with keeper of information than leader, as a Priest/Priestess would be. Mundane examples would be those who bring messages of comfort, relief, spiritual impact, such as a hospice worker or caretaker, or one who brings affirmations, such as a therapist.

Spirit or animal guides offer insights through their characteristics, behavior, mere presence or direct communication. A Spirit Guide can be unique to one individual or a guide to many. The phenomenon of animal whisperers or animal communication is a mundane example of this archetype. Animals can take the role of guide or companion. For example, dolphins rescuing humans, or in some stories, communicating to them, animal familiars, and even the interaction with domestic pets can serve as a relationship where the animal as guide, messenger, or teacher can thrive.

The Guardian typically holds the position of keeper of mysteries, secrets, and sacred wisdom and knowledge, but also protects the ego and provides means of psychological defenses inherent in all people. The Guardian may be given the form of a protective animal, like a dog, wolf, or snake, or may appear in a way that is aversive to others, such as spider or snake, or may be a spirit or creature like a dragon. Usually possessing qualities of determination, self-sacrifice, strength and patience, withholding judgment and focusing on their solitary task of guarding the person, function or information, Guardians are charged to protect. Whether a knight or a three-headed dog, the Guardian's life purpose appears singular, and their view of future benefit outweighs their personal gain.

The Guardian may appear in a dream as a soldier or uniformed guard, security guard or security system, electronic forms of protection such as passwords or programs implemented as e-guardians. Consider baby sitters, and those in positions of custody over people, animals, or even information or objects, as guardians. Characters in dreams standing at the gates, who moderate entry to buildings or events for instance bouncers or even crossing guards; those who are in positions of observation, discerning and protection of people and things represent the Guardian archetype. The Guardian may appear as a gatekeeper and, in a dream, may manifest as anything from ticket collector to random characters whose purpose is to provide oversight and crowd control, or those whose position is to weed out the chosen from the masses.

This archetype may be an individual or even an animal that accompanies the dreamer throughout the dream or through several dreams. It may be a presence felt, but not seen. The key here is that you perceive this being as benevolent and protective as opposed to a teacher archetype in which case the figure instructs or mentors you. Thus, the Guardian has an objective or distant presence in the dream. The figure holds back opinions and does not tell you what to do or where to go. Instead, you get protection and accompaniment. The Guardian is a protector and possesses patience to wait for the correct time and place for the revelation of knowledge or opportunities.

Dream Meaning

When a messenger appears in your dreams, it could mean you will be dealing with upcoming messages in the mundane or you could soon receive spiritual messages of considerable importance. The message you have or will soon receive can have a major impact on the status quo in a given situation. If it's important enough for a messenger to appear in your dreams, then the message is apt to have a life-altering effect. If the Messenger communicates with you directly and you recall the message, consider the context of what the messenger tells you. If you do not remember the dream message, but do recall a dream messenger, look for synchronicities in your waking life that might signal to you the meaning of the Messenger's appearance in your dreams.

If you see animals in the role of messenger, consider the traits of the animal to determine its meaning. For example, squirrels are messengers of readiness and preparation, since they prepare for the winter months in advance. Likewise, the raven represents messages from the realm of spirit. The animal you see can serve as a totem for you in your waking life.

The Messenger can bring positive or negative messages into your life. Remember that just because you don't want to hear a certain message doesn't mean it's not suppose to be given to you. It doesn't mean that ignoring the message will make the potential problem in a situation disappear. Bear in mind that if you ignore enough messages from your subconscious, you could have greater difficulty getting more messages in the future. Finally, messages are useless unless you act on the information you receive.

The Angel archetype is the messenger of the higher self. It's the wise being, the advanced soul, the enlightened master, superman, or the saint. When you connect with the Angel archetype in dreams, you're receiving messages from the divine, higher self, or subconscious or it could mean you're being divinely guided in your life.

The Guardian signifies the entrance of a protector or protectress in your life or that you will soon be taking on the role of guardian yourself.

This archetype can signify the need to increase your awareness in relation to your external environment, the need to prepare for a situation, or the need "to be on your guard." The Guardian might signify that something is amiss and that you should be ready to implement any steps necessary to lessen the severity of any kind of impact or consequence.

Connecting with the Archetype

Are you reflecting on the mundane/spiritual messages you receive?

Are you hearing the guidance you're being given?

Are you acting on the messages you receive?

Are you acknowledging your intuition?

What are the characteristics/behaviors of the animal guide in your dreams?

What are you protecting or what do you have that requires protection?

Are you guarding your emotions and if so, why?

What other parts of yourself are you guarding?

Do you feel your emotional/physical security has become an issue?

Are you soon to face an initiation or rite of passage?

Are you prepared to receive elite, privileged, or arcane knowledge?

Magickal Correspondences at a Glance

COLORS: Yellow, orange, purple, indigo

CHAKRA: Crown, throat

DAY: Wednesday

DEITIES: Mercury, Hermes, all lunar deities

ENERGIES: Neutral

ELEMENT: Air, Water

Incense/Herbs: Angelica, frankincense, myrrh

MOON PHASE: Full, Dark

NUMBERS: 2, 3

PLANETARY: Mercury, Uranus

STONES: quartz, opal, yellow topaz

TAROT: Knights, High Priestess, Temperance

TOTEMS: Birds, horses, fish, aquatic life

ZODIAC: Gemini, Aquarius, Pisces, Cancer, Scorpio, Uranus

The Prophet and Mystic

The Prophet is the visionary and the messenger of spirituality who carries their philosophy to others, but not from the authoritative role of a priest/ess. The Prophet proclaims instructions and declarations with the intent to bring others closer to enlightenment. The Prophet carries a message from the spiritual to the mundane in hopes of improving the lives of others. Spiritual prophets can include missionaries and, in a more secular sense, the modern gurus that hope to spread the revelations they have experienced, be it the experience of spiritual growth, resolution of financial debts, weight loss, or freedom from violent relationships. These advocates and spokespeople typically base their message on a transformation they have experienced personally.

A prophet may interpret the intentions of the Creative Force in the universe and hope to share this message with others. They can be anachronistic and eccentric, such as the town soothsayer, or they can appear to be just like everyone else with the exception of their powerful message wrought of their own crisis and enlightenment. Prophecy was traditionally associated with snakes as well, as it was believed in ancient Greek culture that the snake could give one prophetic abilities by "whispering" in the ears of those who slept.

The Mystic messenger holds esoteric wisdom but only reveals partial truths. They don't open the door and shout the news like the Prophet: they only slide open a small sliver and provide glimpses of what might be. Shrouded in mystery and engrossed in dreamy illusion, the Mystic gives a hint of awareness but forces others to seek through effort to make their way into enlightenment. The Mystic doesn't "lead the horse to water," but rather gives clues, subtle and vague, that the horse must figure out in order to find the water in the first place, and by that time, the drink is not even a question. This is the intent of the Mystic: by shrouding and protecting wisdom in secrecy, the Mystic increases the sacred nature of the wisdom. In essence, if you're willing to work for something, you're far less likely to squander it. Water creatures are associated with mysticism because of the depth that they can travel beneath the surface of the water, an element with subconscious and mystical connotations.

Cassandra from Greek myth represents the Prophetess archetype. As children, Cassandra and her twin sister Helenus, both of whom were daughters of Hecuba and Priam, played in the temple of Apollo; remaining at the temple until it was too late to travel home; the two children slept inside the temple on a couch made of laurel twigs.[23] Nurses went to the girls in the morning only to find two snakes, one beside each girl, licking at their ears. This increased the girls' hearing to the point that they could hear the gods speak.[24] Later in life, Cassandra spent a considerable amount of time in the temple and, in doing so, caught Apollo's eye and adoration; Apollo promised Cassandra he would teach her about the art of prophecy if she would love him in return. Cassandra agreed, but once her curiosity was satiated, she reneged on the agreement.[25] Apollo punished Cassandra by cursing her so that no one would ever believe any of the prophecies she uttered.[26] Thus, Cassandra spent a lifetime knowing things that no one would hear or believe, despite the truthful nature of her predictions.

Dream Meaning

The Prophet and Mystic archetypes serve as messengers involving warnings or communications that signal transitions or transformations leading to enlightenment. These archetypes summon change, and represent intervention, problem resolution, and humility. The Mystic connotes a crossroads, riddle, puzzle, enigma, mystery, or illusion and the need to decipher messages in order to continue or complete a quest. The Prophet or Mystic signifies psychic messages, intuitive communications, or a deep, inner calling from the spirit. When these archetypes appear in dreams, it's time for you to pay heed to your higher self, your subconscious, universal synchronicities serving as life's sign posts, or the divine message you receive.

MUNDANE DREAM MANIFESTATIONS: Forecasters, weather, religious or self-help gurus, spokespeople, pyramid schemes, crusaders, and role models are portrayals of the Prophet or Mystic. Alternatively, an example of the Mystic archetype include the teacher who gives a vague assignment to students who must then research and put the assignment together themselves.

Connecting with the Archetype

What is your spirit trying to communicate to you?
Are you listening to your instincts?
Do you need to free yourself from illusions for spiritual progression?
Are you at a crossroads requiring a life-altering decision?
Are you paying attention to synchronicities?

Magickal Correspondences at a Glance

COLORS: Blue, purple, white
CHAKRA: Crown, third eye, throat
DAY: Monday
DEITIES: Hermes, Mercury, Apollo
ENERGIES: Masculine
ELEMENT: Akasha
HERBS/INCENSE: Laurel leaves, mugwort, peyote, cedar
MOON PHASE: Waxing, Full, Waning, Dark
NUMBERS: 1, 3, 33
PLANETARY: Jupiter, Mercury
STONES: Azurite, citrine, lapis
TAROT: Knights, hierophant, hermit
TOTEMS: Snakes, hawk
ZODIAC: Sagittarius

Divine Beings

The Son and Maiden are youthful archetypes and they sometimes serve as the youthful aspect of a divine trinity. The Maiden and Son are associated with the month of spring, new beginnings, and new wisdom unhindered by self-restraint or social expectations. The Son and Maiden represent new possibilities and births of all kinds.

Maiden

The Maiden is unencumbered by familial responsibilities or the obligations that naturally come with motherhood. The Maiden archetype is active, inquisitive, carefree, and fiercely devoted to her beliefs, as well as the welfare of plants, animals, and children. As a protector, she is fierce and relentless, much like one would see in the depictions of the youthful Amazon warrior who has not yet transitioned into motherhood. This archetype corresponds to the Air element. The Maiden is imaginative, intellectual, and she is associated with the mind and all forms of communication.

When the Maiden is a child, she symbolizes all the magick and wonder of childhood. The waxing moon phase symbolizes the Maiden when she appears with the Mother and Crone as the feminine divine trinity. The Maiden's inquisitiveness and curiosity make her a natural explorer of all that the world has to offer and she enjoys learning, growing, and experiencing life.

Importantly, the Maiden is not always extremely young and her energies are in depictions of young adults. The Maiden is virginal and this aspect of her indicates her innocence. In myth, goddess like Artemis, Athena, Persephone, and Diana represent the Maiden aspect of the feminine divine. The virginal aspect of the Maiden is also in older females, especially if they have made the choice to remain celibate or chaste. She is in the adult woman who is in touch with her inner child or in people who perceive the world with inquisitive, child-like curiosity as well.

The Shadow Maiden archetype is one that is egocentric, self-centered, and might become extremely introverted as she withdrawals from the world. The Shadow Maiden can be flighty, disorganized and have poor communication skills. If the Maiden archetype is tinged with Shadow energies, she might appear as agitated, uninspired, or insensitive to others. Rather than seeking knowledge, the Shadow Maiden might believe that she already knows all that she needs to know about a subject or matter. Her conceit, pride, and boastfulness eventually leads to trouble when experience harshly teaches her that she still has much to learn before she is the master of any situation. This depiction of the Maiden can be seen in stories about Arachne and Athena, where Athena curses Arachne for boasting about being a masterful weaver: one far greater than her teacher.

Son

The Son archetype represents youthful masculine energies and is often heroic, eager to prove his strength and ability, and appears in competition with the Father, King, or elders in his eagerness to compete. He is the young suitor, warrior, or soldier. Sometimes he is mischievous with ample energy and strength, but perhaps lacking ample discretion or judgment: something that he earns through learning, aging, and experience.

The Son is the balance of the Maiden, and they share many representations, including the connection to innocence, virginity, and childhood. This archetype also aligns with the waxing phase of the moon.

The Son represents the wild, untamed nature of youth, and innocence unhampered by experience or imposed societal limitations. In myth, the Son archetype appears in stories of Apollo and Dionysus. This archetype can be a young boy or a young man, but can also be the elderly man in touch with his inner child or emotions.

The Shadow Son archetype can represent the defiant or oppositional side or one who is young, impulsive, and one who walks a fine line between harmony and chaos. Emotional or psychological tides influence the Shadow Son and sometimes he succumbs to the cruel hands of fate or experience as the harsh teacher. The energies of the Shadow Son are visible in those who seek out immediate gratification without consideration of short or long-term consequences.

Dream Meaning

When the Maiden or Son archetype appears in dreams, it signifies the potential for new beginnings, ideas, journeys, or paths. These archetypes can signify abundance, growth, knowledge gained through intuition, or prosperity. If the archetype appears as a young child, your dream might be telling you to reconnect with your inner child or to spend time reflecting on your childhood memories. The Maiden and Son signal the need to tap into your spirituality, your creative forces, and to bring your dreams into manifestation through deliberate action.

If the Shadow Maiden or Son appears in dreams, it represents false hopes or starts; this Shadow archetype represents indecisiveness, uncertainty, ambiguities, and inexperience. If the darker aspect of these archetypes appears in dreams, it could mean you're heeding your superficial desires at the cost of losing yourself, perspective, or integrity.

Connecting with the Archetype

In what ways are you expressing your vital energy?

In what ways should you restrain or moderate your energy?

What causes are you a warrior for and what is your quest?

Where in your life are you experiencing new, untapped creative potential, inspiration, and excitement?

Are you in touch with your inner child?

Magickal Correspondences at a Glance

Colors: White, yellow
Chakra: Heart, soul star, earth star
Day: Sunday, Monday
Deities: Athena, Artemis, Horus, Anubis, Apollo
Energies: Masculine/Feminine
Element: Air
Herbs/Incense: Crocus, lily of the valley, yellow daffodils, tulips
Moon Phase: Waxing
Numbers: 1, 3, 33
Planetary: Sun, moon
Stones: moonstone, sunstone, citrine, opal
Tarot: Pages, The Fool
Totems: Stag, owl, hawk
Zodiac: Virgo, Aries

Father and Mother

The Mother archetype is a protectress, nurturer, and she can be fierce in the defense of her family. The Mother connotes a degree of self-sacrifice or a willingness to set aside her needs for that of her children and family; in this sense, she lacks the freedom experienced by the Maiden or the liberation of the Crone. The Mother archetype is not only one who has given birth to children or who is charged with raising them, but she is also one who has used creative energy to nurture and develop others, whether through leadership, forming a company, caring for animals, or gardening.

While the role of the Mother entails the giving of life and the nurturing of creativity, there are imperfect variations of this archetype. The depiction of the good mother emerges in myth and legend, as does the depiction of the bad or destructive mother: one who is harsh or cruel as seen in the stories depicting wicked stepmothers or in myths involving the distortion of the maternal bond. Most forms of life exist with numerous destructive as well as protective, regenerative potentials, and the archetype of Mother is no different. A mundane example of the destructive Mother is in the harrowing natural disasters that occur that exemplify Mother Nature's unrestrained power, just as the nurturing Mother is seen in nature's regenerative abilities.

The Mother archetype represents both wed and unwed mothers, but it also represents females with or without children who are compassionate and nurturing of others. The Mother is one who offers love without condition; she is resilient with an amazing capacity for both love and forgiveness. Alternatively, the Shadow Mother archetype is one that becomes nurturing to the point of suffocation. She can even become the authoritarian, heavy handed, overbearing meddling mother.

The Father archetype is the regenerative masculine force; it's the male counterpart and balance of the Mother archetype. While the Mother nurtures creative energy, the archetypical role of Father is the enforcer of boundaries, rules, and discipline, and the provider of material structure in which nurturing takes place. The Father archetype sometimes involves the establishing of legacies for children; this energy can manifest in the approving Father whose proudest moment is watching his children inherit the legacy he has built for them.

The archetype of the Mother and Father sometimes overlap, whereas the Mother can be a disciplinarian, provider, and enforcer of structure. This is not a gender bias argument since, in its most basic form, the act of procreation involves these elements. The Mother is the vehicle that carries, nurtures, and births new life, and the Father is the vehicle that carries and transports the seed to the mother for nurturing; therefore, it's not a gender biased argument of who pays the bills and who watches the children, but rather a basic natural process of provision, nurturing and balance.

The Father is archetypically a detached nurturer, and in many ways, a part of the allure of this archetype is his elusiveness and distance. In many stories the Father is a concept of protection, provision and stability, but his role is from afar. Consider in stories like Snow White or Cinderella, the Father is absent, distant or unaware of the danger lurking for the heroine. While he is the protective and wise male figure, he may be detached, unavailable, and unaware of danger.

As with the Mother archetype there is the distortion of the Father role seen in the intimidated King or ruler who fears the rise in power of his own young and so seeks their destruction. Such depictions fall under the dominion of the Shadow Father. He is seen in the stories of Kronos, who seeks to dispose of his young to prevent loss of his own power. In a mundane sense, the Shadow Father is the disapproving father, who watches with grave disappointment as his children forego what he hoped would be his legacy in pursuit of their own independent path, rejecting the kingdom he has built for them.

To dream of the Father or fatherhood calls forth associations with power and authority and may manifest in conflicts or associations with authority figures in daily life. The boss, police, landlord, president, king, ruler, judge, or disciplinarian in the mundane realms calls forth the energy of the Father archetype. With this comes restriction, but also the judicious use of resources.

Dream Meaning

When the Mother or Father archetype appears in dreams, it signals you to question the amount of nurturing you're giving to others. This archetype can signal the need for intentional self-nurturing, since it's difficult to nurture others if you fail to care for yourself. When you see the Mother/Father archetype, it's time to reflect on what you want to nourish or bring into your mundane/spiritual life. Consider if you have issues with authority or rebellion as well, and what you can do to resolve such issues.

This archetype can signal the need to refrain from overzealous care-giving too. While it might sound like a positive thing to be fanatical about caring for another, overzealous care-giving can result in codependency. Thus, the Mother/Father archetype represents the need to maintain a delicate balance, and to strive for moderation in all things.

Connecting with the Archetype

How do you perceive nurturing around you?

How do you nurture others?

Have you spent time nurturing yourself?

What do you hope to nurture or birth in your life?

In what ways do you balance maternal care and are you guarding against the smothering of growth?

How are you handling power and authority?

Is authority a force you respect or rebel against?

Does authority bring a sense of security or confinement?

Do you feel adequately protected, abandoned by those in authority, or left to fend for yourself?

Magickal Correspondences at a Glance

COLORS: Red, blue
CHAKRA: Solar plexus, heart
DAY: Sunday, Monday
DEITIES: Isis, Hera, Osiris, Zeus
ENERGIES: Masculine/Feminine
ELEMENT: Fire
HERBS/INCENSE: Summer-blooms, oak, rose
MOON PHASE: Full
NUMBERS: 1, 3, 33
PLANETARY: Sun, Moon
STONES: Sunstone, moonstone
TAROT: Emperor, Empress
TOTEMS: Bear, lioness, woodpecker, dolphin
ZODIAC: Capricorn, Cancer

Crone and Sage

The Crone and Sage are elder archetypes that represent the wizened individual and the darker side of masculine and feminine wisdom. They are not evil, but they hold an awareness of darkened reality, an understanding of death, and keep safe the hidden mysteries. Both the Sage and Crone archetypes are symbols that connote the waning life force, but this does not mean that the they are diminished or weakened in terms of power or strength.

The elder archetype is sometimes synonymous with fear, as many fear age and the deterioration of the physical appearance or abilities during the aging process. In the Sage and Crone, the tradeoff is in the accentuation of other skills when physical skills or abilities are lost or diminished. An example of the elder archetype with accentuated skills include Tiresias, the blind seer who prophesizes Oedipus Rex's downfall.

The Sage and Crone exemplify the wisdom one can only acquire through time and experience; sometimes part of these archetypes is wisdom that seems arcane or unorthodox; as such, people sometimes dismiss the sacred wisdom of the elder in error as outdated or no longer valuable, easily overlooked or underestimated. For example, in stories and legends, portrayals of the crone are often old and senile. Due to her age and her closeness to death, people often fear her. As the depiction of the crone unfolds, others in the story will discover that she holds secrets that are of great value. One also discovers that it's important not get distracted by physical appearance or assumptions about the value of the Crone's character, or they risk missing valuable discoveries.

Crone

The Crone harnesses the power of destruction, but in its wake, she leaves the seeds of creation. The Crone is seen in moments where wisdom replaces or eradicates ignorance and when experience takes the place of innocence; here, the Crone comes to represent sometimes ugly, painful truths and harsh realities. She is associated with barrenness, the season of winter, and the final harvest.

The Crone is the last aspect of womanhood following the youthful maiden and the compassionate and nurturing mother. Thus, this archetype represents older females who are experiencing menopause or who have already gone through it. Menopause is a transitional time; it's a time when a female moves from the role of mother to crone. The years of bearing children end and are exchanged for experience, wisdom, and personal freedom. Rather than having one's time consumed in the nurturance of others, the Crone is in a position to spend time nurturing the self. She is representative of one who lives life without any preconceived notions or illusions; the veil of innocence is stripped away, leaving only experience and complete understanding in its wake.

The Crone appears in many myths, including the Russian tales of Baba Yaga, an ancient and frightening figure who tests Vasilisa, a maiden, with seemingly impossible tasks. While the Crone Baba Yaga is known for her eccentric abode, as she lives in a house on chicken feet in the forest, stories about her also explain that her house circulates and she flies in a mortar and pestle, thereby suggesting her role as a healer. Her looks may repel or scare others, but the crone's wisdom is of death, the darkness within life experiences and healing. She can be a harsh teacher, but an important one nonetheless.

The Shadow Crone is a symbol of extreme isolation, bitterness and sadness, or regret. Her role as mentor becomes tainted, and she may mislead those who seek out her wisdom. Rather than having grown wise from experience, the Shadow Crone becomes bitter and regrets the loss of her youthful beauty. The Shadow Crone sometimes focuses on her failures or mistakes, rather than her successes in life. She will not see that she has created her own reality, and puts blame on others or the world for her losses or shortcomings; for this, she casts bitterness out into the world: an animosity that sometimes returned onto her through karmic repercussions. The Shadow Crone develops a fixed mind, one not swayed by fact or wisdom.

Sage

The Sage archetype is associated with elder masculine energies. Sages include wizened masters, gurus, philosophers, teachers, and spiritual guides. The Sage is the counterpart of the Crone and is the image of the wizened old man or Father Time; this masculine energy is one of structure, tradition, and wisdom. Unlike the Crone, however, the Sage is more likely to have earned a degree of respect rather than fear, at least in many cultures where age is not yet rejected due to irrational anxieties.

The Sage is often solemn as an individual with great wisdom, superior judgment, and vast experience. It's the experience of the Sage that is most honored since the Sage has weathered much to obtain his knowledge. The Sage acts as a mentor and guide for others since he is both deeply spiritual and philosophical. In some religious systems the Sage is depicted as part of a divine trinity such as the Father, Sage, and Son, with the Sage representing the eldest and wisest aspect of the trinity.

The Shadow Sage is in individuals that become overly dependent on knowledge alone without sharing the knowledge or without wisely applying the knowledge obtained. The Shadow Sage can become didactic, arrogant, authoritative, rigid, inflexible, and can become so closed-minded that his perceptions or ability to empathize are diminished. When the Sage develops a fixed mind, he may base decisions on unsound assumptions rather than wisely sought out facts. Typical portrayals of the Sage reveal a kind, fatherly individual who is at the ready to provide much needed and sound council; the Sage, when shadowed, is one who might have the wisdom to provide advice or solutions, but chooses to withhold such information rather than share it with others. This same dark aspect is in the condescending Father figure or one who, so certain in the superiority of his own wisdom, becomes egotistical, egocentric, and unapproachable.

Dream Meaning

When the Crone archetype appears in dreams, you might subconsciously fear the aging process, but it bears remembering that through the aging process you will have a chance to grow wise through experience. The appearance of this archetype indicates that you might be tapping into the dark feminine energies that the Crone represents. While the Crone is a symbol of death and destruction, she is a reminder of renewal and all the potential that follows in the wake of destruction. The Crone is a representation of endings of all kinds, but she stands on the very threshold of new beginnings. Your subconscious might be bracing you for the ending of relationships, situations or conditions or upcoming cyclical changes, followed by a period of renewal and growth.

The Crone archetype indicates that you are not seeing reality as you need to: free of illusions. Connecting with her archetype suggests that you need to assess your perceptions for accuracy. The entrance of the Crone suggests that you might encounter harsh realities or painful truths, but the Crone is one who has endured much in her life, so connecting with her in dreams suggests that you too can make it through difficulties that might otherwise seem too hard to endure.

If you have connected to the Crone she could signify the final harvest or the reaping of just rewards; the keyword here is "just," meaning that you will not get more than you rightfully deserve. As a symbol of winter, she represents death with the promise of rebirth. Your connection to her might indicate that you're entering an area in your life where you can enjoy more personal freedom or where you're liberated from certain obligations. Seeing images of her or images that allude to her might suggest that you should not dismiss the wise or seemingly unorthodox wisdom of others: within such wisdom you will find something of incredible value.

If you have tapped into the Shadow Crone energies, you might experience a period of self-imposed isolation. Remember that you alone hold the key to your freedom from isolation. The Shadow Crone warns us to avoid becoming bitter or consumed by our own sadness. She reminds us that all things can and do change, and we must accept the changes in our life gracefully in order to make room for new growth and experiences. She reminds us that regret serves no purpose other than to stagnate growth of an individual; to be obsessed with things that cannot be changed is a futile endeavor. The Shadow Crone teaches us that we are the creator of our reality and the karmic ramifications that follow and she reminds us to walk through life with an open mind, for it's in our understanding that we know nothing that we become truly wise.

If you're connecting with the Sage archetype, your dreams might be telling you it's time to engage in the pursuit for greater knowledge or it's time for you to pursue intellectual endeavors. The appearance of the Sage archetype in dreams might allude to the appearance of a mentor type figure in your waking life or it could hint at the fact that you will soon become a knowledgeable mentor for someone else.

The Sage's propensity for contemplation can serve as a cue to consider to all of the ramifications or possible consequences associated with the different events in your waking life. Your dreams may be telling you it's time to turn to an experienced, wizened individual for assistance. The appearance of the Sage in dreams might indicate a need for you to put aside assumptions that hinder your perceptions of events in your waking life; you can benefit from being open to mentoring from another and can learn life-changing lessons from the experience. In dreams focused on the concept of time, dates, anniversaries, and appointments, you might find yourself connecting to the Sage archetype as the Father Time figure as well.

A connection with the Shadow aspect of the Sage is a warning indicating that you should avoid the dependence on knowledge absent of wise application. You will want to avoid focusing too much on thought while avoiding necessary action; the key to mastering the Sage's energies is to find a balance between both. Assess your waking life, events and behaviors to see if you're taking on some of the attributes of the Shadow Sage; question whether or not you're becoming rigid, inflexible, authoritative, closed-minded, or arrogant. If you find that the Shadow Sage energies are present in your life, it's time to make drastic changes, so do not intentionally or unintentionally distance yourself from others or make yourself unapproachable.

Connecting with the Archetype

Do you need to break out of a cycle in order to grow?

What can you release so you can allow growth?

In what areas of your life do you need a fresh start and what can you do to instigate necessary change?

What emotions arise when you consider the Crone's dark power? Do you have the wisdom and solitary reflection of the Crone or do you fear her destructive power?

Do you perceive the Crone's energies as a threat to youthful priorities?
Do you fear the responsibility she carries?
Do you seek an understanding of the mysteries, death, and change?
What are you clinging to that no longer serves you?
Are you open to the wisdom of those who have experience or do you tend to reject such wisdom while insisting on blazing your own trail?
Are you comfortable with your age or your level of responsibilities?
Who in your life represents the Sage or Crone and what kind of wisdom can they share?

Magickal Correspondences at a Glance

Colors: Black
Chakra: Crown, soul star
Day: Saturday
Deities: Baba Yaga, Ceridwen, Hecate, Kali, Chronos
Energies: Feminine/Masculine
Element: Earth
Herbs/Incense: Evening primrose, water lilies, moon flowers
Moon Phase: Waning, Dark
Numbers: 0, 1, 3, 10, 13, 33
Planetary: Saturn
Stones: Onyx, jet, obsidian, apache tear, bloodstone
Tarot: Death
Totems: Raven, cat, wolf
Zodiac: Capricorn

Divine Couple

The Divine Couple represents the union between masculine and feminine energies serving as the perfect complement of strength and vulnerability. This union results in the coupling of direct, active, light masculine energies with receptive, deep, absorbing feminine energies. The Divine Couple archetype is an alchemical combination of spiritual and personal energies representing yin and yang, and the perfect balance in intimate partnerships. In a mundane sense, a Divine Couple can be the ideal business pairing or entertainment duo; the pair will seem so natural that they do not even seem to have their own name or brand without being joined to their ideal partner.

Within the Divine Couple archetype, the mystique of the twin phenomenon exists, although this is a divine union absent of the romantic emotions. When viewing twins as the Divine Couple the energies of this archetype come to represent a special symbiosis uniquely belonging to twins. This archetype represents the pairing of soul mates as well.

Although this archetype seems to represent the perfect relationship, for something to be perfect it must embrace imperfection. The shadow aspect of the Divine Couple, starts out as an ideal pairing but results in imbalances between the couple, jealousies, codependency, infidelities, disloyalties, abusive relationships, or unrequited love.

In myth, the alchemical union of the Divine Couple includes pairings of lovers as well as siblings. Representations of the Divine Couple in Egyptian myth include Isis and Osiris as brother and sister, but also lovers. The same union is found between the twin sister goddesses Isis and Nephthys.[27]

Some myths portray the deities as destined for one another, as is the case with Isis and Osiris, having fallen in love while still in the womb of the goddess Nut. When Set, the Egyptian god of chaos, kills and dismembers his brother Osiris, Isis mourns her husband; She sets out to find his body parts so that she can resurrect him;[28] In this endeavor, Nephthys, The Benevolent One or Savior Sister, assists her.

In Greek myth, the Divine Couple exists in the pairing of the goddess Artemis and her twin brother Apollo or the coupling of Apollo and his brother, Dionysus.

In the case of Artemis and Apollo, Artemis is the first born child of Leto and Zeus, who then serves as the midwife who helps Leto bring Apollo into the world.[29] In the case of Apollo and Dionysus, both are Greek gods of creativity and the arts; Apollo, a sun god, is associated with the arts, medicine, light, order, harmony, rationality, and individuality,[30] while Dionysus, the god of vegetation, wine, drunkenness, and ecstasy, is associated with the illogic, disorder, chaos, and the unification of all with the loss of individuality. Thus, the pairing of gods represents opposite extremes and epitomizes completion/totality.

Dream Meaning

The Divine Couple is The Syzygy or a pairing of opposites as identified by Carl Jung: it's a coupling of the anima and the animus with the result of completeness. On an unconscious level, the anima is the feminine personality within the male and the animus is the masculine personality within the female. When the energy of the Divine Couple connects with you in your dreams, your subconscious might be hinting at your desire for wholeness, completion, satisfaction, and personal happiness.

The story of Isis and Osiris suggest the longing one has to be with another who offers a sense of completion. When the Divine Couple archetype appears, it might be time for you to connect/reconnect with your feminine/masculine unconscious, or you might desire a deep and meaningful connection with another. Consider the concept of "As within, so without," and you can begin to understand that a meaningful and ideal unison with another can be achieved only if you manage to become complete or fulfilled within yourself first.

Apollo and Dionysus, when viewed as extreme opposites, teach the lesson of balance; both light and dark aspects are necessary, in fact vital, for a complete understanding of the self and the world. In this light, your dreams might be telling you that you need to willingly face and embrace the shadow aspects of yourself to become spiritually unified, and through unification, certain aspects of your individuality will be lost through the process of minor or even major change.

If your dream imagery is connecting to the darker aspect of the Divine Couple, your subconscious might be trying to warn you not become prisoner to your jealous feelings or that you should avoid becoming codependent. Your dream might be warning you to avoid events that can lead to disloyal or unfaithful behaviors. If you fear that someone is being unfaithful to you in your waking life, your subconscious could be reiterating these fears in your dreams.

Connecting with the Archetype

In what ways are you vulnerable?

Are you seeking out others whose strengths balance your vulnerabilities?

Do certain types of partners, friends, or lovers naturally attract you? What do these connections say about your willingness to allow reciprocal give and take in relationships?

Do you feel the need to control, rescue, or enable others and how might this be evident in relationships?

Do you feel the need to depend on others for guidance/direction?

Are you not asserting yourself enough?

Are you avoiding the declaration of your independent preferences in relationships?

Explore the state of balance in your relationships and reflect on the dual nature within yourself; in what ways can you strive to achieve greater balance and reciprocity?

Magickal Correspondences at a Glance

Colors: Black, white, gray

Chakra: Heart

Day: Friday

Deities: Isis, Osiris, Nephthys, Set, Zeus, Hera

Energies: Neutral

Element: Akasha

Herbs/Incense: Dong quai, evening primrose, white willow bark, calendula

Moon Phase: Full Moon

Numbers: 2, 4, 11, 22, 33

Planetary: Venus, Neptune

Stones: Snowflake obsidian, rose quartz, malachite, tourmaline

Tarot: Lovers

Totems: Goose, swan, wolf, bald eagle

Zodiac: Libra, Gemini, Pisces

CHAPTER 7

TAROT ARCHETYPES IN DREAMS AND DREAM WORK

After exploring some of the main dream archetypes, here you will find a listing of the Major Arcana Tarot cards and dream work correspondences. Refer to the listing to learn how the messages of such cards might actually manifest in dreams. A brief description of the suits of the Minor Arcana and their correspondences is also available.

Select a card from the Major Arcana corresponding with the specific issue you are concerned with or choose an appropriate card to use for dream understanding intuitively. When you have selected your card, spend time observing and reflecting on it. Journal about all the symbols that catch your eye and any thoughts you get from your observations. Do not worry about analysis at this point. Just take the time to jot down ideas that come to mind.

When preparing for sleep, place the card at the head of your bed or beneath your pillow so it's close to you while you sleep. Consciously ask for deliberate guidance on the issue at hand and proceed to sleep as usual. Do not disregard any dream material that seems irrelevant. Remember, dreams work in symbolic ways. If no dream emerges, repeat the process again in the next sleep cycle or during meditation.

0 The Fool

The Fool corresponds to risks, faith, spontaneous change, new beginnings, adventure, and independent endeavors. This card signifies the wisdom of innocence, youth, seeking, quests, and missions. The Fool represents impulse, actions, the season of spring, and corresponds to the astrological sign of Aries. The color white (for new beginnings) or red (action), signify The Fool's energies. This archetype corresponds to Tuesdays and Wednesdays as well as the planetary influences of Mars and Mercury.

Meditate on this card and the energy of unencumbered new beginnings with spontaneity. Creative acts before dreamtime such as writing, artwork, music-making, or drumming can help invite spontaneity.

DREAM MANIFESTATIONS: The Fool energy corresponds to heroes in myth or pop culture or one who is in a heroic role. Dreams involving journeys, flight, falling, leaping to new heights, crossing roads, new beginnings, and dreams with a carefree air all relate to The Fool. Dreams involving wandering or being lost relate to this archetype. Therefore, adventurous dreams, exciting expeditions, risk taking, and quests are representative of The Fool. Since The Fool represents innocence, dreams of children or of childhood signify The Fool's energies.

CONSIDERATIONS: When working with this archetype, note the receptivity to spontaneous beginnings in your dream. Do you feel fear, resistance, or excitement? Note whether you feel confused or lost in your dream. Consider any new projects or adventurous situations in your life and how the message of The Fool relates to new beginnings in your waking life.

1 The Magician

The Magician relates to magickal workings of all kinds and synchronicity. This archetype's energies signify the power of the mind, attraction, self-discipline, and personal will. The Magician represents the will of the individual connected with the energy of the divine in order to manifest on the physical plane. The card often depicts a Lemniscate, symbolic of infinite potential and accessibility of sources that allow transcendence into higher planes, while bearing a cyclic component. The burden of ethics lies herein, for the magician is held to the rules of karma and "As above, so below."

The Magician corresponds to the number one: the number of beginnings, and the act of bringing intentions into manifestation. The number one signifies rites and initiations as well. The Magician corresponds to the planetary influences of Uranus, Jupiter and Mercury and the zodiac signs of Aquarius, Sagittarius, and Gemini. The color white (representing purity), orange (attraction), and purple (for Akashic or psychic energies) all relate to The Magician.

DREAM MANIFESTATIONS: The Magician's energies appear in dreams where you're taking control or in any dream of involving supernatural or magickal abilities. The Magician's energies sometimes involve lucid dreams or visions of manifesting money, jobs, or desired outcomes. This archetype communicates through dreams of getting what you want or dreams in which you manifest thought for good or ill. The Magician rules dreams of control, therapy; coming to terms with one's strength and mental abilities, creating music, art or literature, or dreams involving building things from the ground up. The Magician governs dreams of wizards, historic occultists, magicians (both real and illusory), and dreams superheroes or of mythic magickal phenomenon, like Excalibur, the philosopher's stone, or alchemy. Dreams of construction workers, builders, entrepreneurs, and visionaries hold this energy. This archetype can involve visions about initiation, starting phases, physical or mental attraction, rituals, and both sacred and mundane ceremonies.

CONSIDERATIONS: When working with this archetype in dreams, note whether negative thoughts are manifesting as reality or whether the manifestation feels in control, surprising, excessive, or out of control. If your dream is of desires pending but just out of reach, note what is prohibiting you from the acquisition of your desires. For more information on the Magician, see the chapter Common Dream Archetypes.

2 The High Priestess

The High Priestess relates to the feminine divine, guidance, therapy, intuition, counselors, and counsel from subconscious or esoteric channels. It corresponds to spirituality, passive messages or support, unlocking unconscious/subconscious secrets, balancing opposites, and revealing hidden drives or agendas. This archetype represents the dream world unperturbed by one's acts or will, receptivity, psychic phenomenon, and inspiration from within. The High Priestess signifies the divine feminine or the goddess in numerous guises. In dreams, she represents subtle cues, passive guidance, and the duality of the inner/outer world, but where acknowledgement of the exterior world is often ignored; this archetype corresponds to the influences of the moon, Venus, and Neptune and the astrological signs of Cancer, Libra, and Pisces. The color silver and blue (representing goddess energies) and white (feminine and moon energies) signify The High Priestess in dreams. Finally, with this card falling under the influences of the moon, The High Priestess corresponds with Mondays.

DREAM MANIFESTATIONS: The High Priestess archetype appears in dreams involving encounters with enchantresses, powerful or wise women, priestesses, spiritual teachers, or deceased loved ones (especially mothers, grandmothers, or female guides), all of which typically carry important messages. This archetype communicates through dreams involving the act of encountering bizarre or disguised spiritual guides. The High Priestess' energies may appear as dreams where you're given hints about the future, but where you must make your own decisions; dreams about nurturing spiritual development, mentors, teachers; dreams of harnessing the energy of opposites, or in dreams reflecting ambivalence or confusion.

CONSIDERATIONS: Note any emotional or behavioral reactions in your dream. Are you ignoring subtle cues or messages? Are you doubting or second-guessing the guidance you receive in dreams or in your waking life? Does your dream involve a spiritual guide presenting as a figure in your belief system or as a part of a foreign belief system or culture? How receptive are you to taking the advice of the guide?

3 The Empress

The Empress relates to maternity, fertility, growth in family or business, motherhood, finances, generosity, abundance, productivity, expansion, nurturing, or being nurtured. This archetype's energies represent material growth, expansion, feminine, earthly energy, and wealth. The Empress corresponds with the planetary influence of Venus and the astrological sign of Taurus. The colors green and brown are representative of The Empress' energies. Venus' planetary influence makes The Empress' energies correspond to Fridays.

DREAM MANIFESTATIONS: The Empress communicates with you in dreams of promotion or dreams involving conception/motherhood and pregnancy. Dreams of business development, gardening, watching the growth of children, animals, and plant life; dreams involving the forest or outdoors; dreams of female power and abundance; visions of winning the lottery, or visions of economic boons are associated with this archetype. The Empress' energies translate into dreams of pregnant people or animals, farmers, cooks, business people, gardeners/landscapers, or dreams of bulls, cows, large herds of animals, and livestock. The Empress translates into dreams of recovering material inventory, products, sales, investments, or antiques. Dreams of finances, profits, crafts, home furnishing, or dreams of going to the theater, the fine arts, cultural events, material luxuries, and generosity.

CONSIDERATIONS: Note the pace of growth in your dreams. Is it normal, too slow, or too fast? Is the growth/birth or presence of a baby/child/young animals or plants welcomed or shunned? Is there secrecy surrounding the new life? Your responses to such questions could suggest a budding idea that you feel the need to protect. If the dream features pregnancy, what is your reaction? Unwelcome pregnancy or children may correlate to new or growing abundance that comes at a cost to you in your waking life, or could signify new responsibilities that you feel you're not quite ready to embrace.

4 The Emperor

The Emperor relates to rulership, authority, power issues, territory, fatherhood, and father figures. This archetype represents paternity, stability, protection, discernment, property, resources, government leaders, advancement, and projected power or sources of power/authority. This archetype is under the planetary influence of Mars; the astrological sign of Aries, and its planetary influence aligns the archetype with Tuesdays. The Emperor associates with the color red.

DREAM MANIFESTATIONS: The Emperor's energetic influence appears in dreams of the father, fatherhood, or father figures; dreams of male bosses or authoritative figures; dreams of power, territory, protection; dreams of appealing to powerful people for help or dreams of being commanded by authority (like dreaming of military service or working under domineering powerful people). The Emperor rules dreams of controlling others or being controlled by others or dreams of unfinished business with a father or father figure, (which can include dreams of other authorities suggesting paternal links). The Emperor's energies sometimes appear as dreams of defense, invasion, or dreams where you or someone else commandeers a project. Dreams of celebrities or people in your life who present with a natural air of authority are representative of The Emperor's energies as well.

CONSIDERATIONS: Note how you interact with power or those holding it in your dream; is there fear of the authority figure or is there a competition for victory? Are you hiding your own power or hiding from the power of others? Are you expressing anger at the powerful figure concerned, or are you grateful for the guidance and protection provided?

5 The Hierophant

The Hierophant represents higher education, advanced learning, institutions and bureaucracies, government agencies, large, impersonal structures, social hierarchies, and clergy. The Hierophant represents higher learning, higher philosophy, detachment, oppression, and organized religion or society. This archetype signifies support, structure, resources, greater emphasis on policy over individuality, governing, organizations, and placing one's needs behind the needs of the greater good or self-sacrifice. The Hierophant corresponds to the colors brown, purple, and black. This archetype corresponds with the planetary influence of Saturn and the astrological sign of Capricorn. The influence of Saturn aligns the archetype with Saturdays.

DREAM MANIFESTATIONS: The Hierophant reveals itself in dreams of higher education, government work, secret societies; dreams of being a drone in large systems or dreams of conformity, uniformity and dependency on tradition. Dreams of working for large hierarchies like the government, religious or educational institutions; dreams of challenging long held establishments, and dreams of being confined by bureaucracy are representative of this archetype. When out of balance, your dreams may include visions involving rebellion within a group, escaping from group dynamics, running away from a job or college; challenging authority on religious matters such as a priest/ess or pope, or balking at bureaucracies or religious dogma. This angle may suggest a feeling of suffocation or conformity in waking life that restricts individual expression. If you're restricted by the external system, this may suggest a need to refrain from flaunting opinion and individuality in order to allow the support of the larger group, but if you're actively trying to break free from routines tailored by traditions in culture, religion or society, this may reflect a need to do so in waking life as well. Dreams of rituals such as baptisms, initiations, marriages, and dreams of organizations, brotherhoods, gangs, mafia, or large corporations, all fall under the dominion of The Hierophant.

CONSIDERATIONS: Consider the following: If your dream symbols signify an institution, how does the institution present to you? Do you find it welcoming, or threatening? Do you anticipate growth and wisdom as a result of being engaged in this institution? Do you anticipate loss of individuality or powerlessness? Do you regard this institution with absolute faith or mistrust? Notice how the institution regards your individual needs and how this feels to you emotionally. Do traditions comfort you in the dream, or are the customs outdated?

6 The Lovers

The Lovers relate to balance, harmony, interconnection, interdependence, unifying opposites, alchemy, and partnerships of all kinds. The archetype relates to compromise, boundaries, confronting issues of vulnerability, openness, and dependency, fair and even exchanges, allegiances without identity loss, the ideal couple or partnership, complimentary pairings, and masculine and feminine energies. The Lovers corresponds with the planetary influence of Venus and Mercury as well as the astrological signs of Libra and Gemini. Being influenced by Venus and Mercury, The Lovers corresponds with Friday and Wednesday.

DREAM MANIFESTATIONS: The Lovers energy appears in dreams of partnerships, intimate dreams (even those that do not pertain to present partners); dreams of having a twin or any work in pairs or couples, or dreams of collaboration with another. If out of balance, The Lovers energies may manifest as dreams of dependency or where another victimizes you. Dreams of rescuing another from their own decisions or circumstances or of being rescued relates to the Lover archetype. Dreams in which a partner or guide advises or completes a puzzle or provides the missing piece to a mystery; a dream where another helps you achieve what you could not on your own, dreams of pairs, the number two, or collaboration, all relate to the archetype of The Lovers.

CONSIDERATIONS: Are you dreaming of a pair or partner familiar to you? If so, what does this couple or person represent to you in mundane life? What is your emotional reaction to this pairing? How does it feel to share responsibility and power? How does it feel to be yourself in this partnership? What do you most like/fear/dislike in this pairing?

7 The Chariot

The Chariot relates to vehicles, journeys, voyages, crossroads, indecision, self-doubt, polarity and self-sabotage. This archetype relates to situations where careful self-evaluation is required. The Chariot signifies refinement, a daring journey, a serious commitment, or the choice to embrace change by facing your flaws lest you run the risk of stagnating in ignorance. The Chariot corresponds to situations where you face self-sabotage versus overcoming doubts and insecurities, dual drives, or ambivalence. The planetary influences of this archetype include Mercury and the Moon, which link the archetype to Mondays and Wednesdays; Astrologically, The Chariot aligns with the signs of Virgo and Cancer.

DREAM MANIFESTATIONS: The Chariot's messages are identifiable in any dreams of transit via car or small/personal vehicle, especially when such vehicles suddenly break down or stall. Any dream references to dead ends, crossroads; a car or vehicle that drives itself or drives without the direction of the dreamer, and dreams of being in the driver's seat yet powerless over the direction/speed of car all share the message of The Chariot. Dreams of loss of control of a vehicle; dreams of sabotage or ruin near completion of a goal or task, and dreams of arrival or plotting/planning one's journey or arrival fall under the dominion of The Chariot. Dreams that entail fear of journey or fear of a road traveled in pursuit of goals, and dreams of conflicting self interest, ambivalence reflected by chasing something in circles; circular or futile motion, treadmills, escalators, or motion in which one is travelling, but not progressing should bring to mind the archetype of the Chariot.

CONSIDERATIONS: How do you respond to beginning the journey in your dream? What is the condition/quality of the roadways and the vehicle in the dream? What is the nature of your journey? What does the type of vehicle in the dream suggest about the journey you face? Do you feel ambivalent about change? In your waking life, what are the pros and cons of doing nothing versus the pros and cons of accepting changes? What is your excess emotional baggage doing to benefit you?

8 Strength

Strength relates to personal emotional tests and challenges, reason trumping emotion, patience, keeping one's head in difficult situations, keeping destructive thoughts/emotion under control, and moderating strong instincts or impulses. The Strength archetype relates to issues involving logic, maturity, tolerance; maintaining integrity in the face of adversity, and situations where patience prevails over emotion or impulse. This archetype corresponds to the influence of the Sun, Sunday, the astrological sign Leo, and the color yellow.

DREAM MANIFESTATIONS: The archetype of Strength is behind dreams involving wild animals and interaction with them on a personal level such as discovering one has wild or unorthodox pets; dreams of displays of aggression or repressed aggression; dreams of strength showing via physical power or an uncanny ability to withstand physical pressure and visions where you demonstrate unusual physical feats. Dreams of one's uninhibited wild nature; dreams of cats hunting for prey, prowling, stalking or activities reminiscent of survival in the wild, but requiring stealth and patience, as well as visions of the steadfast pursuit of goals are under the rulership of the Strength archetype. Dreams in which emotional or physical strength seems to be tested or dreams of heart disease, heartache, or heartburn and dreams of being crushed, bitten or attacked by animals reflect messages from the archetype of Strength.

CONSIDERATIONS: In what ways do you perceive your own strength? How do you convey your power to others? What emotions surface to convey this? What do you notice about your physical condition in these dreams? How are you overpowering your adversary? What is the role of intellect versus physical abilities? What is at stake if you lose control of your emotions?

9 The Hermit

The Hermit relates to lone journeys, a lonely path, spiritual quests, transcendence through receptivity to unusual guidance, and striking out on a journey away from conventional wisdom. This archetype relates to the eclectic, unusual spiritual quest; progressing spiritually or away from the status quo; challenging mundane beliefs and limitations; embracing guidance from unusual sources, or following intuition and inner light/ guidance. The Hermit signifies wise counsel from an esoteric or unusual source, isolation, contemplation, and eventual transcendence. The Hermit corresponds to the color orange (representing fortitude and energy). The archetype corresponds to the planets Saturn and Mercury, Saturday and Wednesday, and the signs of Virgo and Aquarius.

DREAM MANIFESTATIONS: Messages from The Hermit archetype are in dreams where you're alone but reflecting on relationships with others not present, and dreams in which you're moving away from social ties or breaking with social conventions or traditions. Dreams of converting one's religion or changing cultures, isolation, quarantine, or exile, (all of which insinuate the lone pursuit of spiritual or physical purification or the banishment from society), fall under The Hermit's rulership. Dream encounters with unorthodox spiritual teachers or guides, especially of an eccentric nature; visions of pursuing purification, transcending boundaries/ obstacles via a road less traveled, or visions of aspiring to ideals in spite of social expectations, share the message of The Hermit.

CONSIDERATIONS: Do you long for solitude? What could you gain from following your own path? Who is inspiring your unorthodox choices? What goals are you striving for that set you apart from the crowd? How will you know when your own path has led where you need to be? What social expectations stand in the way of your growth? How would your path be different if others' opinions didn't matter? If you didn't listen to the crowd, who would inspire you? Who are the unorthodox mentors providing enlightenment for you at this time? Are you feeling like an outsider in your life? What is your reaction to your solitary path?

10 The Wheel of Fortune

The Wheel of Fortune relates to situations involving fate, openness to change, or divine intervention. The Wheel of Fortune signifies the message of good fortune, release of expectations, and a positive, unexpected turn of events. This archetype signifies the act of letting the Powers that Be take control of one's life, acceptance, the release of the ego, surrendering to a greater power/the universe, and the act of being open to new opportunities that will prove positive markers of growth. The Wheel of Fortune corresponds to the color purple, the planet Jupiter, Thursdays, and the astrological sign Sagittarius.

DREAM MANIFESTATIONS: The Wheel of Fortune's message appears in visions involving unexpected changes in events or scenery that prove fortunate, the role of fate and dreams presenting synchronistic turns/twists that land you in the right place/time to achieve your goals. The message of this archetype is found in dreams of surrendering control to your own advantage; visions of fruitful, advantageous, fated encounters or in dreams of "king for a day" positions/role reversals inspiring empathy, awareness, and the reversal of power. Dream imagery of cycles, wheels, shifting, turning, things turning upside down, or dream references to fate, divine intervention, or controlled intervention issued by a mundane or spiritual authority, as well as dreams of the legs and movement, all share the message of The Wheel of Fortune archetype.

CONSIDERATIONS: Are you trying too hard to get your way? In what ways could you invite spontaneity into your life? Are you trying to cover too many bases? Are you responding to opportunities or turning them down? How would you know if opportunities presented fateful intervention?

11 Justice

The message of Justice relates to karmic returns for gain/loss and a time to balance karmic debts. The appearance of this archetype in dreams relates to the repercussions of your actions, the advocacy of righteousness, higher order, and higher spiritual laws. This archetype's planetary influence is

Saturn and Venus; aligns with Fridays and Saturdays, and it corresponds to the color purple, black, and green. The signs Libra and Capricorn represent this energy.

DREAM MANIFESTATIONS: Dreams involving any and all aspects of the legal system, parole, probation, punitive measures, judges, juries, court rooms, being judged or being the judge of others, fairness, equality, and balance or law, all share the message of Justice. References to any types of punishment, consequential events, or issues brought to mediation in a dream. All matters of karma, retaliation, vendettas, or settling scores; dreams of retribution for past acts positive or negative; dreams of past life events related to present life karma and dreams of damage to or in general reference to the kidneys or lungs, all share the message of Justice.

CONSIDERATIONS: Are you in tune with balance in your life? What governs right from wrong in your current situation? Are you following your highest ideals? Are you bending the rules, thinking no one is watching? Are you feeling that life is unfair? What beliefs do you have about justice, penalty and fairness? Are you willing to let the universe manage justice or are you seeking revenge?

12 The Hanged Man

The Hanged Man is an archetype representing suspension, stalemate, sacrifice, scapegoating, spiritual healing accomplished through surrender of control, or the act of being forced to adopt a different view. The Hanged Man expresses the lack of control over the ego or the assertion of will or being forced to remain in a difficult situation in order to gain greater strength from confronting what would otherwise be avoided. The Hanged Man's planetary influences include Neptune and Saturn; the archetype corresponds to Saturday, the astrological sign Pisces, and the colors blue, purple, and black.

DREAM MANIFESTATIONS: The Hanged Man's message will appear in dreams of being stuck. This archetype's message is in dreams of punishment, martyrdom, or sacrifice, especially when you're a scapegoat. Dreams of paralysis or being frozen in time or space; dreams of futility or the inability to move, control events or changed views; dreams of being suspended, on hold, or of things being upside down represent The Hanged Man's energies. This archetype will appear in dreams that force you to take on a new viewpoint, either from being underground, having your head underground or having your head in a separate realm or location from the body or rest of society. Dreams of serious illness and life altering, incapacitating illnesses or injuries; dreams of stagnation through illness, loss or malformation of the legs or feet, and visions of immobility due to illness or injury share the message of The Hanged Man.

CONSIDERATIONS: In what ways are you feeling stuck in spite of your own efforts? Are you feeling helpless about your situation or is there detachment or acceptance in the dream? Notice the reactions of others to your dilemma in the dream. Notice in what ways situations worsen with resistance or improve with acceptance. What could you stand to learn from accepting the present situation for just a moment? What views are challenged by the situation in the dream? What are you resistant to seeing?

13 Death

The Death card relates to endings, transition, transformation, change, and the potential for new beginnings stemming from recent endings. The Death archetype represents a transitional phase where one is undergoing symbolic death and rebirth; this archetype signifies a maturation process, a bittersweet transition or transformation and dramatic change; the archetype's planetary influences are Pluto and Mars. The Death card corresponds to Tuesdays, the sign of Scorpio, and the colors red and black.

DREAM MANIFESTATIONS: The message shared by The Death card is identifiable in dreams involving your own death or of someone close to you or dreams in which death is a factor. Dreams about metamorphosis, either through eggs hatching, butterflies emerging from cocoons, or snakes shedding skin convey the message of this archetype. Dreams of the underworld, death related places like Heaven/Hell or Hades bring up the message of The Death card. Visions of limbo, purgatory, or dreams of ghosts (see ghost archetype) that lack the sense of true spirit communication suggest a resistance to change of some kind. Dreams of revisiting adolescence, early childhood times, maturation, or the transition in the lifespan, as well as dreams of loss but also of new beginnings, hatching, or births, all fall under this archetype's domain.

CONSIDERATIONS: In case of a birth/new beginning, what is your emotional reaction? Are there aspects of change or ending that you're resisting? Are there parts of your identity that seem vested in change or staying the same? Are there losses implied in this dream that threaten your sense of purpose?

14 Temperance

Temperance relates to situations involving teamwork, cooperation, assembly, alchemy, combinations, and walking in both mundane and spiritual worlds. This archetype relates to balance, moderation, teamwork, synthesis, combining spiritual with practical applications, artistry and creativity, and healing. When the messages of Temperance appears in dreams, you're being called to modify plans, surrender complete control in order to collaborate with others for optimal results or you will need to implement self restraint in some situation. The planetary influences of this archetype include Mercury and Uranus. Temperance corresponds to Wednesdays, the astrological sign of Virgo and Aquarius, and the color brown.

DREAM MANIFESTATIONS: The message of Temperance comes through in dreams of painting, craftsmanship, the assembly of crafts, objects or projects requiring several stages to manifest, building, working with your hands, and collaborating on an assembly line or working as part of a team. This archetype appears in dreams about conflict between your personal desires and limitations imposed by your environment, dreams about having to overcompensate for the lack of effort by teammates, dreams about creative processes and hands on work, or visions representing conflict over wanting to do everything by yourself. Temperance rules dreams of conflict demanding your patience in order to achieve resolution.

CONSIDERATIONS: In what ways does the dream suggest need for moderation and cooperation? What reactions are invoked by the notion of restraint, or collaboration rather than control? What role do you have in expressing yourself creatively in this dream? Is this role a burden or an outlet? How does patience factor into this dream? What is your reaction to situations in which patience is required?

15 The Devil

The Devil archetype relates to obsession, compulsions, and actions that are rewarding but lack heart and soul. This archetype relates to addictions of any kind including relationship addictions (codependency), compulsive work habits, eating disorders, obsessive compulsive rituals, and compulsory business moves where one feels they are "selling their soul to the devil" to advance in career or money matters. The archetype relates to temptation and seduction without substance. This archetype represents the shadow self, the darker part of personality that longs to satisfy base cravings with instant gratification, but with a lack of long-term planning, foresight or stability for long-term sustainability. The Devil signifies unhealthy or imbalanced relationships and routines. The archetype's planetary influences include Pluto and Saturn and The Devil corresponds to Tuesday's, the color red (representing sensual desires, lust, and base instincts or impulses) and black (representing the extreme nature of desires and darkness). This archetype corresponds to the signs Capricorn and Scorpio.

DREAM MANIFESTATIONS: The messages of The Devil archetype come through in dreams of addictions of all kinds, obsession, stalkers or stalking in dreams; dreams of drug abuse, alcohol abuse, excessive eating, spending, or other behaviors; dreams of indulgence or indulging in guilty pleasures and dreams of pleasure-seeking, especially through that which feels forbidden. Other dream imagery related to this archetype include dreams of temptation, seduction, illusion; dreams involving sex without emotional connection; dreams where you feel enslaved, bound, or obligated to act against your true desires, and visions where appearance trumps substance. Dreams involving loss of balance in relationships by either being too controlling or being controlled by partners; dreams where there is too much of a good thing leading to loss of control or perspective; dreams of an adversary or of the dreamer's devious side taking charge, and dreams of sexual behavior, especially those which deviate from your usual behavior or preference, or dreams of genitalia/reproductive organs all carry the message of The Devil archetype. For more information on The Devil, see the section Common Dream Archetypes.

CONSIDERATIONS: What addictions or obsessions are manifesting in the dream? What routines have become habitual, even if destructive or illogical? In what ways are relationships fostering dependency? In what ways are instant gratification or avoidance surpassing your integrity? Where is temptation and false seduction surfacing in waking life? What objects symbolize temptation or obsession in the dream? Is it a forbidden love, taboo behavior, drugs/alcohol or indulgent food? Explore the link between the source of temptation and your own reaction; how does this connect to temptation, obsession and restriction in waking life?

16 The Tower

The Tower card relates to destruction, release and stagnation, potential fallout, loss of illusion, loss of stability or illusion, chaos, and awakening from illusions that are comfortable but no longer sustainable. This archetype signifies the loss of grounding or security. The Tower's planetary influences include Pluto and Uranus; the archetype corresponds with the astrological signs Aquarius and Scorpio, Tuesdays and Saturdays and the color black.

DREAM MANIFESTATIONS: The message of The Tower is identifiable in dreams of crashing, falling, earthquakes; severe weather causing damage to land and home; severe crises effecting stability such as a house fire or dreams involving collapses or being bombed. The Tower archetype communicates through dreams of transportation against one's will; dreams of being kidnapped or having one's vehicle hijacked;, dreams of being dethroned, dramatic loss of power or autonomy and dreams where one is travelling and the road disappears or you encounter a chasm or void. This archetype's message is found in dreams where a death takes place or that involve one's perception of reality. The eyes, vision or ability to see objectively, and diseases of the eyes or brain portrayed in a dream all fall under the dominion of The Tower.

CONSIDERATIONS: What are you defining yourself by? What would happen if this were to change? If you couldn't hang on to this source of security, what is the worst that would happen? How do you respond to change, collapse or loss of control in the dream?

17 The Star

The Star represents the ideal, hope, light, dreams within reach, high integrity and standards, and striving for the ideal. This archetype signifies a perfected image: one that is achievable but perhaps out of immediate reach. This archetype's planetary influence is Uranus; The Star corresponds with the colors blue (peace and harmony), white (purity and light), and gold (the Masculine divine, prosperity and health). The Star corresponds to the sign Aquarius.

DREAM MANIFESTATIONS: The Star's message appears in dreams of accomplishments, accolades, honors and awards; dreams featuring a celebrity or dreams in where you encounter personal role models or heroes. Dreams of heroic or larger than life figures from myth or society; dreams where you travel into outer space or visions pertaining to stars, planets, astrology, the cosmos, and radical breakthroughs, fall under the rulership of The Star. This archetype communicates through dreams inspiring hope and providing epiphanies; dreams where you arrive to a conclusion based on information that seemingly comes out of nowhere; dreams of comets, meteors or other space related phenomenon; dreams where messages emerge from the sky, or dreams where you suddenly know what action to take without consciously being aware of it.

CONSIDERATIONS: What is your guiding hope in the dream? In what ways are you closer to your goal than you think? Where do you find inspiration to proceed in the dream? Where do you find inspiration in waking life?

18 The Moon

The Moon card corresponds to deceptive illusions, urges, cravings, or signifies the desire of the subconscious. The Moon represents the act of nurturing creativity and intuition, the more productive and nurturing aspects of the inner/subconscious/shadow side, and nocturnal or mysterious processes. This archetype signifies mysterious, not-yet-realized aspects of the self, mystical pursuits, intuition, psychic phenomenon, weighing the subconscious desire against conscious diplomacy and maternal energies. The Moon is its own planetary influence so this archetype corresponds to Mondays, the astrological sign Cancer, and the colors blue, silver, and white.

DREAM MANIFESTATIONS: The Moon's message appears in dreams about the moon, the mother, maternity, pregnancy, dreams of business enterprises, entrepreneurship, dreams of the home, native family, motherland, native land, family home, family heirlooms, family legacies or traditions, and dreams where one is near the sea. Dreams involving crustaceans, sea travel, being beneath the sea, personal finances, financial security measures, bank accounts, savings accounts, one's earnings, the home or house, cooking, food, and erratic or extreme emotional displays signify this archetype's message. Dreams involving intuitive hunches or visions involving the breasts or stomach and their illness/health are all representative of The Moon archetype at play.

CONSIDERATIONS: In what ways did the Moon feature in your dream? What emotions seem to lie just below the surface? Explore subtexts and insinuations when the Moon archetype presents: a strong but evasive undercurrent is at work. What parts of the dream triggered strong emotional reactions? What actions or situations are being nurtured in the dream? What signposts of security and emotional attachments surface in the dream? Where do you find home base? Are you being prompted to reconsider what you bring home with you? What cycles of time references are suggested by the dream? Consider the subtext of 28-30 day cycles or a period of 28-30 years. Consider the suggestion of cyclical changes implied by the lunar archetype. How do instincts play into the dream?

19 The Sun

The Sun relates to situations involving health, wealth, success, joy, celebration, love, individuality, personal expression, creativity, and accomplishment. This archetype represents the life force, energy, active processes, vitality, influence, fortune, positive omens, and the expression of individuality and personal strengths. The Sun signifies leadership, and masculine or projected power that is not overbearing. With the Sun as a planetary influence, this archetype corresponds to Sunday, the astrological sign Leo, and the colors yellow and gold (both of which represent the colors of the Sun).

DREAM MANIFESTATIONS: Dreams of lions, leaders, kings, leadership, authority, fathers or father figures; dreams of bosses, actors/celebrities, or entertainers; dreams where grandiosity or a "larger than life" presence is displayed by you or others; dreams involving recreational interests and pursuing luxury or dreams where one lavishes generously upon others, are messages of The Sun archetype. Dreams concerning heart disease, heart health or the heart in general; Dreams of cats or members of the cat family including panthers, tigers or lions; Dreams of the Sun, sunflowers, and lighting of all kinds; dreams involving blood or diseases of the blood, or visions where success and advancement plays a role, all share The Sun's archetypical meaning. For more information on The Sun archetype, see the section on celestial bodies.

CONSIDERATIONS: How are you handling leadership responsibilities? What is the status of your health? In what ways is this dream relating to your successes and vitality? In what ways is this dream encouraging you to share the wealth or extend hope and light to others? Are certain aspects of your personality grandiose in the dream?

20 Judgement

Judgement is an archetype that corresponds to discernment, discretion, a major transition approached with rational appraisal and caution, or the act of outgrowing one phase of life and transitioning into a new one. This archetype signifies graduation, accomplishment, reaching desired heights, and closure on one area of life with openness to new opportunities. Awareness from a global, holistic perspective corresponds with Judgement. The planetary influence of Judgement is Mercury; the archetype corresponds to Wednesday, the astrological sign Virgo, and the colors orange (symbolizing youth and transitioning) and black (representing possibility, the mysterious, and potential).

DREAM MANIFESTATIONS: Dreams where one is graduating or about to retire or dreams of major life milestones (such as purchase of property, marriage, divorce, relocation, movement from one job/career to another), are messages of the Judgement archetype. Dreams involving sorting, evaluating or preparing a will, estates or yard sales; dreams of the process of selection taking place; visions of judgment of others or of self, and dreams of evaluating what will be packed in preparation for travel or a move all share the message of Judgement. Report cards, weigh-ins, measurement-related tools or practices, analytical processes, and categorizations apply to this archetype as well.

CONSIDERATIONS: What major transitions are you considering? What aspects of your lifestyle are you outgrowing? Analyze your current preferences and priorities. Which ones feel most important? Which priorities or goals seem to have lost their importance? How are you reacting to others: are you being critical of people and situations that may be helpful to you? Are you being a harsh judge to yourself? In what ways do you feel prepared for transition into a new phase in life? In what ways does fear keep you from making significant changes?

21 World

The World card relates to graduation, finality, promotion, a successful and significant ending, elevated status, transition, and closure, and new processes pending. This archetype signifies completion and transcendence. The World is associated with the planet Saturn, as well as the four fixed signs of the zodiac: Leo, Taurus, Aquarius, and Scorpio, but by its meaning, corresponds to Pisces.

DREAM MANIFESTATIONS: Dreams of ascending stairs, ladders or climbing up; dreams of traveling to heights, either astral projection or travel in planes; ascension dreams, including those about flying, climbing buildings, trees or mountains; dreams of standing on plateaus, mountains, or high places; dreams of finalizing projects, promotion at work, or dreams of promotion in family or relationships are representative of The World. Having an elevated perspective or looking down or looking at maps or pictures or having an external/holistic view presented in the dream are all visions sharing the meaning found in The World archetype.

CONSIDERATIONS: What are major accomplishments presented in the dream? Notice the perspective you have in the dream; are you looking down from above, or able to see into the future? Are you able to see through situations so that you know the underlying factors of what is taking place? Take note of the broad perspective the World suggests: from your point of view, are you able to cover more ground, or are you missing details? Consider what variables suggest an ending, completion, or resolution. What emotions greet this potential ending? What needs to happen or change in order for you to embrace a new beginning?

Minor versus Major Arcana Tarot Symbolism

Minor Arcana imagery reflects elemental correspondences and mundane situations. Additionally, the symbolism in the Minor Arcana sometimes signifies people, seasons, and time.

Wands/Staves

Wands/Staves represent ideas, inspiration, communication, the element Air, and Eastern corner of the Pentacle. Faeries, angels, maiden goddess energies, new beginnings, initiation, and the dawn are all associated with wands or staves. Wands signify creativity and written, oral, or telepathic communication. Wands correspond to the color white and yellow (both representing the air element), and the zodiac signs Gemini, Libra, and Aquarius. Wands correspond to masculine energy and the planetary influences Uranus and Mercury.

DREAM MANIFESTATIONS: Dreams of pens/writing instruments, computers, phones, faxes, messages, signs, communications of all kinds, bells, instruments of music, art, new beginnings, births, babies, spring, leaves, incense, smoking, smoke, air quality; the ability to breathe vs. suffocation or respiratory systems or illnesses share the message behind the Wands archetypes. Maps, thinking, planning, studying, school, cognitive activities or abilities, confusion, disorganization, miscommunications, words, or the inability to "find the right words," are ways in which the message of Wands appears in dreams.

CONSIDERATIONS: What is the main message you need to send/ receive? Are communications clear? What new beginnings are brewing? Are you open to them? What are you being asked to learn?

Swords

Swords signify action, energy, vitality, passion, will, force, aggression, masculine energy, integrity, and motivation. Swords can signify movement of thoughts to will, and sometimes swords indicate potential strife, conflict, discord, or dissension. Swords correspond to the mother aspect of the divine feminine, guardians and the cardinal direction of south, as well as the planetary influences Mars, Jupiter, and the Sun as well as the zodiac signs of Aries, Sagittarius, and Leo.

DREAM MANIFESTATIONS: Dreams about sex, sexuality, fire, gasoline, food, fuel of various forms, burning, desire, drive, driving or activity such as running, walking, exercise, or biking all relate to Swords. Visions of warriors, being on a mission, soldiers, military, purpose, spontaneity, impulse; dreams with rapid changes of scenery or dreams involving chaos, hectic changes, or rapid movement fall under the rulership of Swords. Masculine, father or paternal themes; dreams of blood and the vitality of the physical body, or dreams of motion, action, intensity, anger, passion, energy, vitality or the lack thereof, all relate to the Swords.

CONSIDERATIONS: Reflect on the pace of the dream; how do you respond to such action/intensity? Where are you being called to take action in waking life? What movements or actions need to happen in order to reach your goals? Do you perceive this as exciting or stressful? Are you getting all fired up, or burned out?

Cups

Cups correspond to the element of water, intuition, receptivity to feedback and signals, mother goddess energies, creation, psychic phenomenon, the cardinal direction of West, sea creatures of all kinds, nymphs, sea deities. This archetype relates to the moon and feminine energies, relationships, and since water is the universal symbol of the subconscious, Cups rule dreams of all kinds, especially psychic or precognitive dreams. Cups correspond to the planetary influences of Neptune and the Moon; the astrological signs Pisces, Scorpio, and Cancer. Cups correspond to the color blue (representing water, the feminine divine, and psychic communications).

DREAM MANIFESTATIONS: The messages of Cups cards are in dreams about emotional displays, relationships, marriages, births, family, loved ones, friendships, intuition, creativity, and the mother or maternal themes. Dreams about bodies of water, oceans, water in general, swimming, drowning or of rain, tears, and bodily fluids all related to the Cups. Dreams about being creative or psychic; dreams of intuitively knowing something without understanding how or why, or dreams about the subconscious are connected to the message of Cups archetypes.

CONSIDERATIONS: What emotions predominate in the dream? Are you riding the wave of emotion or being overcome and drowning in feelings? What is the dream asking you to nurture in waking life? What relationships stand out in the dream?

Coins/Pentacles

Coins/Pentacles cards represent the earth, the cardinal direction North, the crone aspect of the divine feminine, healing, cleansing, purifying, stability, money, material goods, and the manifestation of desires. Coins/Pentacles signify profit and karma, the dark aspects of life, the state of being well-grounded, feminine energies, and materialism. Coins correspond to the planetary influences of Saturn and Venus, the astrological signs Capricorn, Virgo, and Taurus, and the colors brown (representing earth) and black (representing power). This Tarot suit corresponds with the color green (representing prosperity and abundance).

DREAM MANIFESTATIONS: All burrowing creatures or creatures residing in caves or underground are associated with the message of these cards. Dreams of profit, money, financial material wealth and resource or dreams of salt, dreams of physical body and physical health share the message of the Coins/Pentacle archetype, as do dreams of bones, animals close to the earth or earth/ground related disasters such as earth quakes. This archetype corresponds with dreams of caves, mountains, rocks, and natural earth related items. Finally, Coins/Pentacles correspond to dreams of stones and minerals of all kinds.

CONSIDERATIONS: How do you feel about your financial security and work? What does the dream suggest about career and financial status? Does the dream reflect profit or deficit? Does the dream show ways to achieve security beyond material resources? What fears or hopes are reflected by this dream? Does the dream connect financial stability to physical health in any way?

Numbers in Dreams

When numbers appear in dreams, pay attention to them and note how many times specific images or themes appear in your nighttime visions. Numerical references can allude to possible dates and times for events to occur or can reference specific milestone markers. For instance, if you have a dream with repetitious references to the number three, it could mean that the dream pertains to the third of the month, three weeks from present time, or it could suggest that a situation will unfold or conclude in March. Finally, you can use references to numbers to make decisions about what deities to invoke in Magickal applications, rites, and rituals.

Numbers can connote specific themes you will face or need to address and each number has positive and negative connotations. You can determine the nature of a number's connotation by the tone or atmosphere of your dream. If your dream makes you comfortable, or happy, then any number associations are positive, but if your dream disturbs you or makes you uncomfortable, then you will need to consider the negative connotations of the numbers your dream reveals.

Any number you see in a dream or the amount of image or symbol repetitions you come up with can be broken down to a single digit from one to nine. For example, if the number 361 appears to you in a dream, you can add all of the numbers together to come up with a two digit number ($3 + 6 + 1 = 10$). You can then take the sum and break it down further by adding the two digits together ($10 = 1 + 0 = 1$). Once you break down the number to a single digit, you can use the following references to interpret your dream's meaning. Bear in mind there are some double-digit numbers that have an extra layer of meaning before they are reduced to a single digit, like the numbers 10 and 13. Some numbers are master numbers that you do not have to reduce, like the numbers 11, 22, and 33. However, if desired, you can view the latter numbers as a magnification of the sum of the digits within the number under analysis; for instance, $22 = 2 + 2 = 4$, so the master number 22 is a magnification of the properties found in the number four.

(0): If you see dream references to the number zero, the imagery could relate to cycles, circulation, completion, absence, or unity. Additional themes include that which is undefined, lacks definition, or defined by ambiguity. The number zero corresponds with The Fool in the tarot. In references to time, zero can represent a time outside of time, no time at all, or the continually shifting, ever-changing present moment. Adversely, the number zero can signify hollowness, emptiness, superficiality; a lack of purpose, faith, or vision, and coming full circle without gaining any wisdom from the experience.

(1): This number represents new beginnings and starting points. The number one symbolizes the ego, self, identity, self-centeredness, internal motivations, consciousness, external intention, and action. The number one corresponds to The Magician in the tarot. Adversely, the number one connotes a singular enemy or advisory, single mindedness, or a fear of new beginnings. In a negative sense, the number signifies the fear of being alone, the fear of your own power, or the fear to stand on your own.

(2): The number two represents pairings, duality, compromise, connections, balance, things that complement each other, and the unity of opposites; this number invokes the power and reference to various opposing forces found in nature, such as day/night, black/white, male/female, or yin/yang. The number two corresponds to The High Priestess in the Tarot. Astrologically, duality is expressed through Gemini and Pisces. Adversely, two signifies broken partnerships or the fear of a broken relationship. In a negative sense, the number two signifies the loss of power in partnerships, the loss of balance, and the suppression of one's duality.

(3): This is the number of creation, expansion, Magick, and the birthing process or the manifestation of creative energies. Three is the number that corresponds to the divine trinity, fertility, growth, and abundance. In the tarot, the number is assigned to The Empress card. The number corresponds to the element of Air. Adversely, the number three signifies love triangles, jealousy, a threat from magickal sources/actions, a threat multiplying behind the scenes, or a multiplication of problems.

(4): This number associates with stability and balance of all the meanings implied by the number two or the pair, but to a greater degree. Four corresponds to the household, property, family, and traditions, as well as contentedness, but also relaxation, reprieve, and complacency. In the tarot, the number four is linked to The Emperor. Astrologically, the number is linked to the sign of Cancer and the influences of the Moon as well as the element of water. This number's planetary influences make it relate to the feminine aspect of the divine, womanhood, emotions, compassions, maternal matters, and the memory. In a negative sense, the number four represents chaos, stress, disruption, aberration, or something unnatural. Adversely, the number four signifies enforced or chosen complacency and something that begins natural, but becomes grotesque and monstrous.

(5): The number five corresponds to Akasha (the combination of air, fire, water, and earth), Magick, alchemy, creativity, recreation, procreation, and the manifestation of one's will and talents. This number represents minor conflicts and challenges that strengthen the spirit and bring the opportunity to expand experience and awareness. In the Tarot, this number links to The Hierophant. Astrologically, the number five links to Leo and the influences of the sun. Adversely, the number five signifies black magick, danger coming from unseen realms, a mysterious or hidden threat, fear of persecution, and the pervasion of the sacred. Adverse connotations of the number five imply the misuse of sacred power, the use of power to manipulate others, chaotic change, disruption, disconnection, and dissolution.

(6): This number is the magnified power of the number three. It represents stability, resolution, balance, service, work, ambition, health, and the combination of masculine and feminine energies. Six corresponds to unification of receptivity and action, service and gain, and it connotes maturity. In the Tarot, the number six is The Lovers card, which links the card to the sign of Gemini. In a negative light, the number six signifies false endings, false security, illusions, self-deception, and solutions that lead to greater difficulties.

(7): This number links to the concepts of effort, stagnation, and reaching a plateau. The appearance of the number seven in dreams challenges you to find inspiration or to free yourself from tedium. This number corresponds to selflessness and the place of being consumed by what is outside and opposite from the self. The number represents the need to open yourself to alternative perspectives and to restraint your desire or your need for immediate gratification. Seven corresponds with The Chariot. Astrologically, it corresponds with Libra. Planetary influences include Venus. In a negative light, the number seven signifies being stuck, moving and getting nowhere, futile efforts, stagnation, and the number relates to dreams of being buried, suffocation, or drowning.

(8): This number is associated with the infinite, breakthroughs, abundance, fruitfulness, and prosperity that is close at hand. Eight signifies renewed inspiration, the expansion of belongings and property to include the shared money or resources of a partner. This number corresponds to regeneration, renewal, death, and rebirth. The eighth card in the Major Arcana is the Strength card, and therefore corresponds to the sign of Leo the Lion along with the planetary influence of the Sun, but also to the sign of Scorpio and the influences of Pluto and Mars. The number corresponds to the elements of fire and water. Adversely, the number eight signifies narrow-mindedness, lack of vision, a lack of completion, going around in circles, a lack of readiness, short-sightedness, and a loss of resources. The adverse connotations of the number eight might manifest in dreams about infinite suffering, falling without landing, or being stuck in an infinite loop of some kind.

(9): This number represents things nearing completion, inspiration, and the power of three trebled. It represents idealism and philosophical, judicial, or benevolent humanitarian quests. Nine signifies metaphysics, the sciences, and human potential. The number corresponds to the ninth month and the sign of Sagittarius, and is connected to The Hermit card. Adversely, the number nine signifies a lack of contentment, bad karma, backfired success, and wish fulfillment gone wrong. The number nine might manifest in dreams about contracts, something coming to you at a cost, get rich quick schemes, mafia imagery, or genies.

(10): This number represents ten and one, since the sum of all its digits equals one. The number ten is a symbol indicating something has come full circle only to begin again or anew. When viewed as the number ten, it represents endings, but when viewed as one, it represents beginnings. Ten connotes status, public image, career, opportunities, new growth, and fated transitions. The number links to the sign of Capricorn and the Wheel of Fortune Card in the Tarot. The adverse connotations of the number ten include incompletion and endings that fall short. Possible dream manifestations include broken items, death, and the loss of your home, job, or relationship. This number's adverse energies can manifest as a broken dream continuum or the sudden arousal from sleep.

(11): This number doubles the energies of the number one, but it also adds the extra dimension of pairings or balance. Where one stands alone and represents beginnings, 11 brings an element of unity or balance to the concepts of identity, self, consciousness, and fresh starts, where one has balanced footing or stable ideas. This same balance is found in the number two, which is the reduced sum of the digits in the number eleven, so this master number magnifies and expands on all things that the number two connotes. This number relates to Justice in the Tarot, the sign of Aquarius, and the planetary influence of Uranus.

(13): This number represents the lunar months in a year, and is a Magickal number as well. Some people choose to view the number as lucky, rather than unlucky. Only you can determine the meaning of the number when it appears, but this number connotes death, rebirth, and regeneration. Reduced, this number has a meaning similar to the number four, along with the same astrological and planetary associations. However, viewed as a two-digit number, this number associates with the Death Tarot card. The zodiac sign of Scorpio and the planetary influence of the moon correspond with the number 13.

(22): This number doubles 11, so where 11 serves as the stage where one learns to tap into greater energy, the number 22 is the stage where one seeks to bring that heightened energy to others, thus this number is one belonging to partners and teachers. This is a number of balance, leadership, intuition, inspiration, creativity, and unity of dreams and ambition.

(33): This number trebles 11, but is reducible to the number six: a number that already magnifies the number three. Like the number six, 33 connotes resolution and completion, but the number differs in that rather than focusing on ambition, will, and manifestation in the physical realm, 33 connotes spiritual attainment, enlightenment, and the outreach to others in order to spread spiritual understandings and knowledge.

CHAPTER 9

DECODING THE DREAMSCAPE

Dreams are today's answers to tomorrow's questions.
Edgar Cayce

All aspects of the dream contribute to the greater meaning. The archetypes in this book and the magickal/astrological correspondences lend depth to your ability to work with the figures and themes your dreams present.
Consider how your subconscious stages the dream content and the possible meaning this implies: There are no coincidental or unimportant details included in the vision. The setting in your dream conveys meaning as well. It's easy to presume your subconscious chooses a particular setting by default.

Remember, anything is possible in dreams: this makes it more likely that the scene/setting you see has a symbolic purpose. As a comparison, consider all the work a film director and crew put into staging the settings in a movie. There is often symbolic meaning conveyed through different settings and symbols. Thus, if your dream takes place in the early morning, during a specific season, or in a particular landscape, you should make a note of it.

Understanding Time in Dreams

Dreams can sometimes give you cues about when things will happen. If you suspect that you have had a precognitive dream, you should look to time-related symbols to see if you can get an indication as to when something might occur. It will be up to you to determine how to apply the symbols in relation to time to your dream interpretation; you will need to use your intuitive abilities to see if your interpretation feels right to you. It may take some practice in interpreting dreams before you begin to understand how your subconscious communicates time factors or allusions to time.

Time indicators can appear as references to seasons. If you see a repeated reference to numbers or if dream images appear repetitiously a set number of times, this can be a time reference; numbers can related to days, weeks, months, or years. For example, if you see the repetition of the number three, this could mean that whatever information is shared in the dream will happen at three o'clock on a given day, three days from the time you have the dream, on the third of the month, or it could even suggest a time span of three years. As mentioned earlier, if you see references to specific astrological bodies, some planets are associated with days of the week; thus, planetary imagery can serve as time indicators in dreams.

In some cases, time references are symbolic of other concepts or ideas, and this is evident in correspondences associated with various times of the day like morning, noon, twilight, and evening. The seasons are also larger archetypes that represent ideas or concepts. Below are some of the symbols associated with seasons and times of the day when you want to view your dream imagery symbolically instead of literally.

DAWN IS A BETWEEN TIME. A dream scene that occurs during dawn represents waxing conscious energy, but also represents transitional periods or times of change. If you experience a dream that occurs in an early morning setting, it could symbolize openness, exposure, health, vitality, growth, or masculine energies. The morning is associated with the element of air and cardinal direction of east.

MORNING OR DAYLIGHT: Daytime in a dream suggests the yearning for open, outward expression, for things to be brought to light, and for conscious insight. Consider your own patterns of activity; if you're more productive or active in the daytime, your dream is emphasizing this fact. If not, perhaps the dream is suggesting that you express more of your identity in public, in view of others, or in daily routines. This is a time of projection of plans, attitudes, identity, and is associated with Gods and masculine energies.

NOON: Dream scenes occurring at noon are set at a between time; thus, the dream symbolizes transitional periods, change, and transformation, The sun is at its greatest power at noon, so this time period corresponds with masculine energies, the Sun, and The Sun card in the Tarot. Noon corresponds with fire and the south.

TWILIGHT: This time connotes a plateau, indecision, ambivalence, or a period of stagnation that results in a lack of movement or a failure to transition from one stage/condition to another. Twilight is a symbol suggesting a neutral zone where illusions might blur clear boundaries. Dusk corresponds to west, the element of water, and it's a between time.

NIGHT: Dream scenes occurring at night symbolize the subconscious, unconscious desires, hiding, hidden truths, secrecy, mysteries, illusion, psychic abilities, intuition, and receptive feminine energies. The night signifies the mystical or the act of covering actions/awareness under a shroud of mystery. Consider the content of the dream to see if it seems unusual for the activities to take place at night; for instance, if you work a day schedule but dream that you're at work at night, consider the implications of this unusual setting for the corresponding activity. Night is a receptive time corresponding to Goddess energies and of understanding the hidden or esoteric. On a more basic level, nighttime is the conclusion of day, so dream narratives set at night connote endings, conclusions or the approach of a cycle's ending. A dream with a night setting indicates waxing, full, or waning power if you identify a specific moon phase. Night corresponds with the Earth element and the north.

SEASONS IN DREAMS CAN BE TIME MARKERS in the mundane as well as symbolically significant. Consider the symbolic meaning behind a holiday represented in the dream and how this relates to the greater dream messages and themes. Apply your personal association with any holidays, seasons or times as paramount, but consider symbolic or cultural meanings as well.

Seasonal references offer you some clues to the potential timing of prophetic events in dream narratives. If you dream of a snow covered landscape, it might suggest that events will unfold in your waking life sometime during the winter. In contrast, if you dream of reaping the harvests from your garden, predicted events might unfold toward mid-summer or in early fall. As a general guide, when dealing with seasons, consider the following:

SPRING: This season associates with new beginnings, birth, life, regeneration, renewal, awareness, and consciousness as well as the cardinal direction of east, and the element of air. The season symbolizes initiations and the maiden aspect of the feminine divine.

SUMMER: This season corresponds to the cardinal direction of south, the fire element, will, ambition, drive, and manifestation. The season signifies growth, nourishment, maternity, nurturing, and the mother aspect of the feminine divine.

AUTUMN: This season corresponds to the element of water, the cardinal direction of west, endings, cleansings, conclusions, harvesting, karmic issues, and the subconscious. The season signifies abundance, gratitude, harvest, transition, and the crone aspect of the feminine divine.

WINTER: This season corresponds with the element of earth, the cardinal direction of north, death with the promise of rebirth, the attainment of wisdom, and spiritual illumination. The season corresponds to barrenness, loss, scarcity, hardship, hope, sacred births, light, waning strength, and rest.

Dreams and Symbolic Spaces

An integral part of dream scenery is the setting where the dream takes place: it is no easy task to monitor as dream settings can change rapidly, you can forget the setting, or you might not remember it clearly. Nevertheless, you will be able to gain greater wisdom through the extra measure of noting settings and their significance whenever possible.

Outdoors versus Indoors

As a general indicator, consider indoors as reflective of the private or internal nature. The indoors represents the personality, drives, and inner workings of the mind or spirit, or hidden, private matters. Consider outdoor scenes as symbolic of outward, public, and conscious expression. Add to this any personal reactions or preference; for example, an avid camper responds differently to a forest scene than a staunch urbanite not fond of wilderness. Compare your preferences in waking life and in the dream, as there may be discrepancies. The dissimilarities might be your subconscious' way of encouraging you to look beyond your comfort zone.

Take note of scene details and question if the space is open, cramped, crowded or desolate. Notice other inhabitants, whether human, animal, or fantastic, and compare these figures to the archetypes in this book. Analyze the setting based on your cultural and personal reactions. For instance, do you regard a wild animal with fear or admiration? Do you regard a specific person with familiarity or suspicion?

Combination and Fantasy Landscapes

Take into account whether or not a setting that involves multiple elements, like the beach and a volcano, is trying to communicate to you the need to balance multiple elements in your own personality. For instance, a volcano suggests the need to ground otherwise vital and fiery energy to avoid an explosion. In contrast, the beach connotes grounding emotions and not getting carried away by the tide. Thus, any dream landscape can have more than one symbolic meaning.

Part of the joy of dreaming is visiting places that are not accessible in the mundane. Consider how you would interpret any landscape even if it were known to be fictitious. Ask yourself:

What is your knowledge of this setting in the dream?
Does the dream give you reference points of where the place is located?
How does this place compare to your native land in waking life?
What are your feelings and reactions to the location?
What is the location teaching you?
How are you expected to act in the location?
How do you feel about other inhabitants of this place?

BUILDINGS: In general, a building represents form given to a concept. A house therefore symbolizes the form given to the concept of security, safety and self expression, since home is where you can be yourself. Inside the home is more private than a view of the outside of the house, thus, such images suggests public image versus private life. Buildings represent aspects of the body, self, and identity. A workplace office is a representation of your work role manifest in the physical, a tangible representation of what you do, and for many, part of what defines identity.

The family home suggests roots, traditions, and heritage or these aspects of identity, and points to past lessons and starting points. Note any emotional reactions to the building(s) you see in your dreams. A disdained workplace and a warm regard for a family home are images with two very different meanings.

The size and condition of the buildings are important. Tall buildings suggest grandiosity and transcendence or the act of trying to reach into infinite space to expand awareness and identity by striving upward. Small buildings suggest simplicity, introversion, humility, or passivity. Buildings that are new or made over suggest a positive change in your identity or in the aspects of life suggested by the meaning of the building; For instance, a new office building with state of the art equipment suggests brushing up on work skills or pursuing a career makeover. In contrast, a home that is falling apart on the inside, but is well-designed on the outside, suggests appearances to the public that are pleasingly united with chaotic forces or the potential neglect of an area in your private life.

Consider the function of aspects of landscape and setting. A window provides insight and enlightenment, doors provide opportunity, but also blockages if closed or locked. Stairs suggest movement, transition, progress or potential regression, particularly progress if ascending or deep exploration if descending, but also regression if you're moving backwards on the stairs. Tunnels and subterranean passages suggest exploration of the depths, past, or hidden pursuits undertaken alone. Porches or structures that blend indoor and outdoor scenes suggest transitions and balance between internal and external life, but also connote exposure and lack of privacy. Temporary shelters like shacks and tents hint at primitive survival and minimal security, but also being closer to nature. Such structures can suggest loose boundaries and the intrusion of external influences. With this basic understanding of dream settings, you will be able to apply symbolic meaning to any structure just by reflecting on what its general purpose is and what it means to you personally.

Rooms in the House

KITCHENS represent nurturing, healing, and maternal Goddess energies. The kitchen suggests nourishment of the self or others, creative endeavors, family, alchemical processes, and transformation.

BEDROOMS signify intimacy, rest, and unconscious processes. Since you sleep in the bedroom, the appearance of bedrooms in your dreams can connote relaxation, natural healing, and tranquility.

BATHROOMS signify isolation, release, cleansing, privacy, and the riddance of physical/spiritual toxins or negative energies. This room connotes the renewal of the body, self, or inner spirit.

LIVING ROOM/FAMILY ROOMS connotes communal gatherings, celebration, shared identity, commonality, recreation, casual identity, and the sense of belonging.

DINING ROOMS suggest a formal celebration, the identity constrained by social norms, traditions, culture, the nourishment of self and others, socialization, and the act of bringing people together.

BASEMENTS signify hidden areas, secrets, foundation, ancestry, and physical energy. The basement connotes the deep subconscious, inward reflection, and secrecy.

ATTICS connote the mind, conscious evaluations, mind over matter, and spiritual transcendence.

CLOSETS signify subconscious processes, plans, cognitive processes, isolation, privacy, secrecy, and automatic processes.

Roads in Dreams

The appearance of roads in your nighttime visions suggest the journey. Consider the quality of the road as well as the speed on which it can be travelled as having symbolic significance. A dirt path or rocky road implies slow movement and a lot of physical effort, especially if you compare the rough road to a paved highway. Accessibility and the ability to progress correspond to the appearance of roads in dreams. Consider infrastructure such as bridges or other assistive means that appear in the dream: this might indicate assistance from external sources or from those who have "taken this road" before. Roads that are blocked, closed, or end suddenly suggest a need to look for alternatives or reconsider your path.

Maps and Road Signs

Consider maps and road signs symbolic of the nature of your journey and how best to proceed. Red lights indicate obstruction or the need for caution or to stop. Green lights suggest movement, approval, permission to proceed, or an easier transition or progression. Maps indicate overviews of your plans for pursuing your path and goals. Apply your new understanding of symbolism to help read the dream map and compare it to your journey, both in your dream and waking life when applicable. Easily read maps and directions indicate a path that is clearly communicated by guides; a confusing map therefore suggests uncertainty about your path in spite of any available guidance.

Wilderness versus Cityscapes

Think of URBAN SETTINGS as hinting at situations influenced by humanity, culture, others, and of conditions significant to human-generated culture. Pressures, influences and resources will be of the human-made kind when urban settings are present in your dreams. Identity as intellectual and merit-based will likely prevail and the theme implies asserting human potential and will over the natural elements and therefore, making urban settings a masculine, projective, and expressive scenes. Problems may be more human-induced and less natural when such settings appear.

NATURE SETTINGS suggest instinct, natural cycles, and energies of the Earth and elements. If one element is dominant in the scenery, note the symbolic nature of the element. Receptivity, feminine energies and forming individual identity around the resources at hand are suggested here. Survival is implied: In some way, you're being asked to make the most of your surroundings and natural resources, rather than asserting dominance or expecting efficiency to match human-made standards. Powerlessness or acceptance are suggested by urban settings; In the wilderness, humanity is part of the whole or nature. In the city, humanity dominates the landscape.

BODIES OF WATER are symbolic of emotions, depths, mysteries, absorption, assimilation, the feminine, passivity, and things hidden. Bodies of water are reflective surfaces and therefore connote reflection and illusion. Note the movement of the water and its purity or contamination. Notice whether it's salt water thereby signifying protection and security. Water is indicative of maternity, motherhood, and nurturing. Meanwhile, if you're underwater in the dream, this is a symbol indicative or warning of being emotionally overwhelmed or consumed or it can suggest your ability to freely and bravely dive into a situation or emotional issue. Are you able to swim and breathe easily or do you feel like you're drowning? Are you "fighting to keep your head above the water or are you carefree as you swim around in the water?" See the archetypes for Cups/Tarot and water signs for more information.

LAND signifies stability, security, profit, groundedness, and material wealth. Try to remember the entire dream landscape. Mountains suggest grandiosity, foresight, power and possible obstruction of movement. Valleys imply hitting a low point, but also indicate intuition and depth of understanding. Apply your understanding of symbolic meaning to the quality of the landscape by asking yourself is the land a rocky passage or smooth road? Compare the extent of the land's development to the progress of idea or a project in your waking life. Raw undeveloped land symbolizes fresh beginnings and lack of personal power.

CAVES signify the Mother archetype, solitude, reflection, hiding, mystery, limited vision, and intuition. Caves connote internal wisdom, the shadow self, the female womb, sanctuary, safety, and protection, but a darkened cave signifies potential danger, enclosure, captivity, limbo or the Underworld. Consider your position in the dream: Do you stand at the opening of the cave about to enter or are you inside looking out? Do you fear what is inside the cave or have you already entered and begun to explore it?

SKY/ELEVATION suggests intellect (see Wands/Tarot archetypes for more information) reaching ideals, plans, losing touch with material limits or transcending obstacles. Note the quality of the air and the level of security you feel from your elevated position. Is it frightening or do you feel secure? In dreams involving flight, consider the level of autonomy as it relates to your ability to fly without external instruments or vehicles.

Movement and Parts of the Body in Dreams

Regardless of the nature of your dream, if the physical body or condition affecting the body is represented, take note. The body can contain both literal and symbolic meanings in dream narratives. Of course, this does not mean all messages are not of literal significance. Assume that both the symbolic and literal dream meanings are of equal importance.

Consider a dream in which one's foot is in immense pain. Literal interpretations of the dream can suggest it's time to pay attention to foot care, or in a precognitive dream it could indicate the potential for systemic or organic problems affecting the feet. By paying closer attention, you might be able to catch a health problem early if you do not ignore the symptoms. At the same time, consider the symbolism of the foot: independence, direction, action, firm grounding, movement, progress, burdens, carrying the weight of the body, busy routines, "doing the footwork," and maneuvering through difficult situations or "fancy footwork": all are messages that come into play.

An author of this book had a diagnostic dream where she saw herself walking around the library with two friends. She was walking slowly because her right heel was burning and throbbing with pain. She attributed the pain she felt to an accident she had in her waking life a few years prior. When she described the pain and burning sensations to her friend in the dream, he tells her that it's because her spine is "leaking" something. He also explains that the leakage means her spine is out of alignment and affecting the nerves in her feet. He describes it as being crooked or crushed/leaning on something. Once awakened from the dream, she finds that her foot is actually throbbing and burning in the same place it was in the dream.

Another one of the authors of this book had a dream where she had entered into a first-floor apartment she had never been in before, only to find a Hindu healer sitting in the lotus position on the floor. The healer looked at her and told her, "You have a black hole in your aura right here," while pointing to her left cheek. The healer then touched her cheek and she woke up. (When black holes appear in the auric field it can suggest bodily imbalances). A few weeks later she went to the dentist, had an x-ray, only to show a painless infection in the same location touched by the healer in the dream. The infection showed up like a large black hole in the x-ray film.

Consider the implication of illness/injury in the body; in general, take note of the condition's implication for functioning. A broken limb suggests disruption in the area the limb represents, whereas an infection or swelling suggests too much energy, attention, or anger ("heated situations"). Frostbite or freezing suggests a lack of attention. The loss, dismemberment, or absence of a limb suggests becoming disconnected from the area of life that limb or part represents, but always consider context. For example, if a body part is lost in an accident, the contextual meaning is different than if the limb is sacrificed to rid the body of a cancerous tumor. If a body part is cut, consider whether external forces are penetrating the private aspects of life represented by the body part, or if others are crossing into your private life. If a body area is crushed, enlarged or shrunk, consider how this relates to the amount of attention (too little versus over-attentiveness) is given to the area.

Sometimes dreams about body parts do not seem significant at first because they appear too abstract or easy to dismiss. An example of this is a man who recounts dreaming repeatedly of his grandfather. He tried the suggestion of asking his deceased grandfather to let him know what he was trying to tell him in his dream. Later, the man falls asleep for a nap and dreams that his grandfather appears and pulls out a rectangular light brown object resembling a wallet and places it right up against the man's chest while saying, "Here, now you have it." Within a few days, the man fell off his motorcycle and broke a rib right at the spot where his grandfather had placed the wallet. One interpretation of the dream, for this individual, was a potential warning of pain/injury, as when asked about his memory of his grandfather, the man replied he had a striking image of his grandfather coming into the house and asking for a "mustard plaster" on his side to alleviate pain when he was alive. The connection to the grandfather, whose memory conjured the image of needing relief for a painful injury, can then relates to the passing along of the brown object right over the spot where in a matter of time a painful injury would occur.

In dream interpretation, it's important to consider the symbolic meaning of parts of the body or bodily systems that seem to garner attention in a dream. How can you determine a noteworthy symbol in a dream? Consider how you recall your dream. For example, if dreaming about a person invokes the statement like, "I dreamt about a pretty girl," the stand out feature that your conscious memory registers as significant is the girl's hair color and attractiveness, then these are hallmark features that you should reflect on personally, culturally, and symbolically.

Some dreams feature figures and characters do not stand out, but exist as nameless, nebulous faces in your vision; this suggests the presence of another, or quite literally *an other* (other perspective/voice etc.). The nameless or faceless people/characters in dreams are important, but not in the same way when you dream about a person whose appearance, body or mannerisms, since such dreams involve the subconscious' sharing of specific traits. For example, dreaming about a pretty girl who turns out to have an unusual birthmark on her shoulder implies the need to pay attention to the significance of whichever shoulder has the birthmark. If you focus on the girl's left shoulder, this equates to receptive, passive, feminine, and goddess energies, but if you focus on the right shoulder, it represents projective, masculine, assertive energies. Within this same paradigm, when you dream there is equal emphasis on both of the girl's shoulders, it would suggest a balance of the feminine/receptive and masculine/projective energies.

When viewing your dream, examine whether or not the people you encounter in the vision are people you know from your waking life. Do you recognize them immediately or are they the people you know with a different physical appearance? Perhaps the people you see look like a blending of two or more people you associate with, thereby suggesting a mixture or blending of characteristics, traits, and behaviors. If the people in your dreams are people you recognize from your waking life, but their outward appearance is different within the dream, this connotes that you're not seeing the person for who they really are. Make note of the surprising traits and explore the symbolic meaning these qualities may represent.

In the example of the dream of a pretty girl with an unusual birthmark, you should note the shape, color, and type of birthmark if you recall it. Consider the dream giving an added layer of meaning by drawing our attention to anomalies, exaggerations, and other noticeable, unique physical traits. Take note of whether certain body parts are disproportionate, unusual, abnormal, diseased, injured, or demonstratively excessive in some fashion. Note things like excessive hair, height, girth, or flexibility. Consider if there are unexpected and surprising qualities related to the dream imagery you see. Now, imagine the same pretty, dark-haired girl who suddenly reveals a mouthful of sharp teeth. The stark contrast between the pretty girl and the alarming display of teeth is, undoubtedly, surprising, and you should consider the message that such transformation suggests; perhaps, in your waking life, something that looks good is not what it really appears to be or maybe you're not seeing things for what they really are in a situation.

If your awareness focuses on your body in a dream, consider the meaning of what is attracting your attention, especially if your body is experiencing injury, illness, exaggeration, or shocking qualities. For instance, if hair represents power, wisdom, and magick, then consider the meaning of a dream where your hair changes colors. Perhaps it's your subconscious trying to tell you to don on a new color or to change your energy vibrations. Consider how the meaning changes if a female dreams of having a long, lustrous and healthy beard! Take into account how the reactions of others are handled in the dream too. Are they shocked or nonchalant? Is the appearance of the anomaly a reason for panic or concern; do others in the dream treat the situation as normal, or do they even admire it?

Contextual clues provide levels of symbolic meaning. A woman dreaming of having a healthy lock of hair on her face might be shocked or repulsed by the dream content. However, if the context of the dream involves her beard, which others respect and admire, the imagery suggests that the woman is encountering opportunities by extending her personal energy to make magick in the mundane. Further, she is extending her energy in ways that cause her to flex traditionally male muscle and take on noticeable changes. These changes may scare her or feel unattractive, but she may be surprised to find that others respect her sudden display of power. In contrast, a dream where a woman discovers she is growing long facial whiskers and who becomes preoccupied with destroying all traces of unsightly hair, suggests a very different message. In this dream, the woman is experiencing her personal power and magick in ways that cause friction with others or she may be wielding her personal power in social situations aggressively and unethically, which results in an overgrowth of undesirable outcomes. Alternatively, perhaps the dream suggests she should embrace her power and wisdom and wield it mindfully rather than focus her energy on self-disempowerment.

Anomalies may be significant. Consider, for instance, if someone dreams of an eye in the palm of their hand. The message this dream sends relates to perception, action, and manifestation. Consider the actions you experience or witness in a dream. Incorporate context as always, but in general, think about the following:

BIRTH/PREGNANCY signifies conception, the birth of ideas, carrying ideas to fruition, and abundance. Consider the context as well, for example the health of the baby or anomalies.

DYING in a dream signifies regeneration, change, loss, closure, maturation, and the loss of key parts of identity.

FALLING, when not associated with out-of-body experiences, is indicative of a loss of control or the act of surrender. Consider how the fall is broken to derive more meaning from your interpretation.

FIGHTING signifies conflict, tension, assertion of control or power. Consider what you're fighting about in the dream and why you're fighting.

LIMPING signifies impaired movement, a lack of stability or strength, unsteadiness, and a lack of substance or structure.

LOVE MAKING/INTIMACY superficially signifies attraction to a person in the dream, but on a deeper level, you need to consider the symbolism of the person you're with, and what the individual represents. View the act of intimacy as trying to meld qualities with this person or adapt so you can engender the qualities that you associate with this person. Intimate acts symbolize alchemy, balance, and creativity.

MOVEMENT, like walking, running, or jogging, signifies transition, change, and the necessary actions to maneuver through your path. Consider the pace, speed, and any obstacles you encounter along the way as significant. Consider the direction you're headed as equally important.

SITTING connotes casualness, openness, and receptive interactions. It also implies rest, relaxation, and comfort.

SLEEPING is indicative of unconsciousness, lack of conscious awareness, lack of control, passivity, or vulnerability.

SPEAKING/THE VOICE signifies communication and the potential for creative manifestation, the power of vibration, music, and resonance. Consider the tone and the ability to speak versus the struggle to be heard.

STANDING connotes affirming beliefs, solidity, stubbornness, slowness, or rigidity.

SWIMMING signifies pervasive emotional issues, interacting in emotional territory, and striving for survival amidst emotional turmoil. Consider the difficulty or ease associated with how you "manage to stay afloat."

TRAVEL via vehicle signifies travel, change, and action. Consider the type of vehicle you're using as well; for instance, a boat is faster than swimming or a truck is bigger and more powerful than a small car. Travel by vehicle can indicate issues related to control too; question who is driving the vehicle. If it's not you, then who is?

As mentioned earlier, parts of the body have important symbolic meanings in dreams. You must therefore go beyond assessing only action and movement in a dream and give consideration to the message of body parts when they appear in your night visions. When you see various parts of the body, it should trigger you to ask specific questions. Consider the following:

THE HEAD represents initiation, thought, beginnings, telepathy, and power: especially the power through logic versus manpower. This represents authority, taking charge, and spontaneous action. In Tarot, the head corresponds to the Emperor; in astrology, to Aries. The head corresponds to the brow and crown chakras. Ask yourself the following:

What challenges are you heading toward?

Are you running headlong into an ordeal?

Has a situation come to a head and what must you do to head off further difficulties?

Are people looking to you as the head of a group?

Is a conflict all in your head?

Are you having difficulty making sense of a situation or trying "to make heads or tails" of something?

THE EYES signify perception, the key to insight, honesty, the keys to the soul, perception as shaping reality, penetrating through illusion, clairvoyance, and what you're willing to see or not see. In the Tarot, eyes correspond to The Tower. Eyes correspond to Aquarius and the two minor charkas positioned behind the eyes. Ask yourself:

Are you seeing situations as they are?

With reality "in the eye of the beholder," how are you viewing your reality?

Is it time for a new perspective?

Are you open to full awareness or are you "keeping your eyes open?"

Are you looking for something in the dream?

Are you in a situation where you're seemingly "in the eye of the storm?"

Are you or is someone "pulling the wool over your eyes" or engaging in self-deception?

THE FACE signifies expression, confrontation, calling to awareness, and identity. It's synonymous with the various roles a person takes on or the masks people wear. Consider if the face is altered in any way or if the individual is literally masked. The face corresponds with The Emperor and the sign of Aries. Ask yourself:

What do you need to face?

Have you had to "do an about face" or complete turnaround?

Are you "putting on a face for others?"

Can you "face the facts" in a situation?

Are you "trying to save face?"

Are you "ready to face the music" or upcoming outcomes/consequences?

THE EARS signify sound, perception of energy through the sense of hearing, or a subconscious or subtle approach ("putting a bug in someone's ear"). Ears also correspond with the concept of balance, and clairaudience. In the Tarot, ears correspond to The High Priestess. The ears correspond with the sign of Libra, and the two minor chakras located in front of the ears, just below the earlobe on each cheekbone at the jaw line. Ask yourself:

Are you in a situation that requires you be "all ears" or super-attentive?

Are you not hearing what you need to hear?

Are you receptive to others' messages?

Are you careful with your words?

Do you need more experience in a situation or are you "wet behind the ears?"

THE NOSE signifies a sense of smell, sniffing out a lead or smelling trouble. The nose indicates the depth of awareness, the pursuit of issues beyond the surface, and clairolfactory. Due to this depth association this body part can be associated with the energy of Pluto, who delves beneath the surface and is a natural investigator. Consider that in some cultures and even in the animal kingdom, elevating one's nose implies dominance or status. The level of awareness and information gained through the sense of smell makes this body part associated with the ability to keep focused on an issue. Consider that the sense of smell and taste are inextricably linked. Ask yourself:

Are you "keeping your nose clean" in a given situation?

Are you committed to a project or job, focused, and "keeping your nose to the grindstone?"

Do you "have your nose in the air," thereby suggesting your dominance/superiority in a situation?

Are you perhaps "putting your nose where it doesn't belong," and involved in a situation it's best to avoid?

Has your personal taste or style changed recently?

THE MOUTH symbolizes communication via conscious, direct speech, taste/nurturing, and the source or originating point of one's expression. Consider the association of the mouth with superficial communication such as someone paying "lip service" or someone who "mouths" the words to a song or movie, but who is not really using the voice to communicate; for example, someone going through the motions without sincerity. The mouth corresponds with the energies of Mercury, being the planetary influence of communication, and Gemini, the zodiac sign of duality. In the Magickal Arts, words have tremendous power, particularly that of manifestation. If you dream about the mouth or speaking, consider the following:

Are you putting your money where your mouth is?

Are you talking out of both sides of your mouth?

Are you merely "mouthing the words" or lip syncing, but not really saying anything genuine?

Are you capable of backing up what you say?

Are you using your words to manifest positivity in your life?

THE NECK symbolizes the connection between intellect and action, flexibility, movement, extension of will, and bridging thought with intention/action. Therefore, the neck's symbolism aligns with the energy of The Magician and one's ability to bring thought into physical manifestation. The neck corresponds with the sign of Taurus and therefore, with Venus. Consider whether the dream shows disruption in the range of motion of the neck or damage to the neck. The neck is the site corresponding with vampire bites, so consider the possibility of psychic/spiritual attacks that potentially bleed you of your energy. The neck, being a bridge between the head and body, symbolically represents the unity of mind, communication, learning, passion, and motivation; thus, showing the meeting place between idea and action. It corresponds with vitality, as severe enough damage can be life threatening, and the neck, being the point of severance in the killing of some animals, but also in the act of executions. The neck even has associations with status as it can be decorated with fancy collars, necklaces, or tattoos. In some cultures, to extend the neck is a marker of beauty and status. In Tarot, the Hierophant, as the connector between esoteric and mundane, aligns with the symbolic messages of the neck. Finally, the neck corresponds to the throat chakra, the planetary influences of Mercury, and the zodiac Gemini. Consider the following:

Are you in danger of losing your head?

Are you sticking your neck out for someone?

Is something becoming a pain in the neck?

Is the neck damaged or ornamented with collars, necklaces, or tattoos?

Do you feel like situations are squeezing/choking the air out of you?

Are you stifling your voice?

Are you under psychic/spiritual attack?

Are you unifying thought, voice, and action?

HAIR connotes the extension of the life force, vitality, and the spiritual essence. It also corresponds to strength and is a marker of beauty, identity, and cultural affiliation. Hair on the head can express individuality and will mirror a person's state of health or illness; thus, it's a barometer of one's wellness. On the face or body, hair is a maker of age, maturity, and can serve as a marker of one's health since excess hair or absence of hair can signal hormonal imbalances, eating disorders, or other maladies. Consider if the dream shows inappropriate or unusual manifestations of hair. Many practitioners of magick recognize the extension of Magickal energy existing in the hair and are thus protective of this extension of the body. Reflect on the following:

Are you hanging on by a hair or ready to rip your hair out?

Does the hair seem to manifest your inner health or beauty or an inner state of distress?

Is hair drawing attention to part of your life that has grown out of control or become unruly and wild?

Is there something that is bothering you or seemingly "in your hair?"

Are you experiencing anxiety or is "something making your hair gray?"

Are you "keeping your hair on" or remaining patient in a situation that calls for a calm demeanor?

Are you involved in a situation where you or someone is "splitting hairs" or focusing on insignificant details?

SHOULDERS represent how you're carrying your load in life at the moment, and suggest stability, support and strength. Consider Atlas carrying the world on his shoulders for example. The shoulders represent how you're interacting toward others in the world, or how you're expressing your ability to act. There is a minor chakra located at the top of each shoulder. When you dream of the shoulder, consider the following:

Do you have a chip on your shoulder?

Do you offer "a good shoulder for others to cry on" or are you in need of emotional support?

Do you have the "weight of the world on your shoulders?"

Do too many emotions or issues from the past burden you?

Are you trying to "shrug off responsibilities?"

Are you entering into a situation with "a level head on your shoulders?"

Are you giving someone "the cold shoulder" or is someone doing the same to you?

Are you constantly "looking over your shoulder" as if you're fearful of something?

CHEST/BREASTS connote the heart, passion, love, empathy, warmth, nurturing, maternity, and maturity or the lack thereof. The chest is a symbol of abundance, food and nourishment (breasts/milk), as well as the representation of confidence. The chest corresponds with the signs of Cancer, a sign of heart-felt emotions, and Leo, a sign relating to the heart and blood. The Empress in Tarot as a mother, nourishing, and nurturing figure, as well as the Lovers, signifying the heart-felt emotions between two people. The Sun card in Tarot relates to the chest as well as the solar plexus, and heart chakras; the Solar Plexus relating to confidence, self-esteem/respect, and the heart charka signifying warmth, nurturing, understanding, and empathy. There are two minor chakras, one located above each of the breasts. Consider if the dream seems to indicate the heart, ribs, or other specific organs or body parts and what they imply based on their function and context in the dream. Reflect on the following:

Is there something you're trying to get off your chest?

Are you looking for nurturing or to nurture others?

Are you confident?

Are you expressing or living your heart-felt desires?

THE BACK signifies power, support, burdens, (see also shoulder) stance, sturdiness, posture, status, validation, and force of will. This area of the body relates to the unseen, subconscious, unknown, mystery and other realms: those existing, but out of the conscious sight. Consider this symbol connoting the past, but also the act of moving backwards, backing away or regression. Issues arising from beyond your conscious perception/events just out of sight or happening "behind your back" are signified by the appearance of the back in dreams. The Hierophant in Tarot corresponds to this area of the body. Consider:

Are you able to back up your beliefs or personal stance?

Are you putting your back [effort] into your work?

Are you backing down too easily?

Do you feel trapped in a situation as if you're "backed up against a wall?"

Do you have to returning to the beginning of a project or issue or "back to square one?"

Do you need to "bounce back" from a situation?

THE MIDSECTION/ABDOMINALS/WOMB signify the processing of energy, core issues, gut feelings, stability, flexibility, digestion, slow processes, or the procession of options through numerous channels (digestion of one's options or situation). This area body relates to intuitive, motherly instinct's, female intuition, and psychic processes or feelings, and corresponds to Justice and Temperance. The planetary influence of this body area is the Moon. The midsection aligns with the sacral chakra signifying nurturing, emotional wellness, intuition, or gut feelings. The womb corresponds with mother archetypes, nurturing, incubation, and attendance to what is yet to manifest, thereby making this area of the body correspond to the Empress in the Tarot. Consider if situations seem to bring on nausea, or cause upsets to digestion. Are you able to stomach your circumstances? In the dream, does the stomach, core, abs or midsection have abnormal characteristics? Are things emerging from the abdomen, navel or core? Is this part of the body undergoing surgery or injury/healing? Reflect on the following:

Is something making you nervous or inciting "butterflies in your stomach?"

Are you heeding your "gut feelings" or are you tuning into your body's intuitive responses?

Do you have an upcoming decision that requires you to "go with your gut" or to depend upon your emotions only?

Have you suddenly lost your drive, energy, or motivation?

Do you feel like you have taken an emotional "punch in the gut?"

Hips, like shoulders, signify stabilization and act as a bridge between the intuition/gut instincts and internal processes of the core and the ability to take action, achieve mobility and exert one's self. The Chariot in Tarot corresponds with the hips since the card represents direction and movement. The hips align with the root chakra and signify grounding, vitality, life force, passion, and action. Consider the following:

> Are you "shooting from the hip," and expressing something without allowing your heart and mind to
> explore the issue first?
> Do you need more stability in a particular situation?
> Are you moving freely around or through life's challenges or do you feel stuck in place or motionless?

The Genitals symbolize fertility, procreation, sensuality, lust, and gender identity (femininity/masculinity), but also connote passivity or receptivity. Genitals correspond to the signs Scorpio, Pluto, and Mars, death and rebirth, The Devil card, and the Lovers in the tarot. Consider:

> What are you conceiving or in the process of bringing into birth?
> What are the fruits of your labor?
> In what area of your life do you recognize the process of creation?

The Buttocks connote important but forgotten elements in life, taboos, and the process of elimination along with excretion, waste, burdens, old baggage or the dead weight one needs to get rid of (via the process of elimination). This area of the body represents stagnation or issues that you might be "sitting," but not acting on when necessary, but it can signify hoarding, holding onto the past, hiding secrets, and privacy. Consider:

> Is a situation becoming a "pain in the rear?"
> Are you just sitting on mounting issues rather than taking action?
> What excess emotional baggage do you need to eliminate in your life?

The Legs, calves, and knees connote mobility, independence, action, autonomy, spontaneity, and travel. This area of the body relates to The Fool in the Tarot, the planet Mercury, and the sign of Gemini. Bones correspond with Capricorn and Sagittarius, and the planetary influences of Jupiter and Saturn, as well. Knees suggest flexibility, vulnerability, sensitivity, connections, interaction with others, motion, and far reaching/ranging mobility. Consider:

Are you trying to "get a leg up on things?"

Do you have "a leg to stand on" in a given situation?

Is someone not telling you the truth or "pulling your leg?"

Are you moving to your own rhythms?

Do you understand your motivations?

FEET/TOES connote movement, stabilization, burden, martyrdom, balance, and codependency versus independency. This area of the body relates to the Devil and The Lovers in the Tarot. Astrologically, the feet and toes correspond to Neptune and Uranus, as well as the signs Pisces and Aquarius. There is a minor chakra on each of the feet. In the Tarot, feet and toes correspond to The Hanged Man, and the World. Consider:

Are you "standing on your own two feet?"

Can you stand your circumstances?

Does a new situation require you to "get your feet wet?"

Are you hoping to follow someone's footsteps?

Are you trying to break into a new career or "get your foot in the door?"

Are you always putting "your best foot forward?"

Are you living an unbalanced or precarious lifestyle?

THE ARMS signify the extension of will, ability to assert or command, and the extension of dominance. With a bit of word play, "arms" can signify military acts/defense and offense. This part of the body relates to the Emperor or Magician in the Tarot, the sign of Aries, and the planetary influence of Mars. Arms lend you the ability to hold, carry and reach, thus, on a symbolic level they signify the ability to stretch into new territory. Finally, the elbow and wrist both signify flexibility and movement. Consider:

Are you emotionally/spiritually/psychologically armed for a situation?

Do you greet new situations with "open arms?"

Do you feel like someone is "twisting your arm" or trying to make you cooperate?

Are you isolating yourself from others or "keeping others at arm's length?"

Would you "give your right arm" to accomplish/ attain something?

Are you trying to understand a situation fully or attempting to "get your arms around it?"

Are you upset or "up in arms" about something?

Are you embracing change?

THE HANDS/FINGERS connote manifestation, craftspeople, builders, hoarding, facilitating the flow of energy, and material wealth. Receptivity or rejection of wealth/energy (hands open or closed/grasping too tightly/loose), and control, is symbolized by the hands. This part of the body corresponds to the sign Virgo, and Mercury. There is a minor chakra in the palm of each hand. In the Tarot, the hands correspond to The Magician, since it's a card symbolizing physical manifestation. Consider:

Do you have a hand in too many projects?

Are you in need of or offering a hand to others?

Are you handing over what is yours or being heavy handed?

Are others "eating out of the palm of your hand?"

Do you have someone "wrapped around your finger?"

Do you need to get a grip or let go?

Are you acting in an underhanded way?

Is something wrong that you "can't put a finger on?"

Do you feel helpless in a situation, like your "hands are tied behind your back?"

TEETH signify deconstruction, rumination, obsession, delving into the parts of a whole, or breaking things down. Teeth connote eating, digestion, destruction in order to integrate parts of a whole and signify defensiveness, danger or a situation with "bite."

Are you trying to "sink your teeth into something?"

Are you "cutting your teeth" or gaining new experience in a situation?

Do you grind your teeth due to anxiety?

Are you afraid you will complete a project or pass a test only "by the skin of your teeth?"

Are you seeking justice as in a "tooth for a tooth?"

Are you or is someone you know getting "long in tooth," showing one's age, or revealing one's wisdom and experience?

Are you fighting for something with tremendous vigor or "tooth and nail?"

This list of parts of the body is only a starting point and may not encompass every potential body part or function you might encounter in a dream. Use this as a springboard for more individualized exploration of symbolism. Remember, dreams can present infinite symbolic possibilities and the true meaning of any symbol is up to the dreamer to discover.

Improving Dream Quality and Dream Incubation

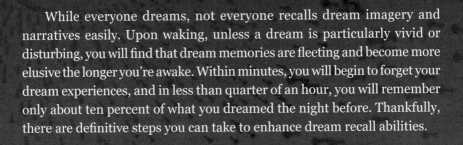

Dreams come true. Without that possibility, nature would not incite us to have them.

John Updike

While everyone dreams, not everyone recalls dream imagery and narratives easily. Upon waking, unless a dream is particularly vivid or disturbing, you will find that dream memories are fleeting and become more elusive the longer you're awake. Within minutes, you will begin to forget your dream experiences, and in less than quarter of an hour, you will remember only about ten percent of what you dreamed the night before. Thankfully, there are definitive steps you can take to enhance dream recall abilities.

Dream Recall Improvement Tips

There are several simple things you can do to improve dream recall. First, try telling yourself that you will remember your dreams just before you fall asleep. Repeat the message to yourself several times each night until you notice dream recall improving. Once you begin to recall your dreams, document as much as you can remember. Make a habit of journaling about your dreams every single day. If you take a mid-day nap and remember your dream, document it. The more attention you give to your dreams, the greater the likelihood of dream recall.

Keep your dream journal nearby, but keep a recording device even closer. You will begin to forget your dreams within five to seven minutes after you have woken up and, by the time ten minutes have passed, you can forget up to ninety percent of dream content. Use a small recorder to record everything you can remember the minute you wake up. To improve the accuracy of your dream recordings, only document what you remember.

The human memory is faulty, and it will begin to piece in information where it might make sense to you. If it didn't happen in the dream or you have a part of the dream you do not remember, do not fill it in with what you think might have happened.

Use meditations during the day to help improve your dream recall at night. Use the meditation in this book or you can write your own. Alternatively, consider preparing a statement of intent before going to bed by writing out your intentions in a journal or on a piece of paper. Make sure you express your intention as simply and clearly as possible. During the day, this written intention can double as a daily affirmation. Repeat the affirmation quietly or aloud regularly throughout the day.

Call upon your patron deity (if you have one) to help you in understanding the dreams you receive. For instance, consider calling on specific deities who rule over sleep, dreams, or deities associated with messages and communications. Lunar deities like Diana, Selene, and Cybele are ideal for dream work as well, since the moon is a symbol of nightly illumination and great mysteries. If you're looking to get quality sleep, you might consider invoking a deity that rules over the night like the Greek goddess Nyx, the Roman goddess Nox, or the Egyptian goddess Nephthys. Appeal to deities that rule over visions and prophecy if you want to summon precognitive dreams.

Deities of Prophecy and Dreams

Keep your dream preparations as simple or elaborate as you like. Some people might be more comfortable with placing a totem, medicine bag, or pouch of herbs under a pillow or nightstand; other people might benefit from carving out a special area for dream preparation. To improve your ability to remember dreams or to have specific dreams, invoke one or more deities to help achieve your goal. Consider erecting a dream altar in your bedroom; it can be a small area on a night table, a dedicated section of your dresser top, or you can set up a standalone altar if you have the extra space. Wherever you establish the altar, make sure that the space you choose is only used for dream-related work. Consecrate the area and consider adding small statues of dream-related deities.

Consider using the altar as a place to make offerings, to center your focus and awareness just before you go to bed every night, or you can set it up in a location ideal for meditating or prayer. The altar is an excellent place to make appeals for divine assistance. Later on in this book, you will find a list of herbs and incense suitable for use in rites, spells, and dream incubation, but the herbs/incense are equally suitable for use as offerings or for invoking an altered state of awareness conducive to dream work. On the altar, you can place statues of the divine, images of dream deities, dream-related imagery, or items that represent totem animals that correspond to specific dream archetypes. If you're artistic, consider creating a mural or dream scene that you place behind your dream altar or headboard.

Alternative offerings can include items you find in nature, stones, or fruits from the harvest. Any item you use as an offering involves gifting the essence of the item to honor the deities. If you use perishable, natural items, you can return them back to nature when they are no longer fresh or useful.

Having some relaxing background noise at night might help in improving your dream recall. If you like the sounds of rain or water, consider placing a small water fountain on your dream altar. The sound of the fountain can serve as white noise, canceling out other distracting sounds, and might help in achieving a trance-like state before you fall asleep. Additionally, water is a symbol of the deep subconscious and has long been considered an oracular element. For instance, in ancient Greece Zeus was honored as a sky god, but votaries also honored him as Zeus Naïos: the god of water and streams. His priestesses interpreted messages from the babbling waters nearby the sacred oak tree at Dodona. To that end, the sounds of nature, including light wind and rustling leaves, were held to have meaning. You can do the same by using natural sounds to serve as calming background noise for dream work.

There are several deities corresponding to dreams, prophecy, and visions. Bear in mind if there is a patron deity you prefer working with, there's no reason why you cannot work with the aspect(s) of the divine of your preference. In the following section, you will find a list of several deities you can appeal to, but the list is by no means all-inclusive.

ANTEVORTA, PROSA, OR PORRIMA, is the Roman goddess of the past, childbirth, and prophecy. She is one of three Carmentes along with the goddess Carmenta and Postverta, all of which have prophetic gifts.[1] As a deity presiding over the past, she is an ideal goddess to work with if you want to dreams about past events or lives.

APOLLO is the Greek solar god of inspiration, truth, soothsaying and prophecy. According to the ancient Romans, Apollo was the son of Jupiter and Latona, the brother of the goddess Diana, and the god who ruled over medicine, archery, poetry, the fine arts and music.[2] In myth, Apollo gives Cassandra, the daughter of Queen Hecuba of Troy and King Priam, the gift of prophesy. After refusing Apollo's affections, the god punishes Cassandra by causing everyone who hears her prophecies to disbelieve them.[3] Apollo is an excellent deity to call upon for prophetic dreams of all kinds.

BRIMO is a title used to call upon the ancient Greek goddess Diana or Hecate; she is called upon alone or when the goddess Brizo is invoked.[4]

BRIZO is the Greek goddess of dreams who was honored mostly in Delos; her name means "to sleep." Those who appealed to her would go to the temple wearing wreaths of laurel and would give offerings; before entering the temple, the supplicant would refrain from eating anything hard to digest, and would refrain from consuming wine, at least three days prior to seeking prophetic dreams.[5] Brizo is an ideal goddess for when you want to improve your ability to interpret your nighttime visions, since she is a goddess associated with the art of dream interpretation.

CARMENTA is a prophetess of Arcadia and the Roman goddess of prophecy. Once called Nico, she was later renamed Carmentis because of the wild appearance she took on when giving oracles. Upon her death, she was elevated to divine status.[6] Call upon Carmenta for all prophetic dream work.

DAMU is a Babylonian and Assyrian goddess of healing and dreams. She brings happy dreams to those who invoke her.[7] Call upon Damu when you want to ensure a night filled with positive dreams or if you're looking to have dream messages of healing.

FAUNUS is the Roman god of the woodland, predictions, oracles and human wit; he was the son of the god Mars and bestowed the gift of prophecy onto his sister Fauna.[8] You can call upon Faunus or Fauna when you're looking to have precognitive dreams.

HERMES is a Greek messenger god. In the Roman pantheon, he is analogous to the god Mercurius or Mercury. Hermes is a god of communication, the inventor of letters, the protector of knowledge, and the god of eloquence and rhetoric.[9] Call upon Hermes for dream work of all kinds.

MNEMOSYNE is a goddess who bore the nine muses. Her name means "memory."[10] Invoke this goddess to help in improving dream recall.

THE ONEIROI TRIBE, (the word Oneiroi is the Greek word for dreams) according to Hesiod, are the children of Nyx, the Greek goddess of the night, and the siblings of sleep (Hypnos) and death (Thanatos). The Oneiroi are portrayed in *The Odyssey* as residing near Oceanus, the land of the dead, and the neighborhood where the sun sets in the far West.[11] According to some writers, the Oneiroi includes Phantasus and Phobetor.[12] Ovid names Morpheus as one of the Oneiroi and offers the name Icelos as an alternative name for this deity.[13] Hypnos is the Greek god of sleep. In the Roman pantheon, he is analogous to the god Somnus, who is the son of Nox and Erebus. Somnus resides in a dark cave where no light may enter. He sleeps on a bed made of feathers, and outside the cave's entrance are somniferous herbs and poppies.[14] Somnus is the brother of death and he bestows the gift of silence, tranquility, peace and refreshed spirit on humanity through his gift of sleep; Some stories portray Somnus residing in a palace protected by the gates of horn and ivory. The gate of horn allows for true dreams to pass through, while the gate of ivory allows for the passage of false dreams.[15] Call upon Hypnos or Somnus when you want to have a peaceful night's sleep or you want to have precognitive visions.

MORPHEUS is the god of sleep. Sometimes stories portray him as a winged, corpulent child holding a vase in one hand and poppies in the other; He is a god of dreams and visions, and he appears in dreams in various human forms.[16] Call upon Morpheus if you're seeking to conjure dreams about specific people or relationships.

PHOBETOR is the son of Somnus and a Greek god of dreams. According to Ovid, Phobetor inspired fear in the minds of humankind and would appear in the shape of wild beasts or serpents. In nightly visions, he appears as animals of all kinds.[17] Call upon Phobetor when you want to keep nightmares at bay or if you want to have specific dreams about animals, familiars, or animal totems.

PHANTASUS is son of Somnus, brother of Morpheus and Phobetor, and he is a god of dreams. He appears as inanimate bodies, mountains, towns, rivers and rocks.[18] Consider working with Phantasus when you want to dream about specific places or if you have questions relating to the natural world.

Dream Work and The Hours

In *The Iliad*, Homer writes of The Hours, Horae, or Celeres Deæ, meaning quick or nimble goddesses, who, as daughters of Themis and Jupiter, rule time and the seasons.[19] The number of Horaes has evolved over time, from just three to as many as twenty-four, with twelve of the goddesses ruling the hours of the night. Below is a listing of the Hours of the night, all of which mythologists depict with wings in the act of flying and wearing different colored robes, that you can call upon in relation to specific dream work.

THE FIRST HOUR of the night, occurring after the sun sets, wears attire the color of twilight. In one hand she holds a bat, and the other the planet Jupiter. Bats are animals relying on the process of echolocation and their sense of hearing to move through the dark.[20] Thus, the bat is an ideal totem to work with when you desire psychic dreams or when you want escape all illusions, penetrate into the very heart of the matter, and to reveal deeply hidden truths. Since bats dwell in caves and move through darkness, you can invoke the First Hour of night to explore the shadow self or maternal matters.

THE SECOND HOUR holds an owl in one hand and the planet Mars in the other. Her attire is gray.[21] **THE THIRD HOUR** holds an owl in one hand and the Sun in the other; she wears black attire.[22] The owl symbolizes wisdom, but the owl can see clearly in the dark; thus, the animal and the Hour that carries it, represents hidden mysteries, secrets, and deep insight.

THE FOURTH HOUR carries an hourglass and Venus. Her attire is light black.[23] Invoking this Hour is ideal for dreams related to relationships or the movement of time, timekeeping, schedules, life milestones, transitions, and rites of passage.

THE FIFTH HOUR carries poppies and the planet Mercury.[24] Poppies signify the god Morpheus and the realm or gateway of dreams. In ancient times, particularly in parts of Germany and Holland, people attributed the poppy with divinatory powers and called the flower the "Confession Rose."[25] Thus, the Fifth Hour can be invoked for dreams about truth, relationships, and when you want to reenter dreams you have already experienced.

THE SIXTH HOUR wears dark black attire. She carries a cat and the Moon.[26] Cats have long been considered an animal of secrecy, mystery, and magick. The moon has similar connotations. Call upon the Sixth Hour when you want to have dreams revealing deep mysteries, secrets, or visions with magickal undertones.

THE SEVENTH HOUR wears a robe of dark blue. She carries a badger and the planet Saturn.[27] Badgers are associated with persistence, perseverance, and determination. Call upon the Seventh Hour of the night when you want greater insight into repetitious dreams or if you seek hidden sources of inner strength and personal power through dream revelations.

THE EIGHTH HOUR carries a dormouse and the planet Jupiter. Her attire is light blue.[28] Dormice are nocturnal and hibernate up to half a year. In fact, the word dormouse comes from the Latin word *dormio* meaning, "to sleep."[29] Call upon the Eighth Hour of night when you're having trouble entering a deep enough stage of sleep to access the realm of dreams, or when you want to tap into deeply buried messages of your subconscious mind.

THE NINTH HOUR signifies the coming of daylight. She wears a purple robe and carries an owl in one hand with the planet Mars in the other.[30] Like the Second and Third Hour, invoke the Ninth Hour for dreams where you seek deeper insight and wisdom or for dreams involving personal introspection.

THE TENTH HOUR wears a light purple robe. She holds a clock with a bell and the Sun.[31] THE ELEVENTH HOUR carries a rooster and Venus. She wears a blue robe.[32] Finally, THE TWELFTH HOUR of night flies just below the morning horizon. She wears a purple, blue and white robe. Her emblems are a white swan and the planet Mercury.[33]

Call upon these Hours if you want to understand more about lucid dreams, false awakenings, or if you want dreams pertaining to the passage of time, spiritual awakenings, and enlightenment.

Dream Incubation

For the moon never beams without bringing me dreams.

Edgar Allan Poe

Dream incubation is the art of conjuring specific dreams. Dreams can relate to anything you desire and as you begin to master the art, you can explore personal issues, problems, or concerns in your night-time visions. The goal of dream incubation is to conjure dream imagery that can provide you with solutions or insight into what concerns you the most. You can practice dream incubation to gain mundane or spiritual insight and the practice has been used for centuries in the healing arts.

The ancients partook of dream incubation to get answers to important questions or to return to specific dreams in hopes for greater understanding of a dream's meaning. Thus, you can use incubation techniques to conjure specific dreams or to intentionally enter into a dream narrative you have already experienced. Incubation not only involves focusing on the dreams you want to have, but also includes preparing for sleep so that you can enter into the dream state with greater ease.

Consider dream incubation like an algebraic exercise: in formulating an equation, the first step involves declaring a variable. Just as the statement "Let 'X' equal the unknown" allows for a mathematician to ascribe meaning to an abstract concept, the active dreamer can proclaim the intent of the journey into the mysteries of the mind, for the purposes of self-analysis, exploration and problem solving. Establishing the purpose of your dream is essential as it allows you to enter your dream with a pre-defined focus.

At first, returning to or conjuring dreams for specific outcomes seems mysterious. Consider dreams are like a wireless connection between your conscious and subconscious mind or higher self and suddenly, it seems natural for you to be able to tap into the conscious/subconscious connection by following simple, but tried techniques. Many of the methods you can use require nothing more than your focused intent.

State your intent quietly to yourself, in meditation, or write it on a piece of paper to place beneath your pillow. Be as elaborate as possible to make your intent perfectly clear. Your goal is to declare your dream intent to both your conscious and subconscious in a pre-dream "meeting of the minds." Art, symbols, written statements, chants, or prayers can prove beneficial in aligning your intent. As you become proficient in dream incubation, you may choose to state your intention aloud before you retire so you can enter the night's dream session.

While relatively simple, dream incubation requires regular practice. Try not to dismiss practices based on one trial run, or worse, without having tried it because the process doesn't seem complex. Begin with a spoken or written statement of intent like "Tonight I will find guidance for my career in my dreams."

Opening Yourself to Dream Guidance

We are not only less reasonable and less decent in our dreams...we are also more intelligent, wiser, and capable of better judgment when we are asleep than when we are awake.

Erich Fromm

The easiest part of dream incubation is asking for guidance. The hard part is remaining open with faith and knowing that your question will be answered: this is not always in a literal sense or in a way you might be accustomed to in waking life.

Dream imagery can be very simple, offering only one or two symbols with a wealth of meanings or you can have many symbols delivering up repetitious themes or several messages through a single narrative. On the other hand, you might receive an answer that seems improbable or impossible or the answer you get might appear to be total nonsense. Remember that dream responses that end with improbable answers might only be dubious because of your current standpoint. In other words, certain conditions or events might need to unfold before the answer you receive will seem less ambiguous. You will have to learn to trust the process and to know that you're being guided. However, the guidance you receive usually needs to be deciphered in order to uncover the dream's meaning.

Consider the following example

During a difficult relationship, you're at a crossroads and you do not know what to do. You sense a lack of communication or possible secrecy.

Prior to sleeping, you ask for guidance so that you can understand what is happening. That night, you have the following dream narrative:

You see yourself preparing to attend a friend's graduation and are holding a place in line for the ceremony while your friend (the person you're wondering about in your waking life) leaves his keys and wallet with you and wanders off. The doors of the auditorium open up. Visitors begin pouring in and soon the line of visitors is wrapping around the corner. You become frustrated because the line is held up. You wait, but your friend still does not return. You leave your place in the line, allowing everyone to proceed without you so you can go and search for your friend. You find him sitting in a child's stroller, engrossed in conversation with someone who works in a nearby store. You suspect that your friend has spent all of his money at the store and his spendthrift behavior is something you plan to speak with him about later.

You and your friend go back to the auditorium to await the graduation. You bring up your suspicions, but he interrupts you by giving you a gift. You feel angry and manipulated. You promise yourself you will not be persuaded to ignore the issue you want to discuss, no matter how thoughtful the gesture. You open the box and find abstract-shaped silver earrings in the form of two small genies. You tell your friend the gift is nice and you thank him. As you remain calm with anger in check, you make your point and tell your friend that you suspect he spent all of his money at the local store.

Your friend becomes argumentative. As he is speaking, you see the genie earrings transform into earrings that look like little bulls. You put the earrings away, and restate your dissatisfaction with your friend's behavior.

Then, the dream ends. You wake up, and you record the dream in a journal.

Initially, the dream seems to have nothing to do with the question you posed before you went to sleep. After you have documented the dream in your journal, go back over the dream's details at your leisure to look for symbolic messages. When you analyze the dream, you soon discover that you indeed receive an answer to your relationship question. It occurs to you that, in the dream, you suspect your friend is being deceitful or manipulative. Your friend's childish or immature behavior is confirmed two times in the dream; first, when your friend wanders off from an important event like a graduation ceremony, and second, when you see your friend sitting in a child's stroller at the store where you suspect he has spent all of his money.

Your dream confirms your friend's deceitful nature when he gives you earrings that look like two small genies. The gift is given to you as a way of manipulating your emotions and the genies represent wishes or "wishful thinking." When your friend becomes argumentative, the earrings turn into two small bulls. The bull carries a deep message for you in the dream. First, on a not so subtle level the dream is implying that your friend is giving you a "line of bull." Second, the earrings only become bulls when your friend becomes argumentative, therefore suggesting your friend's stubborn behavior or indicating that you're dealing with someone who has a Taurus-like disposition. Third, bulls are a symbol suggesting that you remain firm or steadfast in your convictions and to do what you know in your heart is the right thing to do. Finally, the appearance of the bull in your dream might be suggesting that you refrain from "bullish" actions and that you maintain an understanding between aggressive and assertive behavior when sharing your point of view. You realize that your friend never officially makes it through the graduation ceremony: this suggests that your relationship might never reach the point where it can "graduate" to the next level or mature into something more meaningful.

The key to good incubation sessions is a willingness to believe that your questions will be addressed and that you can have the ability to interpret your dreams if you're willing to commit to the practice. Dreams can help you solve problems or make future predictions and can provide clear answers on to handle specific situations in your waking life. Bear in mind that because dream communications stem from your subconscious, you might not always like the answers you receive. Yet, just because an answer makes you uncomfortable, it doesn't make the solution or prediction any less valid or unlikely to occur. Most important, there is little point in mastering interpretation techniques if you don't put the mundane/spiritual messages you receive to good use.

Returning to a Dream Meditation

Review an entry in your dream journal for a significant dream that you would like to re-enter or explore. Use the lessons from this book revealing archetypes and key symbols to list the most prominent dream symbols. From your list, compile a list of your dream signposts: significant characters, or places/objects that connect you to the dream from which you would like to learn the dream's messages.

Compose a list containing at least one reference point or signpost consisting of both human/animal characters (life forms) a setting or place, and an object that helps anchor you to the dream. For example, if your dream involves being in an office with a ruler on the desk and chipmunk that teaches you about German architecture, you can narrow down the dream signposts to a chipmunk, ruler, and office setting. Suppose you note the presence of a grandfather clock as part of the office's décor. The clock can become another signpost for you. The fact that you're being taught architecture and the reference to the German culture are important, but for the meditation you will access meaning by interacting with the most tangible symbols only. A ruler or clock are tangible, whereas the "German culture" is an abstract concept.

You can follow this meditation script by pre-recording it or having a friend guide you through it.

Sit or lie down comfortably, but in a manner that is not conducive to sleep. Slowly close your eyes and allow them the block out the sights of the space around you. Turn your attention inward, away from the distractions of the day—away from the conscious ego and the external stimuli in the waking world. Your breathing slows and begins to relax you as you grow closer and closer to contact with your inner world.

Breathe deeply and slowly. With each breath, you feel yourself more relaxed as you drift further into the realm of your mind and closer to subconscious awareness.

(Pause for 15 seconds)

With each breath, you're continually more relaxed and aware of the internal world: The realm of dreams and intuition. With each breath, you're awakening into the realm of dreams.

(Pause for 5 seconds)

With each breath, you gradually become aware of a hazy, dark, but inviting atmosphere all around you. You can see a dark, velvet, purple and indigo mist swirling about your body as a breathtaking landscape comes into view. Not far off in the distance you can hear the waters of a stream, and in the western sky, the sun is setting. You have no fear of your surroundings and you feel perfectly safe. You become aware of a light shining in the distance. Walk toward the light without fear or hesitation.

(Pause for 10 seconds)

You see the light is coming from a torch held by a benevolent guide who stands before two gates. You can see your guide clearly. Take in the details of your guide's form, size, expression, dress, and stance. Draw closer to the guide and the gates.

"You have traveled far to find this place," the guide tells you, "but before you can proceed, you must tell me your purpose here, for I am the guardian of the gateway of dreams." Respond to the guardian and specify your intentions, revealing your quest to understand your dream messages.

The gatekeeper understands the importance of your mission, smiles, and says, "Before you are two gates, one of ivory and the other of translucent horn. Choose only one."

Surrounding the gates, you see a variety of herbs and bright red poppies swaying in the gentle breeze. You feel a deep urge to explore what lies beyond the beautiful gate of solid ivory, and feel a powerful magnetic force is pulling you toward the ivory gate. You must resist the temptation to enter the gate of ivory; what lies beyond are only daydreams and imaginings never brought into manifestation—things that will remain within the realm of illusions and unfulfilled dreams. Instead, turn away from the ivory gate and tell the guide that you desire to enter the gate made of horn.

Your guide smiles again and says, "You have chosen wisely." He prepares to unlock the gate, but before doing so, turns to you with a final, but gentle word of warning: "Do not lose sight of the world in which you live in by day, but neither should you forget the connection between your dreams and your waking life. Tread carefully, for there is a fine line between dream and fantasy, and good luck on your quest." You acknowledge your understanding of the warning by smiling, nodding, and thanking the guardian. The gatekeeper unlocks the gate and instructs you to place your hand upon it. Gently place the palm of your hand on the gate: the entry to true visions. When you do, it swings open for you allowing you entry.

(Pause for 5 seconds)

You see a scenic landscape with a palace far off in the distance: this is the home of Somnus, the god of dreams and sleep. Just a short distance ahead of you stands a large stone monument. Note the monument's shape and any significant details as you approach it. On the front of monument, you see a list of places you have entered in recent dreams, and you realize that this wall of dream settings is unique to you. Reach into your pocket where you will find a piece of paper containing the list of dream signposts you have compiled. Look down the list until you see the description of dreams and find the listing that matches the dream described in your list. You will notice both good dreams and any nightmares you might have had are both listed on the stone. Do not be afraid to access your nightmares in this realm, for you're here to learn from whatever messages your dreams have to share with you.

(Pause for 5 seconds)

You find the specific entry point you seek with considerable ease. Instinctively you know to place your hands on the engraving of the place you want to visit to re-enter your dream and as you do so, the setting around you changes. You immediately find yourself back in the scene of your dream. Take a moment to reacquaint yourself with the dream setting. If something is missing, allow it to appear or look closer, perhaps it's just hidden in the shadows. If you have reentered a nightmare or bad dream, know that you will remain perfectly safe as you learn your dream messages. When your dream setting is reestablished, call into view a key symbol from your dream with which you want to interact. Whether this is a person or inanimate object, recall to yourself that this is your subconscious awareness and any object or symbol in your surroundings has the power to communicate with you. In fact, simply by willing communication with this person or object, reveals a message to you. Receive your dream message now.

(Pause for 30 seconds)

When you have understood your message, call upon another symbol, then another, until you have the understanding you desire. Repeat this process as often as necessary. If you do not understand the message initially, will it to change and evolve into a symbol and language you can understand.

(Pause for 1 minute)

When you have finished, express your thanks to those who helped you receive this message from within. Prepare to return to the gate, allowing the atmosphere around you to dissolve.

(Pause for 5 seconds)

You're returned to the gate and you, once again, see the gatekeeper. Thank the guardian and bid him farewell. The gatekeeper glances at you knowingly, recognizing that you have been initiated into the world of deeper knowing. You come away from your journey matured, changed, and wiser. You're given one last parting gift from the gatekeeper.

(Pause for 5 seconds).

Examine this gift and secure it for your journey ahead. You will be able to access this gift at any time, while asleep or awake. You thank the gatekeeper and continue on your path, where you will once again return to conscious awareness.

Counting from ten to one, you will be fully relaxed, aware, refreshed, and restored to consciousness.

(Count down from 10 to 1)

Magickally Enhancing Dream Recall

Use the following spell to improve dream recall.

Call upon Mnemosyne (Nee-Moss-See-Nee), the Mother of the Muses and the Greek goddess of memory. For this spell, place a purple or dark blue pouch filled with rosemary and sage under or near the pillow. Say:

Source of inspiration and divine creativity
Mother of the Muses, Mnemosyne,
Come to my aid when I slumber this night
Seeking greater recollection and divine insight.
Allow me to remember all I see,
And to recall, from memory, all of my dreams.
So Mote It Be.

Dreaming of Something or Someone Lost

For this spell place a small magnet, Hematite (for its magnetic properties) in a pouch, as well as sage (to promote clairvoyance), and consecrated sea salt. Write a brief statement about the person/information/object you would like to find or locate and place this in the pouch as well. Considering including a small map or drawing if you have an idea of the general location of the person or object you want to find. Spiritually cleanse the pouch and its contents. While holding the pouch, say:

> *From worlds away, _____ draws near,*
> *Answer my summons, before me appear,*
> *That which is lost, is easily found,*
> *Secrets revealed in nighttime visions abound.*

Place the pouch by your bedside or under your pillow to gain new information in your dreams.

Face Fears in a Dream

Place under your pillow a dark-colored, purple, blue, or black pouch filled with symbols of protection and strength such as images of strong animals, power stones such as hematite, jet, obsidian, or other dark stones, or runes of power or protection. Charge the pouch and symbols in it. Write a detailed summary of the fear/being/situation or quest that you will undertake in your dream, which will bring you face to face with what you fear. The goal of the dream is to confront a fear that may be evident or subconscious and to allow your strength to overcome the intimidation this situation holds over you now. You may choose to place the Strength Tarot card above the bed or to meditate on the images in this card prior to sleep. Other warrior/strength symbols such as the glyph for Mars (the shield and spear or "masculine" symbol) or personal totems can be included.

In circle, picture a strong grounding cord rooting you to the Earth, descending from your root chakra and anchored deep in the ground. You can use the following spell or you can elaborate wording that more specifically addresses the situation at hand if you feel the need to do so. You might want to invoke guardians and guides that can help you in confronting your shadow self or you can call upon the goddess Isis or Maat, both of whom are Egyptian deities of truth and hidden knowledge. Consider adding to the spells wording the names of spirit guides or animal totems you're working with as well.

Say the following words:

Goddess and guardians, here my chant

To me, I ask you, courage grant,

Give me strength to recognize,

The fear that deep within me lies.

With no illusion as my shield.

I bravely face the truth revealed.

Lift the veil on what is dark,

Let me know my deepest heart.

And when I know what I must do at last,

Protect me, Goddess, on my path.

Dream Ritual Using the Tarot to Bring Dream Guidance

Prior to performing this ritual, specify the guidance you seek by posing a concise question or request. Write the request on an index card. For additional power, use indigo or red ink to write your question. Review the list of archetypes in this book and identify which archetypes you feel would best bring you guidance at this time and select from the Tarot deck the cards that closely associate with your current situation.

As an alternative, you can choose a card that best represents you, the situation, and any significant people or factors involved. If you do not own a Tarot deck, you can choose to make a diagram of card names or even draw symbolic portrayals on a piece of paper. You can be as simple or elaborate with your art work as you like, provided you capture the essence of the archetype you want to work with for the purposes of this ritual. If it's easier, you can even choose modern movie and story characters or celebrity pictures that hold the energy of the archetypes in question.

Choose the following cards from the Tarot deck and place them in a horizontal row: The Moon, The High Priestess, and The Star. The order of the cards should be the same as indicated since the ordering is significant, representing the path from unknowing and mysteries hidden in the subconscious (The Moon), to mystical guidance and intuitive instruction (The High Priestess), to enlightenment and clarity (The Star). If needed, add additional cards based upon the archetypes listed in this book that prove relevant to your situation or question. Placement of the cards you choose should signify hidden knowledge/confusion/questions on the left and clarification on the right, but be creative in playing with the cards to create an outline of your mission as you journey into the dream world. Just make sure that you keep the three main cards in their proper places as you make your tarot layout.

Once you have created your layout, keep it near your altar, in sacred space or in a place where it can remain undisturbed overnight. If you will be leaving the layout in a room separate from the room where you sleep, make sure you have time to perform the ritual just before you go to bed. Once you have your layout prepared, put it in the area where you will create sacred space. (If you're new to creating sacred space, check out our book, *Sacred Objects, Sacred Space: Everyday Tools for the Modern Day Witch*, Schiffer Publishing 2013). Cast circle, create sacred space, or declare preparation for ritual according to your magickal tradition Ensure you have summoned the guardians and cleared the working space of any distractions or negativity.

Hold up The Moon card and say:

I begin in mystery, wandering through depths, voyaging into the unknown. I begin my journey in darkness and call upon the powers of the Moon, Goddess Artemis, Cybele, Isis, your beams of light are my only lantern. With your help I seek enlightenment. As your light fills the night sky, fill my dreams with visions of the knowledge I seek. So Mote it Be.

Replace The Moon card into the layout. Take up the High Priestess card. Next say:

Through Divine light emerging I begin to see my path. What I seek begins to transform from what is hidden into revelation. (Speak your original question aloud). Of the answer to this question, I am given full knowledge of in my sleep." I call upon the wisdom of my guides (name your guides if you desire), the Goddesses of the Moon and psychic vision to aid me in my quest and to stand with me on my journey. I recognize your guidance both in my dreams and in my consciousness. Allow me to feel your presence and to gain understanding from the realm of dreams. So mote it be.

Replace the High Priestess card and take up The Star card. Say:

In my quest within my dream, light and guidance I do seek, when my journey in dreamscape is done, answers and wisdom I have won. Connected with the source of all that's divine, understanding will be mine. Enlightenment from the highest source of life, fill me with your inspiring light. I will emerge with my answers tonight, understanding brought forth by daylight. My dream's image and message clear, I will recall what I see and hear. So mote it be.

Replace The Star card in the layout. If any remaining cards are contained in your spread, you can chant over them as well. You can focus your energies on requesting a dream to help in alleviating a situation or providing answers based on the archetypes in the spread. When finished, thank the Divine and any guides, close circle and prepare for sleep.

Astrological Ritual to Bring Dream Guidance

Establish sacred space in accordance with your tradition. Select items to represent the planet/deity/signs that you will call upon for this dream enhancement ritual and place the items in your space or on your altar. See the list below for correspondences relating the appropriate colors, flowers, stones, or fetishes to accentuate the energies of specific planet/deities and signs. You can use any of the correspondences suggested. You do not have to use them all. If you feel creative, you can draw or make collage images associated with the signs and planets.

The point behind using correspondences is to align your thoughts and intent with the magickal working at hand. Consider aligning the timing of this ritual to coincide with specific planetary positions. You can find out more about planetary positions on the Internet or you can access such information from an ephemeris: a book containing details on astronomical events and planetary positions throughout the year. For the planetary and astrological signs to carve into your candles, view the image of the glyphs provided.

MERCURY/GEMINI
DIRECTION: East
COLOR: White or yellow

SYMBOLS: Object symbolizing flight, travel, communication, and intellect. Feathers, pens or chimes. Images of birds, winged creatures, and objects associated with the air element also apply.

SIGN OF GEMINI: ♊

SIGN OF MERCURY: ☿

STEP 1: Carve the signs of Gemini and Mercury into a silver candle. Place the candle in the eastern corner of your sacred space. Surround the candle with symbols corresponding to the god/planet Mercury. Light the candle.

SAGITTARIUS/JUPITER

DIRECTION: South

COLOR: Red

SYMBOLS: The centaur, fire, images of grandeur and abundance, cornucopias, or benign rulers. Images of generous father figures or humane philanthropic leaders are all associated with this sign. Use objects symbolizing diverse cultures, philosophies, or souvenirs from different cultures and foreign lands like small coins or tokens.

SIGN OF SAGITTARIUS: ♂

SIGN OF JUPITER: ♃

STEP 2: Carve the glyphs of Sagittarius and Jupiter into a red candle. Place the candle in the southern corner of your sacred space or altar. Surround the candle with symbols associated with the god Jupiter. Light the candle.

NEPTUNE/PISCES

DIRECTION: West

COLOR: Blue, turquoise or sea green

SYMBOLS: Tridents, mermaid, seashell, starfish, sea glass, chalice, or bowl of water; anything that emulates the energies of water, the sea, mysteries, emotions, and the spirit world are symbols corresponding to west.

SIGN OF PISCES: ♓

SIGN OF NEPTUNE: ♆

STEP 3: Carve the glyph of Pisces or Neptune into blue candle. Place a blue candle and your correspondences in the western corner of your sacred space or altar. Light the candle.

Pluto/Scorpio
Direction: North
Color: Black
Symbols: Images associated with scorpions, fossils, death, resurrection, and initiation into the deeper mysteries.
Sign of Scorpio: ♂
Sign of Pluto: ♇

Step 4: Crave the glyphs of Scorpio and Pluto into a black candle. Place the candle in the North on your altar or sacred space. Surround the candle with symbols corresponding to god and planet Pluto and the sign of Scorpio. Light the candle.

Uranus/Aquarius
Direction: Akashic point (midway between the North and East)
Color: Purple
Symbols: Images of the water bearer, water, amethyst stones, and depictions of creative geniuses or deities of wisdom; you can use images of technology, innovations, or things that represent higher intelligence and advancement.
Sign of Aquarius: ♒
Sign of Uranus: ♅

Step 5: Carve the signs of Aquarius and Uranus in a purple candle. Place the candle in the center of your sacred space or altar, between the north and east cardinal points. Surround the candle with symbols corresponding to Aquarius and the god/planet Uranus.

Moon/Cancer
Direction: Center
Color: Silver and blue
Symbols: Goddess figures, spirals, images of the moon, crab shells, water, moonstones, and pearls.
Sign of Cancer: ♋
Sign of Moon: ☽

STEP 6: Carve the signs of Cancer and the Moon in a Silver candle. Place the candle in the center of your sacred space or altar. Surround the candle with symbols corresponding to Cancer, the goddess, and the Moon. Light the candle.

Cast a protective circle before conducting your ritual. Stand facing East. Say:

Even in sleep my inner eyes are open, ready for clarity, guidance and inspiration. Mercury, divine messenger, carry the message to me swiftly. I am ready and willing to accept knowledge of the obscure.

Stand facing South. Say:

From the warm depths of slumber, awaken my insight Jupiter, Benevolent One. Bestow onto me far-sight, insight, foresight, and awareness of realms beyond the physical. You who are the Great Expander, awaken my consciousness and open my mind.

Stand facing West. Say:

Neptune, Lord of the Deep Waters, Ruler of the Seas and the Mysteries therein, let your currents surround me and cleanse all resistance, that I may be open to sailing into the depths of my own consciousness, where I will find answers and guidance on my voyage.

Stand facing North. Say:

Pluto, Ruler of the Deep, master of death's mysteries, I call upon your wisdom to bring me further into the hidden realms. Allow me to penetrate through all illusions and to expose what is true, real, and hidden.

Stand facing the Akashic point. Say:

Uranus, innovator, holder of futuristic wisdom and the currents of power to break through the surface of all things; Revealer of other worlds, help me transcend the limitations of consciousness.

Face the altar or the center of your sacred space. Say:

Lady of Illumination, Luna, Ruler of the Night Sky, bring me the serene depths of sleep so I may embark on my quest under your watchful and protective light. Touch me with the fine, silvery rays of the moon so I am illuminated and enlightened.

Sit or stand silently in meditation and feel the energies around you. Reflect on the issues or conditions you want to address in your dreams. When you're ready, thank the deities, end the ritual, and close the circle. Extinguish each of the candles, doing so in a clockwise direction. Wait for all of the smoke to dissipate before leaving your sacred space, knowing that as you do so the smoke carries your intentions into the Universe.

Dream Pillows and Dream Catchers

Dream Pillows

The art of aromatherapy involves the use of fragrant herbs and flowers for the purposes of changing your state of mind, mood, or awareness. A dream pillow, also called sleep, dreamtime, or herb pillow, is an object that allows you to makes use of aroma-therapeutic methods for dream enhancement/invocation. You can make your own dream pillow by sewing together two pieces of fabric and filling it with herbs of your choosing. You can use the list of herbs in this book to get an idea about some of the herbs that promote quality sleep and dreams. The pillow does not have to be excessive in size and only needs to be about four to six inches wide. You can make the pillow in any shape you desire. The fabric may be cut into square pieces and sewn together, or may consist of a drawstring pouch or bag that you can open and reseal. If you're not fond of sewing, a pouch or medicine bag can be obtained in most craft stores. Fill the pouch with herbs and fasten the drawstring to enclose your items.

If you want to align the color of the dream pillow's fabric with the intent behind making the pillow, use purple, indigo, deep blues, and black, since the colors are naturally soothing and carry the energy of subconscious states. Lighter or warmer colors may prove too stimulating.

Place the two pieces of fabric together, with the exterior of the fabric facing inward. Use a sewing machine or needle and thread to sew around the exterior of the material. If you hand sew the pillow's seams, make sure you sew the seam tightly to avoid the spillage of herbs while you sleep. Once you have sewn about two thirds of the seam closed, turn the material inside out so that the right side is showing. Finish off the final section of the seam, but leave a small opening so that you can add herbs to the pillow.

To help you choose the right herbs, the next section of this book contains a list of herbs and flowers, some of which are perfect for use in dream pillows. After adding herbs to the pillow, seal off the small opening. Inside the pillow, you might want to add one or two tiny seashells as a symbol of water that represents sleep and the subconscious states. Add a pinch of consecrated sea salt, too, which will help in purifying the pillow. If desired, add one or two small tumbled stones or crystals that have energies aligned with dream work; see the section on Gems for Dream Enhancement for tips on appropriate stones for dream work. When you finish, hold the pillow, and call upon the divine or creator in whatever aspect you're most comfortable with and request a blessing for the object.

Position the pillow under your regular pillow at night. Since different herbs have unique magickal properties, consider making more than one dream pillow. Create a pillow for quality sleep and one to conjure positive dreams. Alternatively, make one for precognitive dreams and one for dispelling nightmares.

Dream Catchers

Dream catchers are a nice alternative to dream pillow and are ideal tools for ensuring positive dreams. You can hang one in your bedroom, nearby or over your bed to help in filtering out negative dreams. You have the option of charging a dream catcher with the intention of making it a tool for inducing positive dreams, or you can even make your own dream catcher with unique decorative beads, crystals, and totems so you can induce specific kinds of dreams too. Consider using a spell to empower the dream catcher you decide to use further.

Incense, Herbals, and Flowers for Dream Incubation

Just before going to bed, lighting incense conducive for dream work and psychic visions can help you in accessing your dream messages more readily. Additionally, you can use herbs for improving sleep quality, preventing nightmares, and psychic dream defense. Following is a list of some incense, herbals, and flowers you can use in dream meditations, ritual, dream incubation, and dream pillows.

When burning incense before bedtime, make sure you use the appropriate censer and that you place the censer on a flame-retardant surface. Do not go to sleep until you have allowed the incense to burn completely. If you have domestic pets that sleep in the bed with you at night and you use small sachets or dream pillows, make sure your pet(s) cannot get into the items you use. Consider placing dream pillows or dream sachets inside your pillowcase for the protection of your beloved pets. Additionally, if you plan to consume herbs, speak with your doctor or an herbalist before doing so; some herbs interact with medications and others may not be appropriate selections for those with certain health conditions.

ANISE was used by the ancients to dispel nightmares; other common herbs used for the same purpose include **FENNEL, CINNAMON, AND MARIGOLD.**

BASIL is suitable for protection, and added to dreamtime sachets, the herb helps to promote quality sleep; some African tribes believe that placing some of the dried herb under your mattress promotes better sleep and protection from evil spirits.

CATNIP OR CATMINT TEA helps promote sleep. The herb helps in dealing with digestive issues that might otherwise disturb a sound sleep session.

CHAMOMILE is a great herbal tea, especially about thirty minutes before bedtime. Consuming it helps you get a more restful sleep.

DAISY ROOTS OR PETALS, when placed under a pillow, are used for divining one's future spouse.

ELM, as identified by the poet Virgil in the "Aeneid," is the tree of dreams.[34] If you want to make a wand for use in magick spells pertaining to dream work, elm wood is ideal.

FOUR-LEAF CLOVERS, when placed under a pillow, induce prophetic dreams. Clovers correspond to positive energies, luck, the sacred trinity, and are believed to protect the carrier or wearer from all evil, but especially during travel (a notion that can encompass astral travel).

HOLLY, in some ancient charms, was worn on the bosom during sleep to cause a person to dream of his/her future spouse.[35] As an alternative, add it to a small pouch and keep it under your pillow, hang three sprigs of holly above your headboard, or place a couple of sprigs on a bedside table for prophetic visions.

HOPS help in natural healing and in sleep promotion. Thus, adding hops to your dream pillow can elicit peaceful sleep, dreams, and healing visions.

JASMINE is a wonderful herb for promoting a peaceful mood; it's ideal for promoting better dream recall, divinatory dreams, and spiritual protection during sleep.

LAUREL was used by the oracle of Delphi for stimulating prophetic visions in ancient Greece.[36] Placing laurel leaves that have been sprinkled with rosewater onto one's pillow at night allows dreaming about a future love.[37] Before going to bed, consider invoking the god Apollo while burning some laurel leaves to increase the likelihood of prophetic visions.

LAVENDER smells wonderful and is an ideal herb for use in dream pillows or sachets. If you prefer, you can use a few drops of lavender oil in your dream pillow or sachet.

MARIGOLDS are great for eliciting prophetic dreams. Dry some marigold flowers and add them to your dream pillow or sachet.

MINT has a pleasant odor and can give your sachet or dream pillow a fresh, clean scent. Use mint for pillows created for lucid dream work. Consume mint tea before bedtime to aid in digestion and to ensure greater quality of sleep.

MUGWORT, called *Artemisia mater herbarum* in Old Latin and so named after the goddess Artemis or Diana, is an herb used in divinatory practices.[38] According to Apuleius, the herb banishes devils and wards off the evil eye.[39] When placed under the pillow, it's said that the herb can bring the dream of a future spouse. This herb's associations with a lunar deity make it suitable for invoking prophetic and spiritually illuminated or enlightening dreams.

PULSATILLA is a purple flower that blooms in April; the Ukrainians call the flower *Son-trava* or the "Dream Herb." Like the four-leaf clover, when placed under a pillow, the bloom is said to induce prophetic dreams.[40] As an alternative, consider drying the plant and placing the dried petals inside a dream pillow.

ROSES are ideal for divining love. Consider placing a single rose in a vase by the bedside, using rose potpourri, or adding dried rose petals to a small pouch and placing it beneath your pillow before sleeping to dream about love and personal relationships. Use red or pink rose petals to dream about love or yellow roses to dream of friendships. A peace bath containing rose petals or using rose oil is an excellent way to ready yourself for a relaxing night's sleep and peaceful dreams.

ROSEMARY is good for divination; sprigs of Rosemary were once used by maidens in dream charms to reveal their destinies.[41] Rosemary has the dual benefit of improving your memory for greater dream recall. Hang a few sprigs of Rosemary in your bedroom for dreams about your fate or you can drink tea for memory improvement. Alternatively, boil some water and put some fresh rosemary in the hot water. Allow the steamy vapors to fill the room where you will sleep.

SAGE has a pungent, but pleasant scent, so a little bit goes a long way if you're using it in a dream pillow or sachet. The herb is ideal for protection during sleep or astral travel. Use this herb to elicit dreams about spirituality and enlightenment.

VERVAIN OR VERBENA is an herb once held sacred by the Greeks. Consuming the herb as a tea will promote sleep.

YARROW is good for use under the pillow to induce prophetic dreams of love.[42] This herb is suitable for eliciting dreams of healing, love, or anything with a fiery association.

Gems for Dream Enhancement

There are many ways you can use crystals and stones to aid in dream exploration and enhancement. Consider placing a few stones inside a sachet or dream pillow to further improve upon the properties of the tool. Alternatively, you can charge stones with a specific purpose or, if you prefer, you can learn how create gem essences. Here are a few stones to consider:

AGATE is said to help in dealing with insomnia and invoking pleasant dreams.[43] You can wear agate ornaments for the purposes of spiritual protection in the dream realm.

AMETHYST was used for inducing visions and dreams by the ancients.[44] The stone is used for clarity of mind, improved memory, serenity, and spiritual connections. Combine amethyst and yellow quartz stones for clear visions, unambiguous dreams, open communication, and understanding.

AZURITE is ideal for eliciting psychic dreams. It's a stone that connects to the mystic archetype (see Mystic Archetype in this book) and the unknown.

CARNELIAN is best for protection during sleep and astral travel. The stone improves creativity and simultaneously helps to release anxiety.

CELESTINE, like the Carnelian, is a stone best used for its protective properties. The stone opens the mind, encourages connection with the deep subconscious, and promotes happiness and joy.

CHRYSOLITE enhances the connection between the conscious and subconscious mind, thereby improving the communication between the two. This stone corresponds to improved spontaneity.

CORAL helps improve your awareness in your waking life, as well as your dreams. Use coral for intensifying your understanding of unity, the web of life, and for greater awareness beyond boundaries, as well as the subconscious. Coral, being derived from the ocean, corresponds to emotions and emotive dream work.

DANBURITE corresponds to expression, clarity, protection, and intuition. Use the stone for eliciting unambiguous dream messages, revealing hidden truths, and for protection during lucid dreams or astral travel.

Diamonds are best for solidifying your intent and purifying your purpose during dream incubation.

Garnets signify unity and serve as a potent protective aid during dream work. This stone represents success, strength, and corresponds with the maiden aspect of the goddess Persephone. Use this stone to elicit dreams relating to feminine energies, maidenhood, and the transition of innocence to experience.

Labradorite helps to improve your focus and to expand your awareness. Use the stone during meditation or in rituals involving dream preparation. The stone can lend to improvements in dream recall.

Malachite corresponds to healing, wisdom, protection, and emotional healing. Use the stone when seeking dreams offering answers on how to balance your emotions.

Quartz is best for opening your mind and improving your ability to receive messages from the deep subconscious. Quartz is perfect for precognitive dream work and it serves as a meditative aid while simultaneously promoting mental clarity.

Sugilite corresponds with spiritual connections and helps to increase your awareness of spiritual guests. Use this stone when you want to have dreams involving spirit communication.

Tiger Eye corresponds with protection and purification. This stone initiates connection between the conscious and subconscious. It aids in understanding, insight, and in seeing beyond the obvious.

Turquoise is perfect for psychic dream work. The stone has protective properties, calms the mind, and strengthens the aura. Use this stone during astral travel, lucid dreams, and to promote quality sleep.

CONCLUSION

Congratulations! You have remained committed to the journey of metaphor, symbol, and awakening that is dream work and are likely reaping the benefit already. To gain the most from dream incubation and interpretation, we encourage you to continue documenting and assessing your dreams in the future. Only through continued practice will you become intimately familiar with the way your subconscious communicates with you, and you will find that the more you pay attention to subconscious messages, the more messages you will receive. As you explore various dreamscapes, you can develop a far deeper understanding of the images and symbols that appear and what those things mean to you on a personal level. Ultimately, you are the best person to interpret the real meaning behind all of your nighttime visions.

ENDNOTES

Chapter 1

1 "Dream," in *Chambers's Etymological Dictionary of the English Language: A New and Thoroughly Revised Edition*, ed. Andrew Findlater, rev. ed. (London: W & R Chambers, 1900), 140.

2 Daniel B. Shumway, "Sagen-und Litterarhistorishe Untersuchungen," *Americana Germanica: A Quarterly Devoted to the Comparative Study of the Literary, Linguistic, and Other Cultural Relations of Germany and America 2* (1899): 94-100.

3 "Dream," in *Chambers's Etymological Dictionary of the English*, 140.

4-5 John Morris, "Oracles and Omens," in *The Religion of Babylonia and Assyria* (Boston: Ginn and Company, 1898), 312-328.

6 Sigmund Freud, "The Scientific Literature on the Problems of the Dream," in *The Interpretation of Dreams* (New York: MacMillian Company, 1913), 1-79.

7 Katherine Taylor Craig, *The Fabric of Dreams: Dream Lore and Dream Interpretation, Ancient and Modern* (New York: E. P. Dutton, 1918), 1-16.

8-9 John Potter, "On Divination of Dreams," in *Archæologia Græca: Or, The Antiquities of Greece*, 7th ed. (London: G. Strahan, 1757), 1:303-314.

10-13 Katherine Taylor Craig, "Dreams That Have Come True," in *The Fabric of Dreams: Dream Lore and Dream Interpretation, Ancient and Modern* (New York: E. P. Dutton, 1918), 91-127.

14 Sigmund Freud, preface to *The Interpretation of Dreams* (New York: MacMillian Company, 1913), 1x-2x.

15 Freud, "The Scientific Literature on the Problems," in *The Interpretation of Dreams*, 1-79.

16 Carl Gustav Jung', "Psychoanalysis," in *Analytical Psychology* (New York: Moffat Yard and Company, 1916), 206-225.

17 Stephanie Poulos, "Computers Draw Images from Dreams," Counsel & Heal, last modified April 5, 2013, http://www.counselheal.com/articles/4747/20130405/computers-draw-images-d.htm.

18 Katherine Taylor Craig, symbolism in dreams to *The Fabric of Dreams: Dream Lore and Dream Interpretation, Ancient and Modern* (New York: E. P. Dutton, 1918), 151-183.

19 Walter William Skeat, "Lucid," in *A Concise Etymological Dictionary of the English Language*, 4th. rev. ed. (New York: Harper & Brothers,

20 Walter William Skeat, "Nightmare," in *A Concise Etymological Dictionary of the English Language*, 4th. rev. ed. (New York: Harper & Brothers, 1900), 360.

21-22 Palmer, "Mare," in *Folk Etymology: A Dictionary*, 231-232.

23 William Dwight Whitney, "Incubus," in *An Encyclopedic Lexicon of the English Language* (New York: The Century Company, 1889), 11:3050.

24 "Succubus," in *The Encyclopaedic Dictionary: A New and Original Work of Reference to All the Words in the English Language, with a Full Account of Their Origin, Meaning, Pronunciation, and Use* (London: Cassell & Company, 1887), 665.

25 "Incubus," in *The Popular Encyclopedia: Or, Conversations Lexicon*, new rev. ed. (London: Blackie and Son, 1862), 4:52.

Chapter 2

1 "Apocalyptic Literature," in *The New International Encyclopædia*, ed. Daniel Coit Gilman, Harry Thurston Peck, and Frank Moore Colby (New York: Dodd, Mead, and Company, 1907), 1:654-656.

Chapter 3

1 Walter William Skeat, "Archetype," in *An Etymological Dictionary of the English Language* (London: Claredon Press, 1898), 32.

Chapter 5

1 "Perseus," in *Dictionary of Greek and Roman Biography and Mythology*, ed. William Smith (Boston: Charles C. Little and James Brown, 1849), 3:205-206.

2 "Polydectes," in *Dictionary of Greek and Roman Biography and Mythology*, ed. William Smith (Boston: Charles C. Little and James Brown, 1849), 3:461.

3 John Lemprière and John Walker, "Perseus," in *A Dictionary of Antient Classical and Scriptural Proper Names* (Burlington, NJ: David Allinson & Company, 1812), 358.

4 Ibid.

5 "Perseus," in *Dictionary of Greek and Roman Biography and Mythology*, ed. William Smith (Boston: Charles C. Little and James

Brown, 1849), 3:205-206.

6 Josephine Preston Peabody, "Oedipus," in *Old Greek Folk Stories Told Anew*, by Josephine Preston Peabody (Boston: Houghton Mifflin, 1897), 59-62.

7 Ibid.

8 Ibid.

9 Ibid.

10 Ibid.

11 1 Kings. 3:16-28 (Revised Standard Version).

12 Earnest Alfred Wallis Budge, "The Judgment," in Chapters I-LXIV, vol. 1, *The Book of the Dead: English Translation in Three Volumes* (Chicago: Open Court Publishing, 1901), 25-40.

13 Ibid.

14 William Smith, "Paris," in *A New Classical Dictionary of Greek and Roman Biography, Mythology, and Geography*, ed. Charles Anthon, rev. ed. (New York: Harper & Brothers, 1878), 604-605.

15 Ibid.

16 Ibid.

17 Ibid.

18 Ibid.

19 Ibid.

20 Friedrich August Nösselt, "Artemis or Diana," in *Mythology Greek and Roman*, trans. Angus W. Hall (London: Kerby & Endean, 1885), 201-207.

21 Ibid.

22 Ibid.

23 Ibid.

24 "Devil," in Oarses-Zygia, ed. William Smith, vol. 3, *A Dictionary of Greek and Roman Biography and Mythology* (London: John Murray, 1880), 347.

25 Ibid.

26 Edward Wigglesworth and Thomas Gamamiel Bradford, "Devil," in *Encyclopædia Americana: A Popular Dictionary of Arts, Sciences, Literature, History, Politics, Biography, Brought Down to the Present Time*, by Edward Wigglesworth and Thomas Gamaliel Bradford, ed. Francis Lieber, new ed. (Philadelphia: Thomas and Cowperthwait, 1840), 4:212-214.

27 Dayna Libra Winters, "ISIS Paranormal Radio and George P. Hansen," *ISIS*

Paranormal Radio, podcast audio, January 10, 2010, accessed March 9, 2013, http://www.blogtalkradio.com/isisparanormal/2010/01/10/ISIS-Paranormal-Radio-George-P-Hansen.

28 Samuel Fallows, "Hermetical," in *The Progressive Dictionary of the English Language: A Supplementary Word Book to All the Leading Dictionaries of the United States and Great Britain* (Chicago: Progressive Publishing, 1888), 246.

29 John Rowbotham, "Monster," in *A New Derivative and Etymological Dictionary of Such English Works as Have Their Origin in the Greek and Latin Languages* (London: Longman, Orme, Brown, Green & Longmans, 1838), 169.

30 John Lemprière, "Medusa," in *A Classical Dictionary: Containing a Copious Account of All the Proper Names Mentioned in Antient Works*, new ed. (London: T. Cadell, 1833), 359.

31 John Lemprière, "Gorgones," in *A Classical Dictionary: Containing a Copious Account of All the Proper Names Mentioned in Antient Works*, new ed. (London: T. Cadell, 1833), 109.

32 John Lemprière, "Medusa," in *A Classical Dictionary: Containing a Copious Account of All the Proper Names Mentioned in Antient Works*, new ed. (London: T. Cadell, 1833), 359.

33 "Cerberus," in *Encyclopædia Britannica: Or, a Dictionary of Arts, Sciences, and Miscellaneous Literature*, ed. Colin Macfarquhar and George Gleig, 3rd ed. (Edinburgh: A Bell and C. Macfarquhar, 1797), 4:295.

34 Ibid.

Chapter 6

1 William Smith, "Hercules," in *A New Classical Dictionary of Greek and Roman Biography, Mythology, and Geography*, ed. Charles Anthon, rev. ed. (New York: Harper & Brothers, 1862), 355-360.

2 Nösselt, "Artemis or Diana," in *Mythology Greek and Roman*, 201-207.

3 Henry Thompson, "Biographical Memoir of Virgil," Introduction to *The Works of Publius Virgilius Maro, by Publius Virgilius Maro* (London: Richard Griffin and Company, 1855), 15-31.

4 Ibid.

5 Ibid.

6 John Lemprière, "Pythia," in *A Classical Dictionary; Containing a Copious Account of All the Proper Names Mentioned in Ancient Authors: With*

the Value of Coins, Weights, and Measures, Used Among the Greeks and Romans, 11th ed. (London: T. Cadwell and W. Davies, 1820), 662-663.

7 J. H. Middleton, "The Temple of Apollo at Delphi," *The Journal of Hellenic Studies* 9 (1888): 282-322.

8 Josephine Preston Peabody, "Arachne," in *Old Greek Folk Stories Told Anew* (Boston: Houghton, Mifflin and Company, 1897), 49-51.

9 Ibid.

10 Ibid.

11 Ibid.

12 Ibid.

13 Sarah Amelia Scull, "Pallas Athena," in *Greek Mythology Systematized*, by Sarah Amelia Scull (Philadelphia: Porter & Coates, 1880), 127-139.

14 Scull, "Pallas Athena," in *Greek Mythology Systematized*, 127-139.

15 Ibid.

16 Ibid.

17 John Lemprière, "Circe," in *A Classical Dictionary; Containing a Copious Account of All the Proper Names Mentioned in Ancient Authors: With the Value of Coins, Weights, and Measures, Used among the Greeks and Romans*, 11th ed. (London: T. Cadwell and W. Davies, 1820), 185-186.

18

19 Hélène Adeline Guerber, "Invention of the Runes," in *Myths of the Norsemen from the Eddas and Sagas* (London, 1908: George G. Harrap, n.d.), 33-34.

20 Guerber, "Invention of the Runes," in *Myths of the Norsemen*, 33-34.

21 Homer, *The Sixth Book of Homer's Odyssey*, ed. Chas W. Bain (Boston: Ginn & Company, 1895), 7-11.

22 Bela Bates Edwards, "Angel," in *The Encyclopedia of Religious Knowledge: Or, Dictionary of the Bible, Theology, Religious Biography, All Religions, Ecclesiastical History, and Missions*, ed. John Newton Brown (Brattleboro, VT: Joseph Steen, 1851), 81-82.

23 "Cassandra," in *Encyclopædia Americana: A Popular Dictionary of Arts, Sciences, Literature, History, Politics, and Biography, Brought down to the Present Time*, ed. Francis Lieber and E. Wigglesworth, 7th ed. (Philadelphia: Carey and Lea, 1830), 2:556.

24 Ibid.

25 Ibid.

26 Ibid.

27 Cornelius Petrus Tiele, vol. 1, "The Religion of Thinis-Abydos," in

Comparative History of the Egyptian and Mesopotamian Religions – Egypt, Babel-Assur, Yemanm, Harran, Phoenicia, Israel (London: Trubner & Company, 1882), 35-74.

28 Earnest Alfred Wallis Budge, "History as Told by Classical Writers," in *Osiris and the Egyptian Resurrection* (London: Philip Lee Warner, 1914), 1:1-23.

29 William Sherwood Fox, "The Greater Gods—Leto, Apollo, Artemis, Hekate," in *Greek and Roman, vol. 1, The Mythology of All Races* (Boston: Marshall Jones, 1913), 174-188.

30 John Lemprière, "Apollo," in *A Classical Dictionary: Containing a Copious Account of All the Proper Names Mentioned in Antient Works*, new ed. (London: T. Cadell, 1833), 172-173.

Chapter 11

1 John Dymock and Thomas Dymock, "Antevorta," in *Bibliotheca Classica: A Classical Dictionary* (London: Longman, Rees, Orme, Brown, Green & Longman, 1833), 704-705.

2 George Crabb, "Apollo," in *Universal Historical Dictionary: Or Explanation of the Names of Persons and Places*, enlarged ed. (London: Baldwin and Cradock, 1833), 1:240.

3 George Crabb, "Cassandra," in *Universal Historical Dictionary: Or Explanation of the Names of Persons and Places*, enlarged ed. (London: Baldwin and Cradock, 1833), 1:151.

4 Andrew Tooke, "The Goddesses of the Woods," in *The Pantheon: Representing the Fabulous Histories of the Heathen Gods, and Most Illustrious Heroes* (London: C. Bathurst, J. Rivington, B. Law, G. Keith, S. Bladon, G. Robinson, R. Baldwin, and W. Stuart, 1778), 209-223.

5 Potter, "On Divination of Dreams," in *Archæologia Græca: Or, The Antiquities*, 1:303-314.

6 John Lemprière, "Carmenta," in *A Classical Dictionary: Containing a Copious Account of All the Proper Names Mentioned in Antient Works*, new ed. (London: T. Cadell, 1833), 381.

7 Theophilus Goldridge Pinches, "The Principle Gods of the Babylonians and Assyrians," in *The Religion of Babylonia and Assyria* (London: Archibald Constable, 1906), 50-106.

8 John Bell, "Faunus," in *Bell's New Pantheon: Or, Historical Dictionary of the Gods, Demi-Gods, Heroes and Fabulous Personages of Antiquity* (London: J. Bell, 1790), 1:307.

9 John Parkhurst, "Hermes," in *A Greek and English Lexicon to the New*

Testament, 4th ed. (London: T. Davison, for G. and J. Robinson, 1804), 259.

10 John Lemprière, "Mnemosyne," in *A Classical Dictionary: Containing a Copious Account of All the Proper Names Mentioned in Antient Works*, new ed. (London: T. Cadell, 1839), 22.

11 Oskar Seyffert, "Dreams," in *A Dictionary of Classical Antiquities: Mythology, Religion, Literature and Art*, ed. Henry Nettleship and John Edwin Sandys, 3rd, rev. ed. (London: Swan Sonnenschein and Company, 1895), 201.

12 Seyffert, "Dreams," in *A Dictionary of Classical*, 201.

13 Ovid, "Story of Ceyx and Alcyone," trans. Dryden, Pope, Congreve, and Addison, in *Ovid* (New York: Harper & Brothers, 1844), 2:45-58.

14 John Lemprière, "Somnus," in *A Classical Dictionary: Containing a Copious Account of All the Proper Names Mentioned in Antient Works*, new ed. (London: T. Cadell, 1833), 29.

15 Anonymous, "Somnus and Morpheus," *Family Magazine: Or Monthly Abstract of General Knowledge*, 1835, 186-187.

16 John Lemprière, "Morpheus," in *A Classical Dictionary: Containing a Copious Account of All the Proper Names Mentioned in Antient Works*, new ed. (London: T. Cadell, 1833), 25.

17 John Lemprière, "Phobetor," in *A Classical Dictionary: Containing a Copious Account of All the Proper Names Mentioned in Antient Works*, new ed. (London: T. Cadell, 1833), 54.

18 John Lemprière, "Phantasus," in *A Classical Dictionary: Containing a Copious Account of All the Proper Names Mentioned in Antient Works*, new ed. (London: T. Cadell, 1833), 39.

19 Anonymous, "The Hours," in *A Classical Manual: Being a Mythological, Historical, and Geographical Commentary on Pope's Homer and Dryden's Aeneid of Virgil* (London: John Murray, 1833), 172-174.

20 Ibid.

21 Ibid.

22 Ibid.

23 Ibid.

24 Ibid.

25 Lizzie Deas, "Poppy," in *Flower Favourites: Their Legends, Symbolism, and Significance* (London: George Allen, 1878), 76-82.

26 Anonymous, "The Hours," in *A Classical Manual: Being*, 172-174.

27 Ibid.

28 Ibid.

29 John Wood, "Dormio," in *Etymological Guide to the English Language: Being a Collection, Alphabetically Arranged, of the Principal Roots, Affixes, and Prefixes, with Their Derivatives and Compounds*, 3rd ed. (Edinburgh: Oliver and Boyd, 1837), 46.

30 Anonymous, "The Hours," in *A Classical Manual: Being*, 172-174.

31 Ibid.

32 Ibid.

33 Ibid.

34 Thomas Firminger Thiselton-Dyer, "Dream Plants," in *The Folklore of Plants* (London: Chalto and Windus, 1889), 103-113.

35 Thiselton-Dyer, "Dream Plants," in *The Folklore of Plants*, 103-113.

36 J. H. Middleton, "The Temple of Apollo at Delphi," *The Journal of Hellenic Studies* 9 (1888): 282-322.

37 Henry Thompson, "Biographical Memoir of Virgil," Introduction to *The Works of Publius Virgilius Maro*, by Publius Virgilius Maro (London: Richard Griffin and Company, 1855), 103-113.

38 Richard Folkard, "Mugwort," in *Plant Lore, Legends, and Lyrics: Embracing the Myths, Traditions, Superstitions, and Folklore of the Plant Kingdom*, by Richard Folkard, Jr. (London: Sampson, Low, Marston, Searle, and Rivington, 1884), 449-451.

39 Ibid.

40 Richard Folkard, "Magical Plants," in *Plant Lore, Legends, and Lyrics: Embracing the Myths, Traditions, Superstitions, and Folklore of the Plant Kingdom*, by Richard Folkard, Jr. (London: Sampson, Low, Marston, Searle, and Rivington, 1884), 105-116.

41 Richard Folkard, "Rosemary," in *Plant Lore, Legends, and Lyrics: Embracing the Myths, Traditions, Superstitions, and Folklore of the Plant Kingdom*, by Richard Folkard, Jr. (London: Sampson, Low, Marston, Searle, and Rivington, 1884), 525-526.

42 Thiselton-Dyer, "Dream Plants," in *The Folklore of Plants*, 103-113.

43 George Fredrick Kunz, *The Curious Lore of Precious Stones* (Philadelphia: J. B. Lippincott, 1913), 52-54.

44 Kunz, *The Curious Lore of Precious*, 275-308.

About the Authors

Dayna Winters

DAYNA WINTERS is a Witch, Priestess, and writer. She earned an Associate in Arts from Hudson Valley Community College, and later graduated magna cum laude from Sage College with a Bachelor of Arts in English. Dayna is one of the former co-founders and co-directors of ISIS Paranormal Investigations in Upstate New York, and former co-host of *ISIS Paranormal Radio*. Her publications have appeared in *Threads* magazine, *The Crescent Magazine, Blood Moon Rising Magazine,* and *The Journal for the Academic Study of Magic.* Her radio interviews include *Alabama ParaSpiritual Talk Radio Show, the X-Zone Radio Show with Rob McConnell, Haunted Voices Radio, The Morning Rush Show on Fly 92.3 FM,* and *Paranormal Radio with Captain Jack,* among others. Dayna was also featured in *Chat: It's Fate, 14 Degrees: A Paranormal Documentary,* and Discovery Channel's *A Haunting.*

Patricia Gardner

PATRICIA GARDNER is a Witch and the High Priestess of the Dragon Warrior's of ISIS Coven in Upstate, New York. She is the former co-founder and co-director of ISIS Paranormal Investigations, and former co-host of the *ISIS Paranormal Radio Show.* She has had publications appear on Isisinvestigations.com, Unexplained-Mysteries.com, Ghost-mysteries. com, and Haunted-Voices.com. Her radio, television, and film appearances include *Alabama ParaSpiritual Talk Radio Show, the X-Zone Radio Show with Rob McConnell, Haunted Voices Radio, The Morning Rush Show on Fly 92.3 FM, The Soul Salon, Paranormal Radio with Captain Jack, Psychic Wisdom with David James, Encounters with the Paranormal,* and *The Gut & Bone Show.* Patricia has also been featured in *Chat: It's Fate, 14 Degrees: A Paranormal Documentary,* and Discovery Channel's *A Haunting.*

Angela Kaufman

ANGELA KAUFMAN is a Witch, Priestess in the Dragon Warriors of Isis Coven, and a Licensed Clinical Social Worker with over seven years of experience working with individuals with mental health and substance abuse issues. She is also a professional Tarot card reader and the owner of Moonlight Tarot. Angela has had several articles published on ISIS Paranormal Investigations, she is a psychic artist for the latter ghost investigation group, and she has had publications appearing in *Wisdom* magazine and the *Magical Buffet*. Her radio, television, and film appearances include *The Morning Rush Show on Fly 92.3 FM*, *14 Degrees: A Paranormal Documentary*, Discovery Channel's *A Haunting*, and *The ISIS Paranormal Radio Show*.

Dayna, Patricia, and Angela are co-authors of *Wicca: What's the Real Deal? Breaking Through the Misconceptions (Schiffer, 2011)*, and *Sacred Objects, Sacred Space: Everyday Tools for the Modern-Day Witch (Schiffer, 2013)*.

You can find out more information about the authors at www.wwtrd.webs.com. To contact the authors with questions or interview requests, use the contact submission form through the website or email the authors at daynawinters@gmail.com.

INDEX